THE COUNCIL OF TRENT

LECTURES

ON

THE COUNCIL OF TRENT

DELIVERED AT OXFORD 1892-3

BY

JAMES ANTHONY FROUDE,

LATE REGIUS PROFESSOR OF MODERN HISTORY IN THE UNIVERSITY OF OXFORD

KENNIKAT PRESS/Port Washington, N.Y.

128614

LECTURES ON THE COUNCIL OF TRENT

First published 1896
Reissued 1969 by Kennikat Press

Library of Congress Catalog Card No: 68-8244
SBN 8046-0159-3
Manufactured in the United States of America

PREFACE

———◇———

THE lectures on the Council of Trent were delivered by Mr. Froude in the Michaelmas Term of 1892 and the Hilary Term of 1893. They formed the first of three courses delivered by him during the eighteen months in which he was in residence at Oxford as Regius Professor of Modern History. Two of these courses, the lectures on Erasmus and on the English Seamen of the Sixteenth Century, have already been published.

Had Mr. Froude lived to publish the present series of lectures, he would no doubt have thoroughly revised and corrected them. They were addressed to varying audiences, and for this reason contain repetitions which will seem unnecessary to the reader. The author would also probably have given, in footnotes, references to the original authorities, as in the published lectures on Erasmus. The quotations are not literal translations, but abridgments or paraphrases, and as their accuracy can, for the most part, easily be verified, it has been thought advisable to publish the lectures as they stood, with only a few verbal corrections.

CONTENTS

LECTURES

ON

THE COUNCIL OF TRENT

LECTURE I

THE CONDITION OF THE CHURCH

IN these lectures I am about to speak to you on the Reformation of the sixteenth century. I need not dwell on the importance of the subject. The Reformation is the hinge on which all modern history turns. Had there been no Reformation, or had the shape which it assumed been other than it was, everything which has happened since would have been different. Yet while it is so important, there is nothing on which opinion is less settled in this or any part of Europe. Authorities violently contradict each other. Catholics give one account of it, Protestants another, philosophers another. Facts are asserted or denied, believed or disbelieved, not according to the letter of the evidence, but according to their antecedent credibility to this or that writer or student. Passion and prejudice still rule the judgment of all of us, and even when we do our utmost to be fair, our points of difference have so changed their shape, so many things are now forgotten which three centuries ago were in the minds of everyone, that we often fail to see what it was that people then were fighting about. Cardinal Contarini, for instance, had to tell Paul III. that if all the Protestant divines, even Luther himself, were converted and reconciled to the Church, the situation would not be affected. The rebellion against Rome would go on as bitterly as ever. Which of you present to-day, which of all the writers who give us their opinion on the matter so fluently, can explain what Contarini meant ?

I have called the subject of my lectures the Council of Trent. The Council of Trent suggests theology, and we all think of the Reformation as a revolution in doctrine. Of the many subjects of which I shall have to speak, the change of doctrine is the least momentous, and I shall touch upon it only indirectly. Erasmus tells us that when Luther first set up his theses, all the intelligent part of Europe, all the most sincere and orthodox of the Catholic laity, were warmly on his side. Erasmus himself, though he differed entirely from Luther in positive theology, yet welcomed the movement at Wittenberg as a providential incident which promised infinite good.

When Leo X. demanded that Luther should be

arrested and sent to Rome, his Nuncio reported that if he wanted Luther's arrest he must send an army of 25,000 men to take him. In that brief time, two years only from the day the theses appeared, Germany, France, and Italy were ringing with Luther's name, and his writings were circulated in tens of thousands of copies through every corner of Europe. New doctrines do not spread with such velocity. Even Mahomet made but one convert in fifteen years, and that one was his wife. Something else must have been at work to kindle so universal an enthusiasm; and my purpose in these lectures is to bring before you what that something was.

It is not an easy task. When we study Greek or Roman history we are dealing with a subject which has no bearing on the world as we know it; there are no surviving prejudices or interests to mislead us. With the Reformation the old names remain, which seem still to represent the same things. A hundred sects or parties, which have grown out of the Reformation, divide us at the present day, and each imagines that the point it is most eager about is identical with one or other of the subjects of contention, which it fancies that it can trace at the beginning of the movement. We read back our own peculiarities into divisions which seem to resemble them. With us the differences are merely in opinion; we conclude that opinions were everything then. All that once lay behind them is passed and gone, and we do not realise that there was ever anything there; we wonder how human beings could tear each other to pieces about speculative formulas; we condemn or we pity the fury with which they wrangled and fought; and we congratulate ourselves on living in an age when men can think differently without quarrelling.

Thus it is no secret that the name of Protestant, once so highly honoured, is no longer respected as it used to be. It is regarded as a polemical word. We are coming, many of us, to consider that the Reformers of the sixteenth century were as narrow-minded and bigoted as their opponents; that they were often contending, as the Greeks said, for an ass's shadow. We see that Catholics, living among us nowadays, are harmless and excellent people, and we think that they were the same then as they are now, and that Protestant writers must have calumniated them. Eminent, well-informed men condemn Luther's violence as needless and mischievous. Goethe says that he threw back the intelligence of mankind for centuries by calling in the passions of a mob to decide questions which ought to have been left to the thinkers. Matthew Arnold finds him to have been a Philistine. An Anglican divine compares him to Joe Smith the Mormon. Our own Reformers come off worst of all; we keep what they won for us, but for the men themselves hardly a good word is spoken. Catholics, High Churchmen, Liberals unite in a chorus of censure. To Macaulay and Buckle, Cranmer is the basest of mankind. Even Lingard has some kind of pity for him; the Liberal philosophers have none. I am not surprised at the rest, but the Liberals, I think, are ungrateful. They are the lineal successors of the Long Parliament. The Long Parliament came straight from Cranmer and his friends, the Marian martyrs. Their existence as a party grew out of the struggle between freedom of thought and ecclesiastical authority, and without the Marian martyrs they would perhaps never have been a party at all.

But the reason of all this depreciation is merely a confusion of the alteration in doctrine and ritual with the immeasurably deeper revolution which preceded it; a revolution forgotten only because the victory of the Reformers was so absolute that the very traces of the struggle have disappeared. The original Reformation was a revolt of the laity against the clergy, a revolt against a complicated and all-embracing practical tyranny, the most intolerable that the world has ever seen. It was based on an assumption, no longer seriously held even by Catholics themselves, that the Church was the source of all authority, secular as well as spiritual; and an historical enquiry into the relations between the clergy and the laity, and the nature of the laity's complaints, will not require me to touch, unless remotely and allusively, upon any dogmas on which conscience is now sensitive.

I intend therefore to put before you as clearly as I can what those relations were at the time of Luther's movement; what the causes were, which made the laity welcome that movement with so much enthusiasm ; and how the ecclesiastical and the secular powers conducted themselves when the popular indignation burst out.

A distinguished Catholic prelate was explaining to me not long ago the tenderness which the Church had always shown for the rights of conscience. The Church, he assured me, never punished anybody merely for his opinions. It had not—would not—could not. Luther and his fellows had been born in the Church, had received the grace of the Sacraments. They were therefore rebels, and as such it was necessary to treat them. Modern Protestants were innocent children born in error for which they were not responsible, for whom the Church had no feeling but of love and pity. We are grateful for the distinction which is made in our favour.

Unquestionably Luther was a rebel against the order of things which he found established. Rebellion against a just government is a crime. Rebellion against an unjust and corrupt government may be a remedy worse than the disease so long as there is any hope that such a government may be brought to mend its ways. But it is also a law of things in this world that corrupt governments shall not continue for ever. They must be mended or ended; and many times in the world's history rebellion has been the only resource. All depends on the facts of the case. A Catiline is justly abhorred; a Brutus, a Cromwell, or a Washington is honoured and admired.

Well, then, for the facts which made a rebel of Luther. In what I am going to say I shall not rely

on the testimony of Protestant writers. Cardinal Newman tells us that Protestant tradition is based on lying
—bold, wholesale, unscrupulous lying. The same has
been said of Catholic tradition. Men under strong
emotion do not measure their words; but I shall accept
for the present Cardinal Newman's assertion. I shall
rely on Catholic documents of undoubted authenticity,
on the testimony of Catholic witnesses antecedent to
or contemporary with the Reformation. I take the
Council of Trent as my first subject, because the moral
condition of the Church comes out with perfect clear-
ness in the discussions in the Council itself. I shall go
on if I can with Erasmus—and Erasmus I may surely
call a Catholic, for he held aloof entirely from the Protestant movement when he had everything to lose by
opposing it. He was, and remained to the end, the
confidential friend and correspondent of Popes, bishops,
abbots, Catholic princes, kings and emperors, who
turned to him for advice in their difficulties. Paul
III., when he had decided that a Council must be held,
so earnestly desired Erasmus's assistance in conducting
it that he was preparing to make him a member of the
Sacred College. The only difficulty was in the want of
fortune, and this was about to be removed when
Erasmus died. Surely therefore there is no room to
challenge the title of Erasmus to Catholic orthodoxy.

Charles V., who will form the subject of the last
series of lectures, was of all the sovereigns of Europe
the most unimpeachably loyal to the Holy See. By
his office he was Protector of the Church. To him

above all the rest the Popes turned for secular assistance in suppressing the Lutheran revolt, nor was any
prince more zealous than he to recover Lutheran
Germany to the papal allegiance. In him were combined all the qualities which the Popes ought most
to have welcomed in their defender. He was personally devout. He was a soldier and a statesman with
a touch of Spanish chivalry. He was constitutionally
conservative, believed in the authority of the wise
over the foolish, and in the difference between right
and wrong. In such a man an honest Pope would
naturally expect to find the help he needed. Charles
shared the prejudices of the time. He believed that
a wilful mistake in religious faith was the worst of
crimes, that it was the magistrate's duty not only to
execute justice but to maintain truth. The only difficulty with Charles was that persons in authority had
their duties also, and that if they were to be supported
they must behave well themselves. Thus when the
Pope cried out that the wolf had broken into the
sheepfold and that Charles must come and destroy
him, Charles answered that certainly he would destroy
the wolf if he could, and if he was quite certain that
it was a wolf, and not a sheepdog driven mad by the
bad behaviour of the shepherds who were wolves
themselves. The morals of Popes and bishops had
been a scandal to Europe. He was willing to use the
power of the Empire to put down heresy, but Popes
and bishops must first reform their own ways.

With the efforts of the Emperor to make the Court

of Rome reform itself, and with the persistent determination of the Court of Rome not to be reformed,
till Charles was dead, and the schism was irreparable,
I hope to deal in the concluding course.

This is my general purpose. I am left free by
the statute to choose my own subject to lecture on.
I have chosen this one, because I still keep to the
belief in which I was brought up, that the Reformation was a great and necessary thing; that it was
brought about by remarkable men who do not deserve
to be forgotten, still less to be traduced. It has been
said that each nation's history is in a sense its own
Bible, its own record of the dealings of Providence with
it. If there be such a thing as Providence at all, we
are bound to try to understand what it may have to
say to us.

I will now sketch in outline the grounds of the
laity's complaints against the clergy at the beginning of
the sixteenth century—we shall see them in detail as
we go on.

There is a maxim now that everyone is equal before
the law. From the twelfth to the sixteenth century
the clergy were a separate caste. They made and
administered their own laws. They could neither sue
nor be sued in any secular court. They had contrived,
under one plea or another, to stretch their privilege till
benefit of clergy, as it was called, extended to everyone
who could read—nay, further, if Father Paul, the Venetian
historian, is to be believed, for he says it had been
ruled to cover priests' concubines. Cardinal Pallavicino,

however, says that this is a calumny. It went far
enough without that. The effect of it was that crimes
of the darkest dye could be and were committed by
clerks in orders with practical impunity. They might
be taken in the act of rape or murder or robbery. The
magistrates could not commit them. The judges could
not try them. They were claimed by the bishop's
ordinary, and were handed over to the bishop to deal
with. By the Canon Law the bishops were bound to
keep one or more prisons in their diocese, where felonious priests were to be confined. But prisons and
prisoners were expensive to maintain; and the obligation came to be universally neglected. A bishop could
not sentence a felon to death, and so get rid of him. A
priest could indeed be degraded and passed back to the
secular arm, but degradation, before the Council of
Trent simplified it, was a complicated and difficult
process, and was rarely or never resorted to except in
cases of heresy. Felons and that description of person
are not frightened by excommunication, and thus
criminous clerks had nothing to fear at all. They
might lose their benefices, but they could not be
hanged, they could not be whipped. To cage them up
for life was costly and inconvenient. They paid with
their purses as much as could be got out of them, and
were turned adrift to go on with their trade.

This extraordinary privilege arose out of the supposed supernatural character which was bestowed in
ordination. *Noli tangere Christos meos* (touch not my
Christ, or my anointed as we translate) was construed

to mean that the grasp of a constable was not to be
laid on the sacred shoulders of a minister of the altar.
The hands that consecrated the Eucharist were not
to be manacled or the body subjected to lash or halter.
That was the argument—you can read it at length
in the letters and discussions about the Constitutions
of Clarendon. Archbishop Becket, who fought the
battle for the clergy and won it, is considered to have
been a champion of the Church's interests, and to be
one of her great saints.   I think, for my own part, that
Becket did the Church a bad day's service when he
secured for the clergy this singular exemption from
justice.   Monks and priests were not all of them
restrained from crime by conscience, and no class of
men can be safely left to do as they please without fear
of punishment.   I have heard experienced judges
express most unfavourable opinions of murderers and
thieves.   Spiritual censures have not the least terror
for such persons, as long as they do not suffer in their
skins, and the effect of clerical immunity was that a
number of dangerous wild beasts were abroad in society
who might be neither killed nor shut up.

That there really were wicked priests of this kind
may be seen in a curious story told in a letter by Sir
Thomas More.   More apparently had been concerned
in the case professionally.   For obvious reasons he
gives no names ; but he says that in a certain monastery
there was a monk who had risen to rank in the fra-
ternity, and might therefore be supposed to have been
a respectable person.   This man took to abandoned

courses, committed crime after crime, and at last, some enemy or rival having to be removed, he came to murder. He hired a party of assassins and concealed them in his cell. Before he set them about their work, he took them into his private oratory, made them kneel before Our Lady, and pray for her favour in the enterprise they were going about, and then dismissed them to business.

More does not say whether the murder was actually accomplished; but the men were caught, and he says that he himself saw them, spoke to them, and heard the whole story from them. They could be hanged, and of course were hanged; but for the monk who had set them on there was no hanging possible. Before he could be brought before a criminal court, he must have first appeared before half-a-dozen abbots, whom, even if they were willing, it was difficult to bring together. If they found him guilty, they would always be reluctant to degrade for fear of the scandal. The process was so tedious and costly that I have rarely found an instance, before the Council of Trent, where degradation was carried out, except, as I said, in cases of heresy.

But if the clergy were exempt from lay jurisdiction, the laity were not exempt from the jurisdiction of the clergy. The law of the land might deal with common rights and obligations definable by statute or precedent. The clergy, as the spiritual fathers of the people, were the guardians of morality. They had courts of their own, conducted upon their own principles, before which clergy and laity were alike bound to appear. They had their own canons, which crown and parliament could not interfere with. They enforced their sentences with censures, fines, imprisonments, and in the last resort with excommunications which carried civil penalties, and deprived a man of his rights as a citizen; and all these penalties had come to be convertible into money payments.

Morality was a word of widest latitude. The law, as we understand it, applies only to injuries to person, property, or character. The spiritual law extended to sins, and not to notorious moral offences only, but to everything which could be construed into sin by the Church's interpretation; men were liable to be summoned before provincial courts far away from their homes, sometimes for looseness of conduct, sometimes for words idly spoken. The judges were the prosecutors. The offenders were fined, and fined worse if they complained. If they resisted further, they were excommunicated, and there was then no resource but submission, or an appeal to Rome, which was so enormously expensive as to be beyond the means of ordinary men. Readers of English history, when they find Henry VIII.'s parliament abolishing these references to Rome, and providing for the determination of suits at home, imagine that the Act of Appeal was passed merely to enable Henry to divorce Queen Catherine. It was to make an end of an intolerable grievance which pressed on every household in the realm.

The clergy possessed a terrible implement by which

to entangle unfortunate men in the meshes of their
courts. Among the offences most eagerly taken up
was heresy or 'matters sounding thereunto.' To complain of the spiritual jurisdiction was itself heresy
of the darkest kind, and through the Confessional
there was a road into the inmost secrets of every home
in the country. Each man and woman was required to
confess to a priest at least once a year, generally much
oftener. Resident rectors and curates who knew their
parishioners personally, might perhaps be safely trusted
with such an office. But by the beginning of the
sixteenth century the general business of religion had
fallen to the mendicant friars. The secular clergy were
said to have been lax and ignorant. The friars had
obtained special privileges from the Popes which had
superseded the parochial organisation. The bishops
had no authority over them. They preached what they
pleased; they taught what they pleased. They claimed
and they obtained a universal right of hearing confessions. They went from house to house. They demanded
entertainment, which no one dared to refuse them.
They were hated. Erasmus says that when a mendicant friar was seen approaching, men shrank from him
as from some noxious animal. But as priests they
were supposed to possess supernatural powers, and
they did possess practical powers which were never
resisted with impunity. To quarrel with a friar
was to quarrel with an order which never died
and never forgave. Introduced into families, these
itinerants gained the confidence of the women, or

worked on their fears. They learnt the character of the husbands and sons. Their rule might forbid the revelation of secrets learned in the Confessional, but all rules could be dispensed with in the interests of the order. Poor men found themselves summoned before the spiritual courts. They were accused of having said this or that. They were cross-questioned. If they were indignant or impatient, their crimes became only more evident. These friars besides watched over death-beds and dictated wills, or if wills were not what the friars approved, the Church courts would set them aside. The whole business resolved itself into an elaborate contrivance for extorting money out of the laity.

You can see how the system worked in the 'Letters of Erasmus,' in the 'Complaints of the House of Commons against the Bishops,' in the first Reformation parliament, and in the 'Centum Gravamina of Germany.' The bishops were so accustomed to it all that they had not the least conception that anything was wrong about their courts, nor could they understand why the laity were aggrieved. The House of Commons charged them with making laws inconsistent with the laws of the realm. The bishops replied that they regretted the inconsistency, but as their laws were undoubtedly in conformity with the will of Almighty God, the remedy was for parliament to alter the laws of the realm, when the desirable agreement would be arrived at. When they were reproached with the expenses of their courts, they answered that the ecclesiastical lawyers were of extreme value to the realm at large, and that high pay was necessary to encourage them.

An appeal to Rome was the only escape from one of these courts. The appeal had been instituted, so its apologists pretended, as a check on the injustice of the local bishops; yet the Court of Rome was the worst offender of the whole of them—*Omnia venalia Romæ* was as true of the Rome of Julius or Leo as of the Rome of Jugurtha. The Church of Rome claimed the two swords of St. Peter. All power belonged to it in heaven and earth. It could make laws and dispense with them. It still pretended to a right to depose kings. Julius II. deprived Louis XII. of France and absolved his subjects from their allegiance. He laid France under an interdict, and a Pope's sentence still excused and encouraged insurrection. Oaths ceased to bind when the Pope pleased. Clement VII. absolved Francis I. from his oath to observe the Treaty of Madrid. There was scarce a duty which did not cease to be a duty if the Pope dispensed with it. Marriage laws were his special preserve and domain. Marriages were encumbered by a list of forbidden degrees extending to the furthest limits of consanguinity or affinity, even to the spiritual affinity of sponsors at the font. The prohibition to marry within these degrees implied that such a marriage was regarded as wrong, but it could always be allowed by a papal dispensation, to be paid for according to the means of the applicant.

The dispensations, again, were not final—for dispensations were only to be granted for a just cause, and
endless disputes could be afterwards raised whether
such just cause had existed. The legitimacy of
children could be challenged, the right of inheritance
could be challenged, with fresh suits before the Rota,
and fresh rivers of gold running into the papal
exchequer.

Every obligation could be dispensed with for a
just cause. It was 'corban' over again. The Canon
Law forbade plurality of benefices, ordered bishops
and clergy to reside, and parish priests to obey their
ordinaries. Cardinals and prelates who would pay
for it were allowed to hold see upon see, and never
attend to any duty save the duty of receiving their
salaries. Cardinal Wolsey, for instance, was archbishop of York, bishop of Durham and bishop of
Winchester, and abbot of St. Albans, though he never
so much as visited either Winchester or Durham, and
was never at York till the last year of his life. All
the cardinals claimed similar indulgences and held
bishoprics when they were not even ordained or when
they were mere boys. Parish priests, again, could
buy exemption from the authority of their diocesan,
leave their work and their dress and follow other
occupations, keeping the profits of their benefices.
The regular orders were answerable only to their
own superiors, and they again could purchase immunities at Rome, forsake their convents, and go
where they would; while for the neglected souls of

the people there were the mendicant friars, with their endless supplies of indulgences, pardons, saints' relics, and lying legends. If this was not enough and conscience was still uneasy, there were pilgrimages and miracle-working images, or masses said by ignorant priests who could read nothing but their own service in the Breviary, and sold their repetitions of it by the dozens, as a cobbler sells his shoes. So Erasmus says, and he adds that the saying of these masses was not confined to the churches: they were said anywhere, without regard to place. He ventures even the extraordinary statement that there was not a private house, not a tavern, *pœne dixeram lupanar*, where these priests were not to be found celebrating. I recommend this passage to those who wish to return to pre-Reformation practices.

I must not omit one little picture of the teaching of a mendicant friar, as it again rests on the unexceptional testimony of Sir Thomas More. Some business or other had taken More to Coventry: on his arrival he was told that the town was in a state of excitement—a certain monk was preaching there that any man who would repeat every day the psaltery of the Virgin was certain of salvation, however wicked he might be. More was asked his opinion. He passed the question off with an ironical answer; but he was not allowed to escape. He was invited to a dinner. The monk was among the guests, a lean, wizened old man with a large volume under his arm, from which he proceeded to read. It was

a catalogue of miracles which Our Lady was alleged
to have performed in the neighbourhood, and More
was again challenged. He said that such stories
were not *de fide*, Catholics were not bound to believe
them, and unless they were true they were nothing
to the purpose. But the company thought differently.
More was left alone in his opinion. The monk went
on preaching, till at last the bishop contrived to
interfere, and silence him.

I need not travel further at present over this part
of the subject. When Adrian VI. wished to reform the
Court of Rome, he was told that the revenues of the
Papacy, then exceeding those of any prince in Europe,
came from four sources, each yielding about an equal
return : the legitimate revenues from the Papal States;
the profits from the Roman courts of law; the annates
and tenths and the Bulls of institution, paid by all
bishops all over the Catholic world; and the sale of
dispensations, pardons, licences and indulgences. It
was represented to Adrian that, if he did not wish the
See of Rome to be ruined, he had better be careful with
his reforms.

The state of things which I have been describing in
outline will come out more vividly as I proceed; but this
was the general aspect of spiritual Europe in the gener-
ation immediately preceding the Reformation. It was
dangerous, for daylight was beginning to dawn. Literature was reviving. The printing press was everywhere
busy. The laity were reading and thinking for themselves. It might have been borne more easily and

have lasted longer if Popes, bishops, priests, and monks had been strict in their personal conduct; but how they stood in the matter of morals I must give you a few instances to show. Again, I am not about to quote Protestant tradition, and no exception can be taken to my witnesses.

First, for the Court of Rome. At the close of the fifteenth and the beginning of the sixteenth century the representative of St. Peter was Alexander VI. It was the era (and it is well to observe this) when Italian art was rising to the meridian and the Virgins and saints were being painted which affect so devotionally the modern mind. That the Pope was Antichrist is considered now an extravagance of Protestant fanaticism. That title was given to Alexander by an earnest Catholic, in a letter to Cardinal Savelli, who was then at the Court of the Emperor Maximilian. The purpose of the letter was to describe the enormities at the Vatican and to invite Maximilian's interference.

The writer says that imagination could not conceive such a monster as Alexander: 'The benefices and offices which ought to be given to persons of merit are offered for public sale to the highest bidder. Men go with gold to the palace to buy the mysteries of the faith. Everything can be had for money—dignities, honours, marriages, dissolution of marriage, divorces—things which our fathers never heard of and which Christian custom forbids. Crimes grosser than Scythian, acts of treachery worse than Carthaginian, are committed without disguise in the Vatican itself, under the eyes of

the Pope.   There are rapes, murders, incests, debauch-
eries, cruelties exceeding those of the Neros and
Caligulas.   None are spared, not even the highest.
Licentiousness, past description, is paraded in contempt
of God and man.   Sons and daughters are polluted.
Harlots and procuresses are gathered together in the
mansion of St. Peter.   On All Saints' day fifty women
of the town were invited to dinner.'   The details of
what followed are totally unmentionable.   ' Gold is
gathered in from all quarters.   Indulgences are sold
in all churches of Christendom to provide a portion for
the Pope's daughter Lucretia.   The son, Cæsar Borgia,
is so like his father that it is hard to say which is the
greater monster.   The cardinals of the better sort, if
such there be, are silent, or affect not to see.   They
bought their rank with money.   They preserve it with
criminal compliance, and continue to speak smoothly to
the Pope and praise and flatter.'

The letter is long, I give but parts of it.   The original
is printed in Burckhard's Diary, which has been lately
published in full.   Burckhard was a high official in the
Vatican, in personal attendance on Alexander.   He
adds a great many disgusting particulars.   The remarkable thing is that he affects neither surprise nor horror,
but relates each abomination as if it was a common
occurrence.

And I would observe that the leading Churchmen,
who had to deal with the Reformation, were trained in
Alexander's court.   Aleander the nuncio, who carried
into Germany the Bull of Leo against Luther, and

himself prosecuted Luther at the Diet of Worms, was Cæsar Borgia's secretary.

I turn to the monasteries. It is now said, and commonly believed, that the monasteries were suppressed in Protestant countries because kings and nobles wanted their lands, and that the charges brought against them were invented to justify the spoliation. In the year 1489 complaint had become loud of the relaxation of discipline in the English abbeys. Cardinal Morton, then archbishop of Canterbury, obtained a legantine commission from Innocent VIII. to examine and correct what might be amiss. It was only as the Pope's deputy that he was able to act. Of his own authority he was powerless. Morton visited, among other places, the great Abbey of St. Albans. The abbey itself was the most splendid in the island. The Abbot was a peer of the realm. Here is part of a letter which the Archbishop addressed to him—a contemporary draft of the original is in Morton's Register at Lambeth—'During the time of your administration you have relaxed the rule of your order. You have neglected almsgiving and hospitality, and other pious offices. Your brethren in the house, whose blood a severe judge will require at your hands, have given themselves over to a reprobate mind, and lead lascivious lives, profaning the holy places, even the churches of God, by infamous intercourse with nuns. Among the crimes for which you are yourself noted and defamed, you have admitted a married woman living in adultery to be a sister in the convent of Bray; of that convent

you have made her prioress. The brethren of the
abbey have resorted, and do resort continually, to this
and to other women at the same place, as if it were
a common receiving house, and they have not been
corrected therefor.'

Minor offences follow: 'You have dilapidated the
common property, you have made away with the jewels,
you have cut down and sold timber to the value of
8,000 marks, &c.'

In this document there can be no suspicion of a
desire to calumniate as an excuse for suppression;
suppressions were not thought of till forty years later.
There could be no question of jealousy between the
bishops and regulars, as the Archbishop was visiting
under order from the Pope. The charges brought
against the other abbeys by Henry VIII.'s visitors were
precisely of the kind alleged by Morton against the
St. Albans monks. The only ground for rejecting them
is the antecedent improbability that men of a religious
profession could have been so loosely given; and how
can we talk of antecedent improbability when the first
abbey in England was in the condition which Morton
describes?

'Why wake up all this?' it is asked. 'Why not
let the dead sleep, good or bad?' Because it is
pertinaciously denied, because in allowing the denial
to pass we are making criminals of a worse kind out
of the statesmen who were obliged to take these places
in hand. To keep back the truth for the sake of peace
is as foolish as it is wrong.

I turn to a letter from Erasmus to an English bishop. Erasmus had keener eyes than were in any contemporary head. He was no iconoclast. He abhorred violence, and wished the Church to stand with undiminished dignity, but he knew that stand it could not unless it set its own house in order. He was eager for timely and quiet reform, and he never ceased to impress on Pope and prelate the faults which required amending, and the need of haste in mending them. I might quote a hundred passages from him, pointing out these faults; a single one will be sufficient.

He had been speaking severely of the scandals connected with the Confessional since it had fallen under the management of the friars. He continues:—

' 'What I have said is not to censure Confession, but to purify the practice of it. Confessions are betrayed. The monks draw harvests from their penitents. They learn rich men's secrets. They stand at their deathbeds and dictate their wills. They rule their families by the knowledge which they have unfairly gained. Reflect seriously on what has grown out of the behaviour of these men, and blame me if you can for denouncing it. Yet it is to these friars that the Popes and princes would trust powers to deal with heresy. Who does not respect a monk who observes his rule? But where are such monks now to be found? What trace have the monks that we now meet of the religious character but the dress

and the tonsure ?   I should be sorry to say that there
are no exceptions.   But I beseech you, you who are
a good pure-minded man, go round your own diocese,
visit the monasteries, examine into the life and conduct of those who are allowed to tyrannise over us.
I am not saying this to hurt the religious orders; my
object is to shame them into amendment.   They are
hated, and they know it, and they know why, but they
will not part with their faults, and try to crush their
opponents by force.

' Augustine says that in his time life in a monastery
was either the best or the very worst.   What would
Augustine say now when so many of them differ
nothing from Lupanaria, when there are so many
sisterhoods where nothing is more rare than chastity ?
I speak of them as they exist at this day among
ourselves.' *1*

1 I have one more extract to give.   It is from the
writings of the great reformer of the Carmelites,
Theresa of Avila.   Theresa says, speaking of the sisterhoods in Spain, as she found them in her own girlhood,
that to many women convent life was rather a pathway
to hell than an aid to infirmity, that parents would
better consult their daughters' welfare by marrying
them honestly than by placing them in relaxed houses
of religion.   ' The girls themselves,' she said, ' are not
so much to blame.   They do only what they see others
do.   They enter convents to serve the Lord and to
escape the temptations of the world, and they find

themselves in the world, with youth, sensuality, and the devil tempting them to evil. In the same house are two roads, one leading to piety and virtue, and the other leading away from piety and virtue, and so little travelled is the road to religion, that a sister who wishes to follow it has more to fear from her companions than from all the devils.'

Once more, I do not quote these passages to revive forgotten animosities, but to show, in mere justice to the Reformers, to what a point the Church had fallen, and how impossible it was to leave things to go on as they were going. It was the time of the Renaissance. The minds of men had wakened up. Great scholars, Laurentius Valla, Ludovicus Vives, Reuchlin, Erasmus, were printing the Greek and Latin classics—printing the New Testament—printing the Greek and Latin Fathers. Of the New Testament the Paris presses alone, in a year or two after its publication, had sold over a hundred thousand copies. The contrast between the Christianity of the Apostles and the parody of it then prevailing in the world was too violent to be denied. The monks recognised their enemy. Making a boast of their own ignorance, they denounced the new studies as heretical, and left them to laymen; and the consequence was, as Erasmus again says, that you heard subjects of serious interest discoursed on at the tables of peers and princes, while at churchmen's tables the talk was ribaldry and licentiousness. What were the laity to do with an order of men whom they still believed to have a supernatural commission, yet who from the Vatican to the secluded priory were living as if right and wrong had no meaning for them? Time was forcing on the question, when the fire was lighted by a spark which was kindled at Wittenberg, in Saxony.

LECTURE II

THE INDULGENCES

IN my first lecture I endeavoured to show you that the irritation of Europe with the Church at the beginning of the sixteenth century did not arise, like the Gnostic or Arian heresies, from a disbelief in its doctrines or from intellectual restlessness. It arose out of natural indignation at the disregard among the clergy of their own teaching and their own canons, at the abuse of the powers and the privileges which had been entrusted to their order, at their own scandalous lives, and the tyranny with which they oppressed the people. The Church had been fighting for centuries for what it called its rights, and it had gained all that it demanded. But men who think much of their rights are apt to forget their duties. The clergy could not excuse themselves by the habits of the age. The natural order of things was inverted. The shepherds of the people had sunk below the level of their flocks. The laity had loaded the clergy with wealth, power and privilege, on account of their supposed holiness, and were startled to find that this favoured order had for-

gotten the meaning of common honesty and morality.
What were the laity to do? They had surrendered
their own rights, and had no power to interfere except
by revolution. They had exempted the clergy from
obedience to the law. They had made over to them
the complete management of their own affairs. Doctrine,
practice, everything which could be called spiritual, or
which affected spiritual men, was the clergy's exclusive
concern. They were stewards of the mysteries of God.
For the laity to interfere with them was sacrilege and
the sin of Uzzah.

For the office of the clergy there still remained a
profound reverence. Salvation was held to depend
upon the sacraments. They alone had power to administer the sacraments. It was a trial to faith to see
Popes and bishops promoting their sons to high offices
in the Church, first under the thin disguise of calling
them nephews, then without any disguise at all. It
was a trial to faith to see lads of fourteen made into
cardinals, or the sons of bishops presented to benefices
when children; and sooner or later a question was sure
to arise whether they really did possess the powers
which they claimed, whether there was any peculiar
gift of the Spirit conveyed by ordination, since there
was such small outward sign of it in life and conduct.

But a reverence which had been long in growing
was slow in passing away, and it was with the utmost
reluctance that the laity found themselves forced into
resistance. The scandals were too gross, the tyranny
too unbearable, something had to be done; but what?

They could not wait for ever till conscience moved the Church to repent. Corrupt bodies are unconscious of their corruption, until it begins to be painful, and the corruptions of the Church had been so far pleasant and profitable.

There had been signs enough of coming storm: a savage satire on Julius II. had been brought on the stage at Paris. Erasmus's 'Encomium Moriæ' and the 'Epistolæ Obscurorum Virorum' had set all Europe laughing, yet no alarm was taken. If complaint anywhere became too noisy, it was silenced with fire and faggot; and there seemed to be no remedy except revolution, to which sensible men can only be driven in the last extremity.

What, in fact, ought to have been done? Goethe says it should have been left to the thinkers; that is, to men like Erasmus. Perhaps so, but how were men like Erasmus, not born to power, to get the management of things? Thinkers are a minority in this world. Thought works slowly, and while the grass grows the steed starves. In whatever way such a problem is dealt with, somebody will find fault. In England the laity, the crown and parliament, took away from the clergy their immunities and privileges, brought them under control of the law, restored and maintained the orthodox faith, and left the clergy reformed and purified to teach and administer it. In England happily the thinkers had the management, and the change was nowhere carried through so peacefully or successfully. Yet that has not pleased people either. None of the

Reformers are more savagely condemned than the English. We see in Germany the majesty of the nation in the person of the Emperor doing public honour to the memory of Luther. Who pays any honour in England to Cromwell or Cranmer or Latimer? Yet Cromwell and Cranmer and many more offered and sacrificed their lives for the liberties which we still preserve and cherish. Cranmer left us as a monument of his services the English Bible and the English Prayerbook. Is that nothing to be grateful for?

The world might have waited till doomsday for any change from within—that is, from the Church itself—yet things are so constructed that injustice and wickedness in high places cannot continue for ever. Indignation accumulates like electricity. The batteries are filled though no one knows it, and some accident explodes the charge.

Alexander VI. had gone to his account, poisoned in a cup of water which had been mixed for another. His body had turned black as a mulberry. They huddled the hideous object into a coffin too small for it. They had thrown a cloth over it, and punched it in with their fists. Julius II. followed, began to build St. Peter's, filled Europe with war and bloodshed, died and went none knew where—as there seemed authentic news that St. Peter had refused to let him into paradise. To Julius had succeeded Leo X., the son of Lorenzo de' Medici, the charming and elegant patron of art and literature, who, as one of his admirers said innocently, would have been a perfect Pope had he known or cared anything for religion or piety. He it was who is said to have remarked that Christianity was a profitable fable. What else could he suppose it to be if a person like himself was at the head of it? It was pagan Rome over again. Augurs meeting in her streets smiled in each other's faces.

The splendid tastes of Leo had emptied the Roman treasury. He wanted money, and he resorted to the time-honoured expedient of an issue of indulgences, to be offered at a moderate price to the faithful all over the Catholic world. What indulgences were, nobody precisely knew. Originally they meant no more than a relaxation of the ordinary Church discipline—permission to eat meat in Lent, and such like. As time went on they assumed a graver character. Plenary indulgences were issued at the Crusades; a sort of papal benediction; an intimation that the buried sins of warriors risking their lives for God and Christ would not be sharply looked after. The practice, once established, was continued as an easy means of raising money, and it was found better to leave the meaning of it undefined. Casuists said that indulgences were a remission of penances inflicted by Church authority on confession of sin. Objectors answered that penances were medicines ordered for the health of men's souls; that it was a strange way of doing good to a sick man to absolve him from the necessity of taking his physic. But the system was popular, and the longer it continued the wider the construction that was placed upon it. The sense of sin was uncomfortable, repentance difficult, and penance or purgatory disagreeable. It was pleasant to feel relieved by a Pope's remission, which could be bought for a few shillings. The authorities perhaps considered that, if the indulgences could do no good, at least they could do no harm. When questions were asked about them by curious persons or councils, the explanation finally given had been that the merits of the saints exceeded what was required for their own salvation; the excess was laid up in the papal treasury for the Pope to distribute. If at any time the supply was insufficient, Christ's merits were infinite and inexhaustible for the Pope to draw upon; and the merits of the saints and the merits of Christ together would be imputed to those who had no merit of their own, if they had faith enough to buy the indulgences.

It is interesting to observe that this was the origin of the Protestant doctrine of imputed righteousness—I mean of the particular and prominent position which it assumed in the Lutheran theology. The Pope's doctrine was that sinners could be saved by the imputation of the saints' merits with Christ's in addition. Luther said that saints have not merit enough to save themselves, that no action of man is good enough to stand God's scrutiny. The work is Christ's alone. He found the belief in substitution already established. He accepted it, with a change of persons. The difference was that Luther required faith and repentance and a renewed life, if the imputed righteousness was to be of any avail. The papal method required only a ducat or two.

Naturally, men were glad to save their souls on such easy terms. The practice became so universal that the Jesuit Cardinal Pallavicino admits that it formed a chief source of the Pope's revenue. The disposal of the indulgences became an ordinary branch of business. There were established official collectors, and such situations were so lucrative that they also were purchased at a high price.

Leo X.'s necessities were excessive, and required special exertion. Contracts were entered into for different countries. The contract for Saxony was given to Cardinal Archbishop Albert, Elector of Mentz, a youth of twenty-eight, who resembled Leo in taste and habit. The arrangement was convenient for both parties. Cardinal Albert was in straits for money, having agreed to pay 5,000 ducats for his installation, and having been obliged to borrow of the Fuggers, the great financial agents of Augsburg. The intended issue had been much talked about. It was growing towards daylight in Europe, and the forms of things were clearer than they used to be, and there happened at this time to be a certain monk at Wittenberg teaching theology at the university there, who felt called on to make a protest.

I suppose you all know something of Luther's history. The Luthers (the name is the same as Lothair) were Thuringian peasants. Hans Luther, Martin's father, was a mining mechanic; a skilful, hard-working man, who had raised himself by his industry, had furnaces of his own, and had made himself valued and appreciated by the Counts Mansfeld, on whose territory he lived.

Martin, his eldest boy, was born on November 10, 1483. He was brought up severely but wisely. His father and mother were both of them strict disciplinarians. When nine years old he was sent to a village school, and thence, as he showed talents, to schools of higher character at Magdeburg and Eisenach. He was a serious, earnest lad, who had his thoughts running ever on his soul, and on what was required of him. He had set his heart on being a priest, that he might devote himself entirely to God's service. His father, who knew better how unlike the ideal priest of Martin's imagination was to the real thing, objected and dissuaded, and sent him to Erfurt to study law. But it was to no purpose. The Bible was a rare book in Germany, but Martin found a copy of the Vulgate in the Erfurt library. He devoured it day and night. The world assumed a new aspect to him. A thunderstorm became a preternatural revelation. His eagerness grew unrestrainable, and, to his father's disappointment and sorrow, he became a monk in the Augustinian monastery. His conception of monastic life was of the ideal asceticism of the rule of the founder; he threw himself passionately into the system. Erasmus, like Martin Luther, began as a monk, but saw through it all, hated it, never believed a word of it. Luther accepted it as a counsel of salvation, fasted, whipped himself, wore hair shirts, slept on the bare stones, with the simple and humble consciousness of unworthiness which is almost always most acute in the most innocent.

Such a character was unusual in those days, and drew the attention of the Vicar-General, Staupitz. The excitement wore off as he grew older. He began to see things as they were, and became restless and miserable. His superior saw that his mind required distraction by work. The Elector of Saxony had just founded a university at Wittenberg, and Luther was sent thither to teach. He was still ignorant of the world beyond his own circle. If things were disordered in Germany, he still believed that in Rome, the centre of Christendom, the scene of martyrs' deaths, all was holy and good. In 1511, when he was twenty-eight, he was sent to Rome on business of the order. His eyes were opened and were never closed again. Throughout, his experience was a parallel and a contrast with that of Erasmus. Both visited Italy. Erasmus went with high-born pupils and horses and servants; Luther walked there barefoot and penniless, lodging at monasteries as he went along. Both saw Julius II. Erasmus saw him at Bologna in the splendour of a military triumph, and observed him with amused contempt; to Luther he appeared as a heathen emperor, the centre of a splendid atheistic court. Pope and priest were alike. Luther heard, so Protestant legend tells us, a celebrant at the altar say at the awful moment, 'Panis es, et panis manebis.' Ever after, in his own wars with the Papacy, he blessed God that he had witnessed these things with his own eyes; had he not seen Rome himself, he might have feared that he had done the Pope wrong.

He returned to Germany disenchanted, shocked, but not inclined to rebellion, determined that he in his own department of things would do his duty, whoever failed in theirs. He lectured at the University of Wittenberg; he preached in the great church there, and drew the attention of the Elector Frederick. His appearance was remarkable, especially his eyes, which people called demonic. They were black, with a yellow rim round the iris, such as you see in the eyes of a lion. 'This monk has strange ideas,' the Elector said, after hearing him preach. Among other ideas were reflections on the Pope's indulgences. On hearing what was to be done, he wrote to the Elector of Saxony; he wrote to his own bishop; he wrote to Cardinal Albert, who had taken the contract, to protest against it. The Elector wrote to the Cardinal also. But indulgences were an affair of the spirituality, with which the secular powers had no right to interfere. Cardinal Albert wanted his money, and cared neither for the Duke of Saxony nor for the monk of Wittenberg.

In other parts of Europe the trade went on as usual. The Cardinal put the business for Saxony into the hands of the Dominican Tetzel, whose name has been placed in the historical pillory for his share of the transaction. Tetzel went about his work as if to challenge notoriety, going from town to town with a train of priests and choristers ringing bells and swinging censers, like a procession of Corybantes. The churches were decorated to receive him, a red cross was set on the altar, a silk banner floating from it with the papal arms, and an iron dish stood at the foot to receive the money of the purchasers who came to trade. Tetzel himself, from the pulpit, exhorted every sinner to use his opportunity and come and buy salvation. No sin, he said, was so gross that an indulgence would not cover it. The efficacy of the remedy was proved by one plain argument—that any one who doubted was damned eternally.

It was said, besides, that Tetzel and his companions were dissolute livers, and spent their share of the spoil in drink and debauchery. It may have been so, but such charges are easily brought and easily believed. If Tetzel had been a saint, his errand was an equally disastrous one to his employers. On his way through Saxony he was approaching Wittenberg, and, remonstrance having failed, Luther resolved to speak.

The doctrine of indulgences had never been authoritatively defined. It was a common practice at the universities to hold debates on points of faith or custom which had been left undecided. Some challenger would undertake to defend a particular opinion, not as committing himself to the view which he offered to maintain, but as ready to argue it and hear what could be said on the other side.

On October 31, 1517, Luther set up ninety-five theses of this description on the various features of these papal pardons. He maintained that it was monstrous to suppose that a man could buy with a few coins forgiveness of his sins. God could pardon those who sincerely repented, but only on condition of their repentance. Popes could not pardon at all, nor could any other mortal. The Church might remit the penances which it had itself imposed, but it could not reach to purgatory. Those whom God had condemned must there remain till He Himself took them out.

The spark kindled the powder which was lying everywhere ready to explode. That one act opened the lips of Germany, and from all parts there rose instantly the cry of denunciation against the Church administration. Erasmus, the best of witnesses, for he himself stood apart from the movement, testified to the universal delight at what Luther had done. Kings, princes, bishops, priests, some even among the monks themselves, equally applauded. A brave man at last had been found to utter the thoughts of them all. There was no question of teaching any new doctrine or breaking the unity of Christendom. All honest men knew that the indulgences were a scandal which it was impossible to defend.

Now, how did the Pope and his friends behave? Erasmus says that if they had been in collusion with Luther they could not have acted more foolishly than they did. Leo was at first amused. 'Brother Martin,' he said, 'has a fair wit. It is only a quarrel of jealous monks.' When he read the theses he said, 'A drunken German wrote them; when he is sober he will be of another mind.' But he soon discovered that it was a serious matter. Erasmus thought that he should have employed some learned person to reply to Luther. Instead of this, he took to fulminating and cursing, and set on rabid, violent monks to cry ' Heresy !' and call for fire and faggot. It was an old method. Lucian represents the alarm of Jupiter, that, if the world left off believing in him, he would cease to exist. Jupiter goes with the other gods to hear a philosophic discussion on the subject at Athens, and he says to his own advocate, ' Do not argue. They will beat you at argument. Curse and rail. That is your strong point.' Leo acted like Jupiter. Luther had spoken no heresy. He had not denied any article of faith. The Pope was blinded by his own fury, and he was furious because he knew that his indulgences were indefensible.

Indulgences were but one of a thousand abuses out of which the Roman revenue had been fed. The bishops had their own grievances. They resented the preposterous sums which were extorted from them at their investiture. They resented the oath of obedience to the Pope which they were obliged to swear. They resented the exemptions from their authority, purchased at Rome by the monks and clergy, which made them ciphers in their own dioceses. To some extent the bishops were held to their allegiance by the resentment of the laity against their own spiritual courts, but all around were the dry materials of a conflagration ready to burst out. The agitation spread. In two years Luther's name was ringing in every corner of Europe.

One abuse was taken up after another. The printing-
presses rained pamphlets. Luther published tract on
tract; his own eyes were opening as he went on. The
Pope's defenders in Germany could not get their books
published, as it was observed all the compositors were
on Luther's side. The papal party were chiefly the
monks. The policy of Rome had been from the first
to secure the religious orders by keeping them immediately under the Holy See and forbidding the bishops
to meddle with them. The monks as a body remained
true to their salt, but in the end more to the hurt of
the Holy See than to its advantage. For the monks
were universally hated by the laity and by the secular
clergy too. The celibacy of the clergy, invented to
detach them from worldly interests, became now their
greatest danger. It had destroyed the social and
human relationship between themselves and the rest
of the community.

The fire burnt so fast that they did not try to
reason. The Pope took the position of injured
authority. He called the movement a rebellion. He
urged the secular powers to put it down with force.
He summoned Luther to Rome. It was remembered
how Huss had fared at Constance, and Luther was
advised not to go. Leo wrote to Maximilian, to the
Elector of Saxony, to other German princes, to seize
Luther, and send him to Italy to be tried for his offences; or, at least, to imprison him, silence him, silence
all his adherents, to punish especially the superior of his
own Erfurt convent, who had nursed such a cockatrice.

The princes not complying, the preaching friars cried 'Heresy!' louder and louder. Passion on one side called out passion on the other. The Pope sent nuncios to the German princes to remonstrate. He sent legates, either to persuade the secular powers to crush the movement, or, if that could not be done, to conciliate Luther himself—flatter him, bribe him— at all events, shut his mouth. He selected, says Erasmus, the worst persons whom he could have chosen: Aleander, who went first, had been Cæsar Borgia's secretary, trained in the infamies of the Court of Alexander; Cardinal Caietano, who followed, was insolent and furious; and the monks whom he sent about to preach were wild and blind as their master. Outcries had long been loud against the immoralities of the clergy. A Minorite preacher startled the world by saying boldly it mattered not how immoral a priest might be: salvation depended on the sacraments. 'Christianos ad leones!' was the cry of heathen Rome. Christian Rome had adopted the vices of its predecessor, and cried for stake and gibbet against those who wished to mend it. Again Leo wrote to the Elector of Saxony, sent the letter by Aleander, ordering him at once to seize and deliver up the child of iniquity, and threatening an inter- dict if he disobeyed. The Elector, with convenient irony, told Aleander that he was surprised the Pope should have appealed to a layman like himself to interfere in a spiritual quarrel. With more alarming significance, he refused either to imprison Luther or

to deliver him up till he had been condemned by
a Diet of the Empire. Hitherto the theory had
been that in all spiritual matters, or what they pleased
to call such, the civil power was the servant of the
ecclesiastical. The Church was to judge. The civil
power was merely to execute. It could claim no
opinion on a question of faith or on the merits of
an offender.

Those happy days, it seemed, were ended. Maximilian, the Emperor, gave the same answer as the
Elector of Saxony. A Diet had to be summoned at
Augsburg a year after the storm had begun, and
Luther was required to attend. Maximilian sent
him a safe-conduct, but John Huss's fate was in
everybody's mind. He, too, had gone to the Council
of Constance, with a safe-conduct from Sigismund,
and the council had seized and burnt him. Luther
obeyed, presented himself at Augsburg, and the Legate
Caietano urged that the same course should be taken.
But the Emperor and the Diet had pledged their faith
for Luther, and Caietano was not listened to. Neither
was the Diet inclined to condemn Luther. The subject was new, large, difficult, involving a hundred
questions. The Elector of Saxony, the most powerful
member of the Diet, and respected as the wisest, would
not hear of any summary decision. They must take
time and think. Caietano had been ordered (should
the Diet prove unmanageable) to try what he could
do with Luther himself. He was blamed afterwards
for having managed his negotiation badly. He had

been ordered to bribe and to flatter. He saw Luther and despised him. Luther, as yet a poor, simple man, entirely free from vanity, had written already to the Pope to promise to submit if the indulgences were dropped. He said the same to Caietano. He was very humble. It was not for him to fight single-handed with the head of Christendom. But Caietano would hear of no 'ifs,' and must have instant submission. 'Do you think,' said he to Luther, 'that the Pope cares for the opinion of Germany, or that the princes will take arms to defend such a creature as you are?' Luther says himself that his being so small a creature was a misfortune to the Pope. If the Pope had agreed, there would have been an end of the movement, and all would have gone on as before.

It was believed that Caietano, finding that the secular powers declined to arrest Luther, had formed a plan to seize and carry him off. Luther was warned, escaped in disguise from Augsburg, and returned to Wittenberg. The legate again threatened the Elector with excommunication. Luther offered to leave Saxony to save him from an open quarrel with the Church. The Elector refused to hear of it. Luther so far, he said, had done nothing for which he could be fairly blamed. He declared that he would protect him with all his power till the Wittenberg theses had been argued and answered.

Erasmus, speaking the common opinion of moderate men, declared that the whole business had been miserably mismanaged. In the whole army of noisy

monks, not a single sensible person had appeared.
They had but cursed and thundered: none had hurt
the Pope's cause more than those who had been
loudest in defending him. Luther published an account of his interview with Caietano. Leo, only
more exasperated, again despatched a nuncio with
fresh menaces. The child of perdition must and should
be taken, and sent to him at Rome. The nuncio was
obliged to report that, if the Pope required Luther's
arrest, he must send an army of 25,000 men to seize
him. Three-quarters of the German nation were now
declaring for him. Once more it was no question of
the faith. It was a question whether the Pope, by
his own arbitrary will, was to impose his own pleasure
upon Christendom.

To this it had come in two years. Opinion changes
slowly, and when the creed itself began to be touched
the unanimity ended—the position of parties changed.
It was a serious thing to break the established union
of Christendom. But the laity were demanding, in
a voice not to be mistaken, whether they were to
submit to scandalous impositions, which no serious
Catholic ventured to defend by argument, and whether
the Popes were to be allowed to burn or imprison anyone who ventured to oppose them. The Emperor Maximilian shared the general feeling of Germany. Luther
himself published a tract on the Papal Supremacy,
appealed to a General Council, or, if a General Council
could not be held, professed himself willing to submit
to a synod of German bishops.

The Popes dreaded a council because they could not trust the bishops. The Council of Constance had declared that the Popes themselves were subject to councils, and there was every fear that, if they met again, the bishops generally would be found of the same opinion. There were difficulties about a national synod, because the bishops had sworn allegiance to the Pope, and the laity, who had their own grievances, were certain to claim a voice in it. Something might have been done had Maximilian lived. But he died in the midst of the confusion, and the Imperial throne was vacant.

The Emperor was chosen by the German nation. There were seven Electors; three archbishops—Mentz, Trèves, and Cologne; and four lay princes—Luther's friend, the Elector of Saxony, the Duke of Brandenburg, the Count Palatine, and the King of Bohemia. Every German loved and honoured the Elector of Saxony, Frederick the Wise, as he was called. The Imperial crown was offered to him by the unanimous voice of the Electors. But the times were dangerous. The Turks were threatening Europe by land and sea, and the patriotic Elector considered that Germany would be safer under a prince of ampler independent power. The choice lay between two candidates: Francis I., who had succeeded Louis XII. on the throne of France, and Charles, Maximilian's grandson, sovereign of Spain, of the Low Countries, of Naples and Sicily, and of a new world beyond the Atlantic. Of Charles, I may have more to say to you hereafter; a

few words about him are enough at present. Philip,
son of Maximilian, and of Mary, daughter of Charles
the Bold, had married Juana, daughter of Ferdinand
and Isabella, and sister of our Catherine of Aragon.
Philip died early, leaving two sons: Charles, born in
the Low Countries in 1500, the first year of the century
—a date easy to remember—and Ferdinand, born in
Spain a few years later. Juana, their mother, went
mad of grief, it was said, for her husband, and was
placed in confinement. On Ferdinand's death she
was heiress to the crown of Spain. Many Spaniards,
jealous of Charles's foreign birth, would have had her
queen, spite of her infirmity, while she lived. But
Charles had been recognised as king, and had succeeded,
when no more than eighteen, to his enormous inheritance. He had been brought up in Flanders, under
Adrian of Utrecht, who was afterwards Pope. He
combined the most remarkable qualities of his several
ancestors: from Charles the Bold he inherited the
instincts of a soldier; from his grandfather, Ferdinand
the Catholic, the sagacity of a statesman; from Isabella
the proud genius of Spanish chivalry; from his mother
perhaps a slight touch of madness, for at some moments
of his life he resembled the Knight of La Mancha. He
had a natural piety, which might have become superstition if it had not been checked by powerful sense,
and he had been carefully trained in orthodoxy by his
tutor Adrian.

The combination of conditions pointed him out as
the fittest successor to Maximilian. There was division

of opinion, as it was feared that his independent power
might make him dangerous to German liberty. But
the Elector of Saxony, when refusing the crown for
himself, gave his voice for Maximilian's grandson, and
Charles of Spain became Charles V. of Germany. He
was in Castile when the election was made known to
him, and the first duty which fell to him was to consider
and, if possible, compose the Lutheran excitement. All
eyes and all thoughts were turned to him, and it was
generally expected that he would throw himself on the
Pope's side. He was young—not yet twenty. He was
a Spaniard, and no heresy was ever tolerated in Spain.
He had been trained by a cardinal archbishop, and
surrounded from his cradle with Catholic influences.
It was inevitable that, young as he was, he should take
the colour which had been impressed on him. When
the choice became known, Erasmus wrote to Luther to
tell him that he had nothing to hope from the new
Emperor. Pope Leo was of the same opinion. Charles
had already directed that Luther's writings should be
burnt in Spain and Flanders. Leo, confident of support,
issued a Bull declaring for indulgences and asserting as
a pious Catholic doctrine that the Pope's pardons would
serve the living upon earth and the dead in purgatory.
He went on to condemn Luther's writings, to order
them to be burnt, and to excommunicate Luther himself and all his supporters. He tried one more private
appeal to the Elector of Saxony to withdraw his protection. It was again ineffectual. The Elector said
he found much in the New Testament about Christ,

but little about Popes and bishops. He determined
still to stand by Luther, at least till he was condemned
by the lawful authority of a German Diet.

It was war to the knife now. How could a Pope
who sold indulgences, and anathematised and tried to
murder a man who had dared to remonstrate, be really
a Vicar of Christ? No Vicar of Christ he—but Antichrist. Rome was Satan's seat. Luther understood it
now—wrote his 'Babylonish Captivity,' and, in return
for the burning of his own writings, burnt the Bull and
a copy of the papal Decretals in the market-place at
Wittenberg. In this daring act he was throwing down
the glove to the whole system of ecclesiastical domina-
tion. It was, in fact, a declaration that the claim of
the Pope and clergy to be a superior caste, possessed of
preternatural powers, was an illusion and a fraud. His
thoughts rapidly crystallised, and the Lutheran theology
grew out of the denial of indulgences. The papal
Church talked of the saints' good works: no works of
man were good. All were defiled more or less by
something of sin. Christ's merits alone could save,
and the merits of Christ were secured to the soul, not
by ceremonies and sacraments administered by the
tainted hands of imperfect or wicked men, but by the
faith of the penitent himself. Salvation was no contract
between God and man: so many good works done, so
much merit accrued, and so much reward deserved.
Even between man and man no link could be formed
on such terms as that. The good servant was one who
devoted himself loyally and faithfully to his master;

did not ask for payment, but trusted in his master, believed in him and followed him.

The sacraments, baptism, and the Eucharist had been appointed by Christ; and in the Eucharist Christ was really present. But they were symbols, not instruments, and their efficacy did not depend on vicious or lazy priests, or on any priest at all. The movement, as I have said, was a revolt of the laity against the clergy. They had protested against a practical tyranny. They were now carrying their revolt into doctrine. Luther denied that under the Gospel there was any special priesthood with supernatural powers attached. The value of the sacraments depended on the faith of the receiver. There was no difference between a priest and a layman. Baptism or the Eucharist might be administered equally by either; and the whole fabric of ecclesiastical dominion which rested on the powers conveyed in ordination was declared to be based on falsehood.

His views developed by degrees, but the beginning was the burning of the Bull. He denied that he was teaching any new doctrine. He claimed to be reverting only to the faith of the Apostles, and appealed to the Bible to prove it.

Something had to be done. Every prince and baron, every gentleman, every burgher of the free cities had his grievance against the Church courts. The stir had brought them all to the surface. The Estates of the Empire had to be called together again, and the famous Diet of Worms was summoned to meet on January 21,

1521. The young Emperor was to preside and to meet for the first time his assembled vassals. It was a bitter thing for the Pope and the Church. They had claimed for themselves the exclusive control of doctrine and spiritual administration. That such subjects should be submitted at all to an assembly in which laymen sat and voted was itself as unwelcome, almost as menacing, a novelty as any heresy of Luther's. One more effort was made to avert so fatal a precedent. Luther had been already condemned by the Pope. Erasmus says that Charles was entreated to act in the usual way, and take and execute Luther without further trial. The Emperor refused. Luther, he said, should not be sacrificed till he had been heard in his own defence. He summoned him to appear, and sent a safe-conduct for him to last for twenty-one days. There was a vast gathering—princes, prelates, barons, knights, representatives from all the free cities of Germany. A papal Legate attended, with an array of theologians behind him, Aleander to prosecute and the divines to argue. Once more Caietano protested against the hearing of a condemned heretic. The precedent of Constance was brought up, and the opinion of that council, that in such cases safe-conducts need not be observed, was again alleged in all seriousness, as if it was nothing to be ashamed of. The Elector of Saxony said peremptorily that he would allow no violence to one of his own subjects. Faith given should not be broken a second time, even to please the Pope. Luther himself expected the worst. He was advised to fly. He refused.

128614

He would go to Worms, he said, in words that have
never been forgotten, 'if there were as many devils
there as there were tiles upon the housetops.' He
hoped only that the Emperor would not begin his reign
by a murder. If he was to be killed, he would rather
it should be done by the Pope's own myrmidons.

The crown of Germany was a splendid ornament,
but it conveyed little separate power. The Emperor
had no army, no revenue, no police of his own. The
several States were independent within their own
limits, and all public acts required the consent of the
majority of the Diet. The Emperor was young and
among strangers. The situation was new. The summons to Luther to answer for himself was the first
acknowledgment that a man under the Church's curse
had any civil rights remaining—in itself an enormous
fact. Before Luther's arrival at the Diet there were
seven days of stormy debate. The intention had been
to confine the discussion to the one subject. But
tongues could not be restrained, and the great hall
rang with outcries against a hundred scandals which
the most Catholic princes did not dare to defend.
'The monk makes work,' said a grim baron. 'Some of
us would crucify him, and perhaps we may do it; but
he will rise again the third day.'

Erasmus was not present; he wrote to protest
against violence, yet such was the rage that it was
doubtful whether the 'monk' would reach Worms
alive. Franz von Sickingen said that, if Luther was
murdered, he would not answer for what might happen

to Cardinal Caietano. Luther travelled from Wittenberg in a cart; an escort of cavalry volunteered to
protect him. Enthusiastic crowds met him outside the
gates of Worms, and the young Landgrave of Hesse—
ardent and hopeful, but as yet knowing little—wrung
him by the hand, saying, 'Dear Doctor, if you are right
God will protect you.' As Luther walked up the
audience hall George of Frondsberg touched him on
the shoulder with his gauntlet. 'Little monk, little
monk,' he said, 'thou hast a fight before thee which we
whose trade is war never faced the like of. If thy
heart is sound and thy cause good, go on, in God's
name, and fear not.'

George of Frondsberg, six years later, commanded
the German division of the Imperial army which
stormed and sacked Rome, and took the Pope prisoner.

LECTURE III

THE EDICT OF WORMS

MY last lecture ended with the meeting of the Diet of Worms in 1521. I know of no grander scene in history or fiction than the appearance there of Martin Luther to answer for his life.

A miner's son, a solitary Augustinian monk, had presumed to arraign and challenge a power which had reigned supreme for a thousand years over the fears or the reverence of mankind. Little as churchmen had shown in later centuries of Divine grace in their lives, they were still dreaded as possessed of awful supernatural powers. No one doubted that, however wicked they might be, they had the keys of heaven and hell. They only could bind, and they only could loose; their curse was fatal. To dare the anger of the priesthood was to challenge God Himself. The faith had encountered many a shock. But the storms went by, and it still stood, strong, not in itself (for its independent power was nothing), but strong in the superstition which persisted in regarding its ministers as the representatives of the Divine rule, whom it was impious to doubt or disobey. It held at its disposition the terrors of both worlds. The spiritual censures which affected the soul were supported by substantial and material penalties, which those who incurred them were made to feel to be too dreadfully real. In the world invisible churchmen were the arbiters of the eternal fate of the human soul. In the world visible there was the sword, the stake and the gibbet, for everyone who dared defy them, and the frightful power which they were able practically to exercise gave reality and probability to the spiritual dominion to which they pretended.

The ages, I often say, do not understand each other. If in these days the Church of Rome was able to persuade any secular power to burn a single heretic for it —as it in past centuries burned thousands—I suppose the whole system would at once be torn to atoms. We cannot realise the state of mind in which such things were possible; yet they would not only have been possible, but doubtless have been common as ever, except for individual brave men who dared to encounter the worst that tyranny could do.

The wonder was that any one was still found to dare, so hopeless the struggle had seemed. The Albigenses, the Vaudois, the English Lollards, had advanced in forlorn hopes and had fallen in the breach. The Bohemians had avenged the murder of John Huss and Jerome of Prague on eleven bloody fields; but they too had been crushed, and there remained only Jean Ziska's skin, which he bequeathed to his country to be stretched on a drum, and so keep alive the echoes of the eternal battle-music.

An impression had been made at last, however. Ziska's drum had not sounded for nothing, and there could have been no stronger evidence of the change that was coming than the scene now to be witnessed at the Diet of Worms. A quarter of a century earlier quick work would have been made of such a person as Luther. A Church court would have handed him over to the civil magistrate, and a stake in the market-place would have done the rest. At least a poor heretic could no longer be despatched in this way. He had been able to bring together the Diet of the Empire, and as a more extraordinary innovation, a question of religion, which the ecclesiastics had hitherto so passionately reserved to themselves, was now to be submitted to an assembly where clergy and laity were to sit and judge side by side. Rightly understood, this was the first step in the great lay revolt which was impending.

It was not understood at the time—Luther himself did not understand it. He had not expected to fare any better than those who had gone before him. He had looked for nothing but death, and this was the reason why he had so fiercely and scornfully defied the worst which the Pope could do. His death he supposed would serve the cause better than his life.

Erasmus thought him lost. As long as it was merely a question of indulgences the intelligence of Europe, even the conscience of Europe, had been at his side. But he had since struck the idol in the face.

When the Pope cursed him, he had retorted that the Pope was Antichrist; and it was not to be supposed that the custom of centuries, and the reverence to established authority, however unwillingly conceded, would go down at the first summons. The church-men were fighting for their existence, power, wealth, splendour, dominions—all which made life valuable. The princes and peers, who had so far been the mere instruments of the churchmen's orders, could not be expected to allow a single person, and one, too, who was himself a monk under vows of canonical obedience to fly in the face of the Vicar of Christ.

After the burning of the Bull at Wittenberg, Erasmus says that most moderate men had fallen off from Luther. Erasmus looked to what he considered certain to follow with anxious distress. It was not that he cared much what became of the monk of Wittenberg. In his opinion a great opportunity had been thrown away. The mass of the people, he said, were still on Luther's side, but the intelligent and the wise had withdrawn from his companionship. He could be saved only by civil war, which would not lightly be encountered. His remaining friends would certainly be in a minority in the Diet. He would be condemned, and the good work which he had done at first would be overthrown.

Never had the city of Worms witnessed a spectacle more magnificent than on the occasion when Luther appeared there. Deputies were collected from every part of the Empire; the young Charles, just twenty-one, pale, eager, intense, wise beyond his years, on the Imperial throne; the Roman cardinal in his purple, with his retinue of divines; German prelates in their robes; princes, and barons, with their knights and gentlemen, glittering in their steel coats in the pale light of the April afternoon; burgher representatives from the free cities—all passionate and heated with the seven days' angry debate on the corruptions of the Church, which had preceded Luther's arrival. Before them the mean, insignificant-looking monk in his brown frock, who had brought together that august assembly, standing there under the Pope's curse to be tried for his life.

He was led up the great hall. The usual formalities were despatched, and the legate and the nuncio demanded sentence upon him without debate as an excommunicated heretic.

A pile of books was brought into the court. He acknowledged them to be his, and he was then required to retract. He was nervous, brave as he was, and Charles, who examined him curiously and expected a more imposing presence, was at first disappointed. But he gathered firmness as he went on. He said his writings were of three sorts. Some contained plain Gospel truths which he could not retract. Some were directed against papal canons and customs which had tried honest men's consciences and had been made instruments of fraud and plunder. These, too, he would not disgrace himself by retracting. What he had written on those subjects was true, and he would

stand by it. A third sort had been written in heat,
attacks on particular persons, on the Pope especially;
in these he said he might have been too violent, and
it might be fit and right to retract them. He was
allowed a day to reconsider his answer. The Diet
adjourned, and next day met again. The proceedings
lingered into the evening twilight and the hall was
lighted up with torches. He stood for many hours at
the bar under a storm of cross-questions and reproaches.
He was warned of his apparently inevitable fate. His
mind and his nature rose to the level of the scene. He
gave his answers first in Latin and then in his own
vernacular German, that every layman might understand. There was a difficulty in convicting him of
formal heresy, for the points which he had raised were
new, and the Church's doctrine was undefined. At last
a decree of the Council of Constance was produced
which seemed to touch him, and, form and order all
forgotten in their eagerness, the priests and their
supporters shouted 'Retract! Retract!'

In a clear ringing voice, which still vibrates across
the centuries, Luther answered: 'Councils have erred.
Popes have erred. Prove to me out of the Scriptures
that I am wrong, and I submit. Till you have proved
it my conscience binds me. I can do no other. ('Ich
kann nicht anders.') God help me. Amen.'

Ich kann nicht anders—words for ever sacred in
every German heart when duty calls.

Unreserved retractation had hitherto been the sole
alternative offered to a heretic. When Luther ceased

a loud shout rose from the clergy: 'To the dungeon with him! To the dungeon with him!' But the lay princes and barons remembered their honour, and the Emperor himself said that Germany should not again be disgraced by the breach of a safe-conduct. Amidst a tempest of outcries, which would have passed to blows but for Charles's presence, Luther was allowed to withdraw without immediate sentence.

He had no hopes of acquittal. He was happy only in the thought that he had not disgraced himself. His friends received him with enthusiasm. 'I am through, I am through!' he cried, as the Elector of Saxony took him by the hand, and told him that he had done bravely and well. They were all exhausted. As in most human things, the commonplace jostled against the sublime. Duke Eric of Brunswick drained a tankard of beer, filled it again, and handed it to Luther, that he might refresh himself.

The Diet did not, could not acquit him. A majority in the great Council of the Empire could not, in the first instance, sanction an open breach with the established order of the world. The papal party was unanimous and resolute. The party of reform was divided and uncertain. Many who were delighted at the attack on the indulgences were offended, like Erasmus, at Luther's violence. Authority might be corrupt and might need mending, but for a private individual to fly in the face of it, defy it, and call it names, was to shake the principle on which society rested. All the laity, the Emperor along with the rest, agreed that the safe-

conduct should be respected, but it was to be construed
to the letter. It was limited to twenty-one days.
Luther was ordered home to Wittenberg, there to
remain till the three weeks were expired. If at the
end of them he had not made his submission, he was
placed under the ban of the Empire as an excommunicated heretic. The Elector and all other persons
were forbidden to shelter him. He was to be seized
wherever he could be found, and to be handed over
to justice.

The Edict of Worms was so memorable in Reformation history that it requires a more exact description.

The duty of the Emperor, it said, was to extinguish
heresy. Luther was infecting Germany with false and
pernicious doctrines. Evils of all kinds would follow if
he was allowed to go on. The Pope had condemned
him. A copy of the Bull had been presented to the
Emperor with a demand for execution. The Emperor
had consulted the Diet. Questions of faith belonged
to the Pope. Neither the Emperor nor the Diet had
jurisdiction in such matters. Luther, however, had
been heard in his defence. He had refused to retract,
and must now be dealt with as a heretic convict. He
and his accomplices must be arrested as soon as the
safe-conduct had expired. His writings were to be
burnt and never to be reprinted, and no books were
to be published anywhere touching the faith of
the Church, without consent of the bishop of the
diocese.

Such was the Edict. But to issue an edict was one

thing, to execute it was another. There was as yet
no sharp dividing line in Germany between Catholics
and Protestants. The lay part of the Diet, whether
advanced or moderate, felt that they owed too much to
Luther to consent to his destruction. Charles himself
had no wish to commence his reign with an execution
which would make him hateful to the mass of his
subjects. A way was found out of the difficulty.
Luther on his journey home through the forests to
Wittenberg was waylaid by a party of apparent banditti,
and spirited away to the castle of the Wartburg, in the
Elector of Saxony's dominions. It was given out that
he had been killed, and the secret was so well kept
that for many months no authentic news was heard
of him. Charles made no inquiries. He probably
suspected the truth, but did not wish to be too well
informed. Erasmus, who knew Charles well, said that
he too, like every other noble-minded layman in
Germany, had approved of the attack upon the indulgences, and did not wish to press too hard on a man
whose only fault was to have denounced them with too
much vehemence.

Meantime the movement rushed forward with its
own impulse. The Edict fell unheeded. A revolution
had set in which was not to be suppressed except by
civil war, and a civil war the Emperor early resolved
that there should not be till every other resource had
been tried. The debate in the Diet had opened his
eyes to the enormities of the papal system. He did
not choose to bring armies from Spain and Flanders to

maintain an odious tyranny, and his hands were soon full of other business, which left him no leisure to attend to the Pope's complaints.

Immediately after the Diet, the revolt of the Comunidades broke out in Castile. This was no sooner quieted, than the war began with France, which lasted, with brief intervals, for the rest of his life. Turkish armies came up the Danube. Lewis of Hungary, Charles's brother-in-law, was killed. Pesth was taken, and Vienna was threatened. The Mediterranean was overrun with Turkish and Moorish corsairs, who plundered the coasts of Spain and Italy, carried off Christian prisoners in tens of thousands, sold the poor as slaves and held the rich to ransom.

It was no time for the Emperor to make himself the minister of clerical revenge, or reimpose by force a detested despotism which he himself was rapidly growing to understand.

Luther meanwhile remained at the Wartburg for nearly a year, passing under the name of the Ritter George. By degrees it became known where he was, but it was thought better that he should remain in seclusion till the immediate danger was over. While there, he was engaged in a work which, more than anything else he ever did, immortalised his name and his influence.

The strength of Romanism lay where it still lies, in the craving of human nature for authoritative certainty about religion and our own souls. Death, when our short lives are over, lies before all of us as an inevitable fact—death, and the consciousness of the many sins which we have all committed.

To make existence tolerable, some fixed belief seems necessary as to the meaning of life and as to our condition hereafter. Such a belief, Romanism, with all its faults, professed to give, and if the authority of Rome was overthrown, there seemed nothing before any one but blank darkness. Unstudied, unthought of, except by a few, lay the sacred writings on which Romanism itself depended, where alone the truth was to be found which men were now demanding. Erasmus had published the text of the Greek Testament with a fresh Latin translation, and notes and paraphrases. Luther, while at the Wartburg, translated the Gospels and Epistles into vernacular German, with so much beauty and power that his version, as a mere piece of literary workmanship, has no rival, save in our own English Bible. The Old Testament was added after a year or two, and in this book, or book of books, each humble Christian could find for himself the answer to the eternal question, the account of the nature and responsibilities of human beings, acknowledged by the Church itself from the beginning to be authentic and inspired. Here, and nowhere else, was the authoritative certainty, the essential parts of which could be understood by all, needing neither Pope nor priest to interpret.

The Bible, as the old saying went, was the religion of Protestants. Luther's translation became the text of it for the German nation. Twenty years later came the English version, equally admirable, to spread over the globe, and mould the character of the Anglo-Saxon mind. This it was which did the work of the Reformation, which without it would inevitably have failed. 'The translated Bible,' Cardinal Newman says with reluctant admiration, 'is the stronghold of heresy.' It was the seat and centre of real infallibility to those whose consciences rejected the false infallibility of the Popes.

Erasmus must have his share of the honours. Before Erasmus's edition appeared, there was scarcely a single copy of the Greek Testament to be found in Germany outside the monasteries. A hundred thousand copies were sold immediately on the publication of that edition. It provided Luther with a correct text to work from, and the notes and paraphrases restored life and meaning to words which had become dead in the droning of the Vulgate.

What meaning the monks had got out of the Vulgate, Erasmus illustrates with a hundred instances. He was present once when some of them were arguing whether it was right to put heretics to death. A learned friar quoted from St. Paul 'Hæreticum devita.' He had conceived that by 'de vita' St. Paul had meant an order *de vita tollere*.

All was made clear now, and the Christianity of the Apostles could be contrasted with the vicious lives and tawdry teaching of the Popes and bishops.

Luther having appeared before the Diet, and returned alive from it, the first battle in the war was won. The Edict of Worms was a dead letter. Across the Continent, from Denmark to Switzerland, the people took the work of reform into their own hands in orderly, regular method. The monasteries were either dissolved by the secular authority, or dissolved of themselves. The Church courts were abolished, the bishops silenced or restrained. The images were removed from the churches. The private masses, the occasion of so much scandal, were forbidden, and the mass itself was converted into a decent communion service. The Church lands were sequestrated to the use of the several States; the revenues being employed to maintain schools, or for the modest salaries of the new pastors, who ceased to be regarded as priests, and married, and became like other citizens. All was done with the regulated enthusiasm of a conscientious nation carrying into effect the happy changes which they had so long desired. There was little passion, little violence, because there was generally but slight resistance. The free cities became Lutheran almost without exception. Erasmus himself witnessed, and wondered at, the order with which the city of Bâle reconstructed itself. Again I repeat, it was a revolt of the laity against ecclesiasticism, provoked by the audacious immorality of the secular and regular clergy, and the tyranny and extortion of ecclesiastical rule.

Of course in so vast a number there were many to whom the revolution was unwelcome. I must pause for a moment, for a few general words. In days like ours, when religion has become opinion, it is easy to

tolerate varieties of ritual and belief. At a time
when religion was a rule of life, it seemed as difficult
to allow two or more religions in the same country
as to permit two or more systems of law. A code of
laws grows in every community from the nature of
human society; every nation develops its own by
custom and enactment out of its character and traditions. None professes to be perfect. The best are
but approaches to abstract justice. Men form and
select what is most suited to their temper and conditions, and what practically answers best for the great
ends of equity.

What we mean by *law*, however, covers but a small
part of human conduct, and beyond the sphere of
definite wrongs forbidden by the civil magistrate, there
lies the broad region of moral duties which law cannot
reach. There grow up, therefore, everywhere parallel
to the laws, and by the same methods, what are called
national religions which insist on purity, truth, honesty,
piety, and sense of responsibility to God. Every man,
Plato says, is bound to believe that he is responsible
for his actions, and will have to give account of them
here or hereafter. This is the essence of a religious
creed, and it takes shape like the law, in rules of
action, in ceremonies, and in historical traditions.

These national religions are not perfect after any
pattern made on the Mount. It cannot be said of any
of them that they are abstractedly and absolutely true ;
and Plato again says that, about the traditionary part
of them, conscience ought to be left free. But in noble

nations they assume noble forms, and answer a noble end.   As a general explanation of a man's position and duty in this world, the creed which he finds established in his own country is infinitely nearer the truth than any theory which he could reason out for himself.   A religion which has established itself in usage and conscience is so infinitely precious as a restraint on evil passions, and a stimulus to wise judgment, that no sensible person, save at desperate extremity, will question the truth of it.   The legislator, according to Plato, will hold it his duty to protect such a creed from outrage.   If a man denied that the gods regarded human conduct, or would punish wicked men after death, θανάτῳ ζημιούσθω, Plato would send him to the scaffold.

This is the theory set out in the Νόμοι.   It is a theory which has been consciously or unconsciously held, and acted on, by all wise statesmen, as long as religion is a rule of life, and has not degenerated into opinion, as long as it practically answers its purpose in purifying and elevating conduct.   Unfortunately in the sixteenth century it had ceased to answer that purpose.   The essential conditions had been forgotten. Conscience was bound when it ought to have been left free.   The things insisted on were ceremonies and traditions which had lost their meaning.   The θανάτῳ ζημιούσθω was applied to those who questioned the powers and privileges of a profligate clergy, a clergy who set an example of defying the morality which they were appointed to teach, and who were sending men

to the stake for metaphysical opinions, while they were
outraging the sense of Europe by personal profligacy.

Thus the problem for civil government had taken a
new form. No one doubted that it was the duty of
the magistrate to maintain truth. To allow the practice of more religions than one was as impossible as to
allow the practice of two laws. Toleration would
degrade religion from an authority into a disputed
opinion. What, then, was to be done ? The Emperor
Charles had begun on the old lines. He found the
Roman Church in possession. The faults had been
concealed from him. He had been told that religion
itself was in danger, and that he must extinguish
heresy in the germ. He had tried. He had issued the
Edict of Worms, and the Edict was passed over as
waste paper; but the instinct of order was in the
German heart. The people abhorred anarchy. They
did not want a schism. They believed and hoped that
Christianity could renew its youth and become again
what the Apostles had made it; and in the midst of
the confusion the cry rose everywhere for the General
Council to which Luther himself had appealed. Could
a council meet, the several States were willing to be
bound by it; but it must be a free council, not a
papal one. It must meet in Germany, for in Germany
it was most needed. The trouble had arisen from the
disorders of the clergy. The laity, therefore, must be
represented upon it as well as they. The Emperor,
not the Pope, must summon the meeting; for the Pope
and bishops were themselves to be called to account,

and the Pope in his Bull had prejudged the question of indulgences in his own favour. The wisest and best men in Germany must be called together, whether lay or cleric. Let them decide, and the whole nation would submit to their decision.

It was a sanguine hope, but not an unreasonable one. The doctrinal questions which were to cause such irreconcilable divisions were still in their infancy. The reform demanded was a reform of morals and discipline, a dethronement of an unrighteous tyranny, and a return to justice. In defect of a council, a national synod might be an alternative; but the whole Catholic lay world, even Spain itself, was crying for the same reforms which were demanded by Germany. Let a free council meet, in a free place, freely composed of all the orders. The corruptions of Rome would be ended, and all would be well. Austria and Bavaria, where the Edict of Worms had been partially executed, united in the same entreaty. Charles himself and his brother Ferdinand agreed in thinking that a General Council was the only remedy.

Rome understood the danger. Rome well knew that, bad as her case had been at Constance, she was in worse condition now. Her splendour and her prerogatives would have little chance of surviving in the presence of such a council as was asked for in Germany. Even the bishops she could not trust. The bishops had been among the worst treated of her victims. Left to themselves, even if the council could be confined to them, the first act of the bishops would be to repudiate their oath to the Holy See, and renew the decision of Constance. Among the uncertainties of the Vatican, there was one resolution fixed as fate—that no council should be held of which the Pope had not complete control.

The splendid reign of Leo X. was setting in gloom and storm. If the great Powers deserted him he was helpless; and singularly the only sovereign in Europe who seemed disposed to lend him a hand was the young Henry of England who was airing his theological attainments by writing a book against Luther. The rest were all cold or hostile. The Pope's power had no basis but belief. If his curses ceased to be feared, he was no better than any other man. Distracted, harassed, uncertain what to do or to whom to trust, he died when but forty-seven years old, and left the fire which he had so lightly kindled as a legacy to his successor.

Never had the cardinals more need of the guidance which was supposed to direct their choice than when they met to elect a successor to the magnificent Leo. Perhaps under the personal influence of Charles, perhaps in alarm at Charles's wavering attitude, perhaps to conciliate the Catholic part of Germany, they broke through their usual custom of electing only an Italian. They chose Adrian of Utrecht, who had been the Emperor's tutor. He had been the schoolfellow of Erasmus at Deventer. Adrian was a man who knew much of scholastic theology, and was learned in all the subtleties of the Angelical Doctor. But he was moderate, honest, experienced in public affairs, and had been tried in situations of difficulty. At the time of his appointment he was in Spain, where he had been sent as regent, after the rebellion of the Comunidades. He hurried off to Rome. A few months later he wrote to Erasmus, appealing to their old friendship, entreating his advice and help, praying Erasmus to visit him at the Vatican, and to write a book against Luther.

Erasmus's letters were often written for the world, and were meant to be preserved and published. He says himself that his reply to Adrian was designed only for his friend's eyes. At any rate, he wrote his opinion frankly for Adrian to accept or to leave:

'Your Holiness desires my advice in these confusions, and you wish me to join you at the Vatican. I would go with infinite pleasure if my health permitted, if the road over the mountains was not so long, and if the accommodation on the way was less detestable. Indeed, I should like to speak with you. Meanwhile you shall have my honest opinion. Your eyes and mine will alone see this letter. If you like my counsel, you can adopt it; if not, let it be regarded as unwritten. As to my writing against Luther, I have not learning enough, nor would a word from me any longer carry authority: such popularity as I once had is now turned to hatred. Once I was prince of letters, star of Germany, high priest of learning, champion of a purer theology. That is all gone. One party says that if I do not attack Luther, it is a sign that I agree with him. Luther's followers fall out with me because I have not come forward in his support. I wrote to Luther himself, advising him to be more moderate, and I only added to the number of my enemies; while at Rome and in Flanders, among my own people, I am called heretic, heresiarch and schismatic. I do not agree with Luther on a single point, yet they pick this sentence and that out of my writings to show that I say what he does, as if I could not find a hundred passages where St. Paul seems to teach his precise doctrine.

'Little did I dream when I was engaged with my own early work of the time which was coming. I cannot deny that I helped to bring it on; yet I was always ready to submit what I wrote to the Church's judgment. I begged that any errors that I might make should be pointed out, and nobody then objected to anything. Then there was only approval and encouragement, where now there is a scorpion under every stone. People seem as if they wished to drive me into rebellion, as they drove Tertullian and Arius. Believe me, those are your own best friends who recommend you to try gentle measures.

'The loud, violent champions of the Church estrange those who would otherwise remain orthodox and disgust them into heresy. Alas! that I in my old age should have fallen into such a mess, like a mouse into a pot of pitch. Your Holiness says, "Come to me at Rome, write a book against Luther. Declare war against him and his followers." If you tell a crab to fly, the crab will answer, "Give me wings."

I answer to you, "Give me back my youth and my health." What should I do at Rome? If I went, it would only be said that I was going there for a share in the spoils. If I attacked Luther when I was staying there, it would be alleged that I had been bribed. If I wrote moderately, I should be accused of trifling. If I imitated his own style, I should stir a hornet's nest.

'But you say, "What am I to do? Advise me. Help me." Well, then, some say that there is no remedy but force. That is not my opinion. If you try force, there will be frightful bloodshed. The question is not what heresy deserves, but how it can best be dealt with. Things have gone too far for knife and cautery. It is urged that the Wickliffites were suppressed in England—so they were; but the fire broke out again; and, besides, England is one country under one sovereign, Germany is a bundle of independent States, and I do not see how the thing can be done. If you mean to try whip and stake and dungeon, you need no help from me.

'Your own disposition, I know, is for gentle measures; but you are surrounded by people who think of nothing but their own interests, theologians who care only to keep their authority, monks who are in alarm for their luxuries, jealous and sensitive princes, and all with the bit in their teeth. How, you ask, with such councillors about you, can you arrive at any peaceful settlement? I would answer, "Look for the causes of what has happened and remove those.

Punish no one. Accept the past as a judgment from
Heaven upon our sins and grant a general amnesty."
If God forgives so much, surely God's Vicar can forgive. Entreat the magistrates throughout Germany
to prevent seditious innovations, and restrain the printing presses; and then give the world a hope that you
will reform the abuses of which it so justly complains.
If you ask me what those abuses are, send agents on
whom you can depend through the German States.
Let them consult the wisest men whom they can find,
and you will soon know.'

Adrian never answered this letter. Perhaps he
thought that Erasmus might have been less anxious
about his own skin and more willing to come forward
to help him. But he did what Erasmus recommended
so far as his nature allowed him. He was himself a
systematic theologian. He did not understand Luther.
He could not measure the influence of a free, noble,
original thinker over the imagination of mankind. But
even the Angelical Doctor himself could not have shut
his eyes to the scandals of the pardons and indulgences,
and the first act of the new Pope was to call the
cardinals together and consult on a question which
certainly needed answer—what indulgences were. If
only the remission of canonical rules and penances,
they were licences to a sick man not to take his
medicines. If they were held to extend to purgatory,
was it true that the Pope had any real power over
purgatory ?

He was told that, be that as it might, no one would

buy an indulgence unless it was supposed to benefit a soul in purgatory. A large part of his revenue was derived from the sale of these things. The trade was established, a body of persons engaged officially in the distribution were spread over the Catholic world. These officers had purchased their situations, and if the system was abolished, it would be necessary to reimburse them.

Adrian was not satisfied with this extremely practical view. He argued that if indulgences were legitimate, they were rewards for works of piety. They could only benefit a man to the extent of his own good deserts. To the wicked they could be of no benefit at all.

But it was precisely the wicked by whom indulgences were sought, men whose deserts were not good, and who desired to escape the consequences. Cardinal Caietano, fresh from Germany and his conference with Luther, explained that, however just the Pope's view on the matter might be, it was not a view which could conveniently be acknowledged to the vulgar. The trade would collapse altogether if the efficacy of an indulgence depended on the good qualities of the purchaser.

The Decretals, though vague in their language, implied that indulgences applied originally only to penances imposed in the Confessional. The explanation was at least plausible, and recommended itself to Adrian. He considered that all which would be necessary was to increase the penitential severities, and the penitents would then buy as freely as ever.

He was answered, however, that the time was passed for tightening Church discipline. The Church itself must have returned to purer conditions before it could venture heroic remedies. The laity would not bear them, and if Adrian tried such an experiment as that, instead of recovering Germany, he might lose Italy. Indulgences were an open question in the Church, and Adrian was recommended to leave them so.

He meant honestly. Indulgences were but one of many scandals which opened before him as he looked. The marriage laws, the pluralism, the entire system of dispensations, were contrivances to give rich men advantages denied to the poor. Simony stared him in the face at every joint of the ecclesiastical organisation. He wished to end all that, to do as Erasmus had advised, and show the world that, if he continued the war upon heresy, he meant at any rate to set his own house in order.

Francesco Soderini, an experienced old cardinal, who remembered Innocent VIII., and had served under five successive Popes, was obliged to moderate the zeal of the well-intending Adrian. He applauded the excellence of his purpose, but he reminded him that to encounter Lutheranism with a reform of the Church of Rome would be a confession that Luther had been right. The more he conceded, the fiercer would be the demands. Heretics had always commenced by denouncing the corruptions of the Court of Rome, but nothing had been gained by altering Roman practice to please them. To change established institutions was always dangerous, and the way to extinguish heresy was not by a reform, but by a crusade. Where were the Albigenses? Where were the Vaudois? Let Adrian offer the States of Germany which had taken up Lutheranism to the well-disposed Catholic princes, and he need have no fear that the Church would not find champions. In short, no serious reform could be undertaken without financial ruin. A fourth part only of the revenues of the Holy See came legitimately from the States of the Church. All the rest came from indulgences and dispensations, the Roman law courts, the annates, and the sale of benefices.

Adrian was unconvinced, but helpless. Charles was away in Spain busy with his French and Italian wars. The Turks had taken Rhodes, and were threatening Vienna again. Ferdinand, left to his own resources, was obliged to appeal to Germany for men and money, and at such a moment it was useless to attempt to enforce the Edict of Worms. A Diet was called again at Nuremberg, at which Ferdinand presided, and Adrian, baffled in his reforms, was tempted to try what could be done on the lines advised by Soderini. He sent a Nuncio to the Diet, in the hope that the orthodox princes might be gained over. He wrote a long protest against the disregard of the Worms edict. Luther had returned to Wittenberg. Adrian complained of the insult to the Church of permitting a man, condemned and under the ban, to be at large and unpunished. He said that they ought not to allow a single monk to lead them away from the customs of their ancestors. The interest of the Church was the princes' interest. If the Church was defied, the princes would be defied. If the Church was plundered, they would be plundered. He urged them to use the sword promptly and to save society. Luther was another Mahomet. Scripture sanctioned severity against spiritual rebels. He quoted the familiar illustrations. Dathan and Abiram, Ananias and Sapphira, were signal examples of the fate which overtook the enemies of the Holy Spirit. He was not even ashamed to refer to the execution of Huss as a precedent which the princes might conveniently follow.

With the infirmity of honesty, however, the Pope admitted, and he ordered his Nuncio to admit, that the revolt of Germany had been provoked by the immoralities of bishops and churchmen and the peculiar abominations of the Holy See itself. He protested an earnest intention of reforming the Roman law courts at the earliest moment. The poison had gone so deep that he could only move slowly, but he promised that the extortionate charges in those courts should be looked into immediately: meanwhile he trusted that the princes on their side would check the progress of revolution; especially that they would forbid the scandal of monks and nuns running about the country and marrying, and would send them back into their convents.

Germany was still one in heart on the great question. The division into Protestants and Catholics which afterwards envenomed the quarrel had not yet begun. The contest so far was between the moral sense of the laity of all sorts and the pretensions and scandals of ecclesiasticism. At the Diet of Nuremberg princes, barons, burghers were of the same opinion. They would not be taken in by smooth words and promises. They were willing to vote supplies against the Turk, but only on condition that reform should be taken up in earnest. Even Ferdinand himself was obliged to go with the rest, for half the Privy Council at Vienna were open Lutherans. Perhaps he went with his own will. Of all the princes, except the Elector of Saxony and the Landgrave, Charles and Ferdinand were the most consistent from first to last in insisting on the urgency of reform.

The Diet replied to the Nuncio that the Edict of Worms had not been executed for important reasons. Luther had opened the eyes of Germany. He was respected and admired there and could not be arrested without a civil war. The Pope must begin the purification of his own court and prove that he was in earnest. Meanwhile supplies were needed for the Turkish war, and the annates, which had been originally granted for the defence of Christendom against the Moslem, and which had been so long misappropriated by the papal treasurers, would be applied to their legitimate purpose, and would no longer be remitted to the Pope.

For the rest, the administration of the Church had been so corrupt that it could only be remedied

by a council; a council, not of bishops only and called
by the Pope, but one in which the laity should have
a voice, and which must be called by the Emperor.
Such a council there must be, and it must be called
within a year. If the Pope agreed, the Diet would
undertake that Luther and the preachers should be
silent until the council had sat and given in its
decisions.

This was peremptory enough. The conclusion had
a further sting. The Pope had complained of the
marriage of monks and nuns and other excesses of
renegade clergy. The Diet replied that the marriage of
the clergy was not forbidden by any law of the civil
government. If it was an offence at all, it was a
spiritual offence which the Church must deal with as
it could. The State could not interfere. The immunity
of the clergy from the criminal law was the most
cherished of ecclesiastical prerogatives. The Diet said
that, although they could not interfere with clerical
marriages, they would undertake that if any clerk
committed a felony, he should be punished like any
other offender.

Bitter as aloes to the Nuncio, who did not know
that a page had been turned in the world's history.
The Nuncio protested. At least he hoped that the
Diet would not persist in the rough handling of felonious clergy. They belonged to Christ and the Church.
Apostasy itself could not withdraw the clergy from the
authority of the Church.

The implacable Diet, instead of yielding, replied

with the remarkable address to the Pope known in Reformation history as the 'Centum Gravamina,' the hundred grievances, for which the laity of Germany demanded redress, the catalogue of wrongs which had accumulated for centuries, and were now brought up for judgment.

It was a frightful list, deliberately drawn, not by platform orators or polemical advocates, but by the united council of the Estates of the German Empire. Every gift which the Church had to bestow had been prostituted for money. Its courts had sold justice. It had sold its benefices, sold its absolutions and dispensations, sold its sacraments, sold even baptism and the Eucharist. In a hundred forms the priesthood had plundered and tyrannised over their miserable flocks, and the moral conduct of too many of them had been as disgraceful as their administration had been iniquitous.

Having thus given in their answer to Adrian's demands, and in turn presented their own, the Diet passed the votes for the war and then dissolved. The 'Centum Gravamina' were printed and circulated through Europe as the stern voice at last grown articulate of the long-suffering laity.

Adrian had little thanks at Rome for his honest admissions. In his simplicity he had pleaded guilty to charges which he ought to have denounced as slanders. Too plainly it was foreseen by the cardinals that by his needless confessions he had infinitely increased the difficulty of resisting the demand for reform.

He read the report of his Nuncio, and read in it the utter hopelessness of his own situation.   For him as for Leo there was no resource but to die and escape the shame of leaving promises unexecuted, which he would have been forbidden even to attempt to fulfil.

LECTURE IV

CLEMENT VII

A DRIAN was gone ; and with him had gone the last hope of spontaneous reform in the Court of Rome. The cardinals would have no more foreigners ; one experiment was enough. They fell back upon their own Italians, on whom they could rely to try no rash adventures. They elected another Medici cardinal, known to English history as Clement VII. He had for many years been governor of Florence, and had brought away with him a fair reputation. He was easy-going, witty, humorous, a patron of art like his kinsman Leo X. ; but he had no ostentatious vices. He was hot-tempered but not ill-natured ; he had some Italian patriotism, and a large share of Italian adroitness.

No reforming fervour was to be looked for from such a Pope, but also no violence. Being far off at Florence, he had perhaps heard less than the rest of the cardinals of the German tempest. After his elevation he endeavoured to understand it. He studied the 'Gravamina,' and he perceived that, though Rome did not escape, the weight of the complaints was against the local tyranny of bishops and their officials. He saw, like Erasmus, that it had been a mistake to trust the management of the situation to the over-bearing insolence of Caietano or Aleander. The Diet was to meet again at Nuremberg. He chose as a Nuncio to represent the Holy See there Erasmus's friend, the smooth, good-humoured, moderate, and rational Cardinal Campegio, who was sent afterwards to England to settle, if possible, Henry VIII.'s divorce case. Imperiousness and obstinacy had produced no effect; Germany was practically united in the determin-ation to bring the clergy under the law, take from them their independent jurisdiction, abolish or limit the privileges which they had abused, and compel them to reform their discipline and morals.

But in all movements there is a moderate and an extreme party. Extremes of all kinds have much in common. The clericals called for fire and sword against all who denied the Pope's authority. Extreme Lutherans insisted on clearing violently away every-thing which they called idolatry. There could not be two laws in the same country; both said alike that there could not be two religions; therefore, when the Communion had been substituted for the Mass, the advanced reformers said that the Mass was not to be permitted. Between these, especially among the reasonable and the educated, there was a middle party, who knew that it was neither wise nor necessary to sweep ruthlessly away the customs and traditions of ages. Some of them, perhaps, thought that they had not gained much liberty if, instead of scholastic definitions, they were to be entangled in fresh dogmas on free-will and justification.

To reform practice was one thing. To revolutionize doctrine was another. Pronounced Lutherans said the tree is known by its fruit. Teach a 'pure faith, and abuses will disappear, and a righteous life grow out of it as the fruit grows. Princes and statesmen who were responsible for the peace of the world, Charles and Ferdinand in Germany, Henry VIII. in England, thinkers like Erasmus and Sir Thomas More, said it might be so if the new doctrine was absolutely and exclusively true. But who could say ? The Catholic faith had been taught for a thousand years. It was woven into the organisation of the world. In practice the Church had become corrupt, and must be reformed ; but in principle its morality was pure. It insisted on all the duties which religion had been established to teach. The Catholic Church might be maintained if the abuses were corrected. Customs, if they did no moral harm, need not be interfered with. The new ideas might be allowed to grow, if they were not thrust on other people till it was seen what was in them. This, if you will think of it, was the exact principle of the Reformation in England. It was especially the view of Erasmus and Charles V., and was largely held in the German Diet. It may be called a reasonable view ; one regrets that reason has so little to do with the management of human things. The world is governed by superstitions, customs, passions, interests and emotions ; least of all by reason.

The mission of Campegio to Nuremberg was addressed to the tendency which I have described. Erasmus was eloquent about his fitness for the post which he had undertaken. They were close correspondents, and Erasmus had probably instructed his friend what to do. ' He came,' says Erasmus, ' prepared to make large concessions, to allow the Cup to the laity, and, more important, the marriage of the clergy.' Campegio, as little as Leo, intended to agree to any reform in the Roman papal system, but something had to be done if it was to be avoided. He was extremely skilful, polite, deferential, especially to leading laymen. He examined the new doctrines, made various good-natured remarks on them, and hinted that innovations were dangerous ; but said he had come to consult and not to prescribe. Such an attitude exactly met the feelings of the moderate part of the Diet. They generally agreed with him about the doctrines, but they required an answer to the hundred grievances. Campegio assured them that the Pope had examined into the hundred grievances. He had found some things which required attention, especially in the behaviour of the local Church courts and the bishops. In other points the complaints were less reasonable. The language about the supremacy of the Holy See savoured of heresy. He said he had no commission to deal with the subject, but would willingly talk the matter over privately with them.

Passion was still at spring-tide, and the moderate party were in a minority at the Diet. But all still agreed that there must be a council; a council must meet in Germany as soon as possible. Meanwhile a committee might be appointed to consider Luther's doctrines, and determine what should be taught in the interim. A committee of laymen, or a committee where laymen were to have a voice, struck to the heart of the Roman system. It was almost as horrible as the responsibility of felonious clergy to the criminal law, but Campegio was infinitely prudent. He worked privately on the alarms of the Catholic princes, especially on the Duke of Bavaria and Ferdinand. He suggested a plan of his own for dealing with criminal clerks. He admitted as frankly as Adrian that the clergy had been loose livers, and the ecclesiastical courts extortionate. Thirty-seven articles were sketched out for the restoration of discipline, for the limitation of the bishops' authority to deal with laymen, and other points on which the 'Gravamina' had been loudest. To these he thought that the Church would agree if, on the other side, the innovations could be checked and the printing-presses laid under a censorship.

He could not persuade the Diet to be satisfied. The Catholic princes would have been contented with the articles. But the Lutheran party exclaimed that only the minor iniquities were touched by them. The great offenders would escape. As to censorship of the press and such like, no further restraint could be permitted till the whole Roman system was examined and reformed. They still demanded their council in Germany. A council they must have. These concessions were only excuses to enable the Pope to escape a hateful necessity. The Diet broke up without any step being taken towards reconciliation. But Campegio had not altogether failed. The Catholic princes consented to repress innovations in their own territories on the understanding that the Pope would do what Campegio had undertaken for him ; the Austrian and Bavarian students, who were learning heresy at Wittenberg, were ordered to return to their homes, and Campegio went back, having succeeded in dividing the enemy and introducing a rift into Germany which was to grow at last into the Thirty Years' War.

The Diet had no sooner broken up than another serious misfortune overtook the reforming party. As Adrian had foretold, religious anarchy was followed by social anarchy. The principle of authority had been shaken. Disorder was contagious, and socialism began to show itself three centuries before its time. Under the Gospel it was said that all men were equal. Of all inequalities, the division of mankind into rich and poor was the least endurable. 'La propriété c'est le vol.' Property was theft, and must be divided. A fanatic prophet called Münzer, an Anabaptist Fifth-monarchy man, started up in Thuringia, inciting the peasantry to insurrection. They burnt castles and houses, they levelled fences, committed the usual revolutionary excesses. Thuringia was in the dominions of the Elector of Saxony. The reputation of the

Reformation was at stake. All that its opponents had said of the effects of a change of religion appeared to be fulfilled. The Elector and the Landgrave of Hesse promptly brought a force into the field, and crushed the insurrection before another Diet could meet. Münzer was hanged, and order was restored; but many thousand poor people had been killed. The effect was a serious scandal, and strengthened the Catholic reaction.

More serious still, and more alarming to Germany, was the great victory of the Imperial army at Pavia and the capture of Francis I. The contention between the French and Spaniards for the possession of Italy was of old standing. The Italian States were too jealous and too divided to maintain their own independence. Spain had conquered and occupied Naples and Sicily. The French, having tried and failed to expel them, claimed Lombardy and Savoy as their share of the spoils. Francis I., young, chivalrous, possessing all the fine qualities which disguise and gild ambition, and disappointed in his suit for the Empire, had found or made a pretext for declaring war against his rival, had crossed the Alps with a powerful army, overrun Lombardy, and despatched half his troops to Naples to complete the work and drive the Spaniards out. The King with the flower of his force was ruined by his own confidence. He allowed himself to be surrounded at Pavia. His army was cut to pieces. He was himself taken prisoner and sent to Spain. He summed up the catastrophe in the brief theatrical despatch that all was lost but honour.

The political aspect of this great incident cannot be considered here. The Emperor, it was thought, would now be master of Europe. Universal monarchy was in the air. There was but one sun, people had said, and there ought to be but one sovereign. In Germany the more practical fear was that Charles would use the opportunity to enforce the Edict of Worms; would call a Diet at Speyer, the Imperial centre, and issue his mandate for the restoration of the papal authority and the punishment of the disturbers of order.

The alarmists were not altogether mistaken. Politicians seldom gauge the strength of movements which rise among the common people, especially of religious movements. Charles, however, though still young—he was only twenty-five—was too wise to rush into precipitate measures. More than ever he was convinced of the necessity of a reform of the Church, and convinced too that Popes and bishops must be dealt with sternly, if reform was to be got out of them. He too had consulted Erasmus, and Erasmus had given him the same advice which he had given to Adrian. With Francis a prisoner, the French power broken, and no one to resist him, he felt strong enough to assume an air of authority. He sent to the Diet to ask why the Edict of Worms had not been executed, but he coupled the enquiry with an intimation that he was going into Italy to talk with the Pope, and that he would insist on the call of a General Council.

A council, yes; but what sort of a council? The

Germans wanted a national council, called by the Emperor himself—a council sitting on the Rhine or the Danube where they would themselves preponderate. Neither the Pope nor the Lutherans knew precisely what to expect of him. The Diet stood firm. To his question why the Edict had not been carried out, the Lutheran princes and the representatives of the free towns replied, as they had replied to Adrian, that it could not be done without a civil war. A council would be welcome, but not a council presided over by the Pope. On the other hand, Clement and the cardinals knew too well that they would not find any complaisant instrument in Charles. After Pavia, in their guilty consciences, they had expected to see him sword in hand before Rome, come to call them to account for their misdoings. He might summon a council which would reduce them to shadows. They had left themselves no friends. The laity were everywhere open-mouthed against them. Even Charles's own Spanish bishops would like nothing better than to see him cleanse the Augean stable. The Emperor had even gone so far as to write to the College of Cardinals telling them a council must meet whether they liked it or not, and that if the Pope refused, they must call a council themselves. He even added a menace that, unless they obeyed, he must do what Germany desired, and put the matter into the hands of the Diet, or of a national synod.

Charles, like most other sensible laymen, wished to preserve the established order of things, if he could

make it any way tolerable. He would rather mend
it than end it. Clement and the Sacred College had
no intention of being mended if they could help it.
Pavia had produced other consequences besides the
spiritual, and the fishermen of St. Peter saw a chance
of benefitting themselves by throwing their lines in the
troubled waters.

France had provoked the Italian war. France was
justly to be made to pay for it. Hard conditions of
peace were exacted from Francis at Madrid, conditions
which, if executed, would have crippled the French
monarchy. The balance of power was being disturbed.
Italy, Germany, even England, the Emperor's hereditary
ally, took alarm at the enormous power which Charles
seemed now to possess. It was more in appearance
than in reality. The Empire, in spite of Pavia, was
more a name than a force. Naples and Sicily required
an army to defend them, and rather strained his resources than added to them. The gold-mines of Mexico
and Peru terrified European imagination, but gold-
mines cost money to work and do not permanently
yield much revenue.

The essential strength of Charles lay in Spain and
Flanders only ; but it was magnified by illusion, and
Europe began to think that it must combine to defend
itself. The Pope saw the growing alarm, and took
advantage of it. Terrified at the threat of a council,
he preferred to set the world on fire like Julius II., and
he went to work in the same way as his predecessor.
Julius at his election had promised a General Council ;

when he became Pope he absolved himself from his engagement. Clement ventured to make use of the most insolent and detestable of the papal prerogatives. Francis before he renounced his freedom swore solemnly to observe the Treaty of Madrid. Clement absolved him from his oath. It was the most daring defiance which he could offer to the Emperor; but he looked on Charles as more dangerous to him than Luther or Lutheranism. This was not all. As Pope he was spiritual head of the Church, but he was also temporal sovereign of a large part of Italy. In that capacity he formed a league among the Italian princes, with France for an ally, to resist Charles's further progress. When, as he thought, he had secured himself, he replied to the demand for a council by charging Charles with having caused the miseries of Italy and threatening him with war.

The distinction between the Pope as supreme bishop and the Pope as a temporal prince was intelligible in theory, but was hard to maintain in practice. The Popes themselves never observed it. Julius II. excommunicated Louis XII. when he went to war with him; and to a sincere Catholic prince like Charles, who still regarded the curses of the Church as a thing to be avoided, Clement's conduct was at least embarrassing. He remonstrated, but he showed no fear, and let Clement see that in extremity he could and would fall back on the support of Germany. Again he pressed on the Pope's attention the demand of the Germans for a council of their own. He had refused his consent so far to please the Holy See, but he again insisted that the alternative was an ecumenical council, and again warned the Pope, with significant repetition, that if it was refused he would try other measures. He said that the Germans justly complained of the Pope for having decided the case of the indulgences before it had been heard. ' Just complaints ' was an expression which did not pass unobserved. How far did Charles really mean to go ? It was open to him, if he chose, to do what Henry VIII. did afterwards in England— fall back upon the Diet, as Henry did on Parliament, reform the Church, and maintain the orthodox faith, with the help of his own lay councillors. His own subjects, the Flemings, even the Spaniards, would not have complained, so utterly had the Popes lost the respect of everyone out of Italy. All earthly temptations drew him that way. He had but to place himself at the head of the German movement to be the most popular prince in the world. He could have saved orthodoxy by sacrificing the Papal Supremacy. He might have saved even the priesthood by preserving the form and bringing ecclesiasticism under lay control, as his uncle Henry had done ; and the true and noble features of Luther's creed might have been introduced without hurt into the Church's teaching.

The Pope expected nothing else, and published the Emperor's threats in his own justification. His only hope appeared to lie in the support of France and the success of his Italian League. All that Charles did pointed in the same direction. He was openly at war

with the confederate States of Italy, the Papal States
among them. Notwithstanding his supposed wealth,
the Imperial army had been left without its wages in
Lombardy and had been living at free quarters. A
war with the Pope had been welcomed enthusiastically
by the Lutheran States, and a large Lutheran contingent had joined, led by George von Frondsberg, who
had patted Luther on the back at Worms. So delighted was Von Frondsberg with his occupation, that
it was said he carried a rope about to hang the Pope
with. As there was no money to pay the soldiers'
wages, there was neither discipline nor attempt at it.

Church lands, churches, monasteries, nunneries
were given up to plunder; Spaniards and Germans
alike licentious and equally indifferent to sacrilege.
The Duke of Bourbon, the commander of this motley
host, a revolted subject of Francis, finding he could
only feed them by pillage, undertook to lead them to
Rome. They swept through the country leaving behind
them a black belt of ruin, and in May 1527 came under
the walls of the sacred city. They did not wait for the
ceremony of a siege. The day after their arrival they
stormed the walls, swarming up the ladders, the German
heretics leading the assault in the name of the Emperor.
Never since Attila's time had Rome witnessed such a
scene of havoc. The wealth of the world was gathered
there to become the prey of the spoiler. The splendid
palaces of the cardinals were gutted; the holy men
themselves were mounted on asses' backs in their robes,
with their faces to the tail, and carried through the

streets in mock procession, Clement himself looking on, shivering in terror, from the Castle of St. Angelo. Orthodox Spaniard and heretic German fought side by side as brothers in arms, executing vengeance on the hated and despised oppressor, who was brought at last to a dreadful reckoning.

Charles himself was in Spain when he received the news of this extraordinary exploit. He was called the most Catholic king. The capital of Christendom had been sacked by his troops, and the successor of St. Peter was his prisoner. He was a devout, serious man; and he was agitated, but not perhaps really alarmed. He had now the means in his hand to carry out his long-demanded reforms, and members of his own council advised him to use the opportunity. The plan was to transport the Pope into Spain, keep him there, and either force out of him the necessary measures or else execute them without him. No one could say what the Emperor would do. Perhaps he hardly knew what to do himself. In the universal confusion it appeared likely that Christendom might break up into national churches, French, English, Spanish, German. In the course which he adopted he followed the same principles which had governed him throughout. He was essentially conservative. He wished to preserve the Papacy in spite of itself, purified and reconstructed. To some extent he was perhaps influenced by another incident equally unforeseen.

The Pope, from his confinement in St. Angelo, appealed for help to France and England. Both agreed to go to war for him. Francis sent another army to Milan, invaded Naples, and was proposing to attack the Spaniards in Rome. Henry VIII. professed equal forwardness, but used the occasion to require Clement to sanction the divorce of the Emperor's aunt, Catherine of Aragon, which, under the circumstances, he, and Wolsey with him, conceived Clement would not hesitate to do. The chivalrous element in Charles's character decided him to support Catherine, though politically it might have been an advantage to him to let her go. He insisted that Clement should refuse. The French army of Italy being destroyed by a pestilence, the Pope found prudence counsel him to reconcile himself with his late enemy. The Emperor came to Italy, allowed the Pope to crown him, assured him of his protection, and arranged with him the terms on which he would endeavour to recover Germany to obedience. You know how things went in England. The Pope had appeared perfectly willing to concede the divorce and only drew back at the Emperor's order. The King, resenting the Emperor's interference, threw himself on the English Parliament; and the Parliament and the Crown together did what the Emperor had threatened to do : reformed the English Church, and threw off the Pope's authority. The parties in the game had changed places. The Emperor, who had seemed to be at the head of the revolution, was now the Pope's patron ; and Henry, who had come forward to defend the Pope, had revolted from the papal authority.

It was an extraordinary complication. All Europe was in a ferment, and each disturbed corner of it thought its own affairs required most attention. Queen Catherine in England, with the English clergy who were smarting under Henry's hand, clamoured to Charles to bring an army over and depose the King. Charles had work enough of his own to attend to without undertaking England. The Turks hung like a cloud over north-eastern Europe. He required men and money again from Germany, and at such a moment he could not afford to quarrel with the Diet. He had to manœuvre as he could. The danger from the Turks was immediately pressing. The Diet voted supplies freely. The Elector of Saxony and the Landgrave gave troops, and the Turks were flung back; but more than ever all parties were agreed that there must be a council, and the Emperor said again that there should be one.

In his conference with the Pope he had exacted a promise that Clement should continue to refuse the divorce. Clement had hinted that the English Catholics looked to him for help. Charles had answered that when the Church was reformed he trusted that Henry would return to his allegiance; but that the alterations which he was engaged in were in themselves reasonable, and he would not meddle with him. He required the Pope to follow the example himself. Germany, he said, demanded a council, and a council must be held.

The Pope had perhaps hoped that his complaisance about the divorce might have delivered him from the dreaded danger. No Pope ever faced a council without alarm. The bishops had their own grievances against Rome. The laity were claiming a voice, and were even less easy to be controlled. He pleaded pathetically with Charles. He pointed out to him that it would be safer and wiser to take the course recommended by the Cardinal.

A council, he said, would be the letting loose of a tempest. The German princes cared nothing for religion. Their only object in protecting Luther was to plunder the Church and to assert their own independence. A council, especially if held in Germany, would be the crater of a volcano. The Pope might lose much, but the Emperor and Ferdinand would lose more. It would be better, safer, to use force at once. Peace had been made with France. The Turks had been driven back. Half Germany was still orthodox. Let the Emperor use the opportunity and strike before it was all corrupted, and while he had still friends to support him. A council would only mean delay. In any case it could only be composed of bishops who had sworn allegiance to the Holy See. To such a council the Germans would certainly refuse to submit, and everything would be made worse. There was nothing really to fear. In Clement's opinion the gates of hell would never prevail over the Church. The Edict of Worms should be enforced, and no excuse allowed. The Catholic princes would remain firm in the faith, and with their assistance, and with his own force from Spain and Flanders, the Emperor could do as he pleased.

This advice, or something like it, Clement gave to Charles V., when he went to Bologna to be crowned in 1529; and, as a further encouragement, and in the exercise of his universal spiritual sovereignty, the Pope presented him with a large grant of Austrian and Spanish Church property, professedly as a subsidy for the Turkish war. The conversation was private. The report of it which got abroad was probably incorrect in many ways. It was alleged, and this in some shape was true, that Charles insisted, if he was to act as the Pope desired, on Adrian's reforms being carried out.

Believing the Pope to have consented, the Emperor summoned the famous Diet of Augsburg to meet in the summer of 1530. He determined to be present in person, and set out for Germany, accompanied by the plausible Campegio, who had just come back from his fruitless mission to England. Undoubtedly Charles hoped that, with the help of some concession, he could persuade or compel the Diet to support him in maintaining the Papacy in Germany. The purpose was evident; and as evident was the resolution of the earnest reformers that orthodoxy should not be restored. The Diet opened with a procession of the Holy Sacrament. It was the office of the Elector of Saxony, as first of the princes, to bear the sword before the Emperor. The procession ended with the Mass, and the Elector, when called on to fulfil his usual duty, refused. Erasmian friends of peace reminded him of Naaman the Syrian, who was allowed to bow in the house of Rimmon. The Elector persisted, and was not to be persuaded by analogies. Charles passed it over. Campegio preached a mild sermon, smooth and conciliatory; dwelt upon the dangers of schism, exhorted the Diet to return to the old paths, and promised for the Pope that they should be received back with open arms. Business began. The Lutheran confession of faith, known as the Confession of Augsburg, was to be presented to the Emperor by the Elector, carefully and temperately drawn, and concluding with an appeal to a council. It was read in the Diet, and submitted by the Emperor to the Catholic divines. The divines, after guarding themselves with a protest that points of faith were reserved to the Church, and that lay Diets had no right to meddle with them, examined the articles in detail, and found heresy in every one of them. But Charles did not mean to aggravate the quarrel, and the Pope had agreed to try concession before force was resorted to. Campegio, speaking with the very genius of his friend Erasmus, said that for himself he could see little difference between the Church's doctrine and the doctrine of the Confession. Form was one thing; essentials were another. It was not, he thought, desirable to commit the Church to scholastic definitions and subtleties which only provoked division.

Luther was not present, being excommunicated. But there was a general feeling, even among the

prelates, that he had said much that was right.   The
Archbishop of Salzburg said that he would even allow
a reform of the Mass if carried out properly, only he
would not have it done by a miserable monk.

Since the capture of Rome, the Holy See had
fallen into contempt.   A pert Imperial secretary said
the Germans might have any religion they pleased,
if they would only spend money enough in the Sacred
College.

The Emperor summed up.   He said he had read
the Confession, and had heard the answers of the
Catholic divines.   It was not for him to decide
between them.   The Church of Rome needed reform,
and reformed he undertook that it should be, but
the changes required must be made by order and
authority.   The Lutheran States and cities must
depend on him, and first return to their obedience.
If they submitted, their complaints should be enquired
into and remedied.   If they refused, he must do his
own duty as defender of the faith.

The Emperor might threaten, but he could not
compel, for he had no force behind him for any such
purpose.   The Catholic provinces, the Catholic laity,
were not prepared for civil war.   The Lutherans were
their equals in number, their superiors in military
power, in spirit, force and resolution.   Melanchthon
and his friends, who had drawn the Confession,
were willing to revise the points which had been
most objected to.   There were private conferences.
Seven Catholics and seven Lutherans met to arrange

a compromise. Then three and three tried it. They could not agree. Theologians seldom can. The Reformers were supposed to have been divided. The common danger had drawn them together. The free towns and the barons had borne each other no good-will. Attempts were made to create jealousies among them, but these failed; the free towns could not be shaken. Charles tried persuasion. He appealed to the princes of the Empire. He entreated them not to set up a new religion in the world which had never before been heard of; at least he implored them all to allow Mass to be said in their several States till a council had decided otherwise. They replied that theirs was the old religion, and popery the new. They had gone back to the ancient usage. Mass was not said in the Apostles' time, and they would not have it.

Very intolerant, we think, very unnecessarily scrupulous; but it was through the Mass, it was on the supernatural power of the priesthood, that the entire fabric had been constructed of ecclesiastical privilege. They knew perfectly well that if they allowed the Mass to be restored the superstitions would revive; the roots would throw out shoots again, and in a few years all would be once more as it had been. John Knox, in Scotland, said that Queen Mary's one Mass was more terrible to him than ten thousand armed men; and John Knox was right. The Mass cannot, will not live peacefully beside another faith.

For three months the Diet continued its fruitless sittings, and then broke up. Charles did what he could. He put out another edict confirming the Edict of Worms. He did not try to reach conscience, but he insisted on uniformity of observance. Priests who had married were ordered to put away their wives; the laity were recommended to attend Mass, pray to the Virgin and saints, and restore the monasteries. Each prince was enjoined under penalties to enforce the law in his own province, and Charles undertook for himself that there should be a General Council in six months.

A council—but, once more, what sort of council? A council called by the Pope in Italy would be like Julius II.'s Council of the Lateran—a committee of nominees called merely to register the Pope's decrees. It was to no such council that Germany intended to submit itself. The Lutheran princes and representatives demanded always, with one unvarying voice, a free council called by the Emperor, where the laity could speak and vote on equal terms.

They replied to the Edict of Augsburg with the famous Schmalkaldic League, half of the States and cities of Germany binding themselves to stand side by side in defence of their common liberties, to resist force by force. For the first time was launched into the world the name of Protestant. The Schmalkaldic League protested against being coerced into practising ceremonies which they thought idolatrous, or into professing to believe what they knew that they did not believe, under any fear or any temptation. A noble and honourable declaration, the noblest and purest for which any body of men ever combined in this world. It was the symbol at once of constancy and piety. Martyrs died for it at the stake; heroes laid their lives down for it on the field. It was the Labarum under which the battle was fought and won for European liberty. In the modern crumbling of convictions Protestantism is now spoken of with contempt, but it will be heard of again. All brave men are Protestants who refuse to take a lie into their mouths in the name of religion.

This was the chief result of the Diet of Augsburg. The League sent round a defence of themselves to the Courts of Europe. They dwelt on the iniquities of the papal administration; they said they were quiet people who meant no harm to anyone; but they would not submit to it any longer, and if attacked would defend themselves.

The Emperor had pleased no one. The Germans defied him; the Pope affected to be displeased that he had allowed laymen to discuss points of doctrine, and complained of the public acknowledgment that the Church was corrupt and required reform. The Pope was coquetting with France again. If the Emperor required a council, France might protect him. He raised his tone. The Emperor, he said, had no right to promise reforms, still less to promise a council. The Pope was the superior; the Emperor was only his minister. He was at his wit's end, and

clutched at each passing straw.   At one time he
made approaches to Henry VIII.; then to Francis,
or to Francis and Henry together; or could not
Francis and Charles be brought to unite to crush
down Henry and stamp out heresy everywhere?   The
French Ambassador at Rome pointed out to him that,
with the Turks so near Austria, Charles could not do
it.   Francis could not, or would not, do it either.
In fact, the Ambassador told him, a council was his
best chance after all.   The Protestants would submit
to it, if it was called in a free country and was fairly
composed.   The Pope, perhaps, would have done
better for himself if he had consented.   No one wished
for a schism; the tempers of men had not yet been
hardened by war and persecutions.   If Clement had
complied with the universal demand, and allowed a
free council to meet, with the laity represented on it,
and had submitted himself to its decisions, he might
still have been left with an honourable supremacy.
States where the majority were Catholic could have
kept their Mass; the Church could have been reformed;
varieties of doctrine and ritual could have been comprehended under ambiguous formularies; even the
League of Schmalkald might have been satisfied, and
the spiritual constitution of Christendom might have
remained outwardly unbroken.

One regretfully wishes that it had been so; but,
in fact, nothing could have happened but what did
happen.   Either his own cowardice or the genius of
his office forbade Clement to take the course which

seemed the wisest. He preferred to trust to his
Italian cunning. He affected to yield. The world
wanted a council; well, he said, then the world should
have a council. But it must be called under the
old precedents. It must consist of bishops only;
he would have no laymen on it. Moreover, it must
not meet in Germany. A council sitting in Germany
would only be composed of Germans; none else would
attend. It must be held either at Rome, or at
Bologna, or at Parma, or some other Italian town,
where it would be under his own influence. The
Protestants should have a safe-conduct, and might
be heard in their defence: but they were not to have
a vote, or a place of their own in the synod, and they
must promise to be bound by the council's judgment
before they could be allowed to speak.

The Emperor remonstrated. He might have been
satisfied for himself, but he was loyal to the promises
which he had made when he required German help
against Solyman. The council, he said, was only
needed for Germany; in Germany it ought to meet.
Pope and cardinals were obstinate; they even hinted,
it is curious to observe, that if the Emperor persisted,
judgment might be given for Henry VIII.'s divorce.

There was no moving Clement. Without help
from the German princes the Moslem would be in
Vienna. The Emperor had struggled hard to no
purpose, and he was driven back on what became
known as the Capitulation of Nuremberg. The Edict
of Augsburg was suspended. Toleration of religious

differences had never yet been heard of. It was now to be the rule, till the free council could meet which the Germans demanded. The Emperor promised to do his utmost to make the Pope agree. If he failed, he would lay the whole matter before the Diet, which should decide what was to be done.

This was all which the Pope had gained by shiftiness. Rome was in a fury. The Emperor, it was said, had thrust his sickle into the Church's harvest. The Church had made laws to maintain truth. In suspending those laws the Emperor had broken his oath and incurred Divine vengeance.

Elsewhere, except among the professional theologians, the Nuremberg settlement was received with a sigh of relief. It was felt even by the moderately orthodox that Christians ought not to kill each other for differences of religion. The papalists might say that heretics were worse than infidels, but the sense of mankind declared that men might disagree on points of belief without forfeiting their rights to be looked upon as human beings. Doubtless it was important to hold the true faith, but civil war was worse than toleration of error. Thirteen years had passed since Luther had set up his theses. Through all those years the Emperor had struggled to suppress the movement which Luther had originated. He had failed, and might now try other methods. The world could not be forced into one pattern. Germany was not to be schooled by Italy, and the peace of Europe could not be sacrificed to the pretensions of Rome.

The grateful Diet voted supplies; again a Protestant army was despatched to Ferdinand, and again the Turks were rolled back upon Belgrade. Clement endured what he could not help, but never, according to Father Paul, liked or trusted the Emperor again.

LECTURE V

PAUL III

A MONG the results of the Reformation we used to be told that the best and brightest was the establishment of a purer form of Christianity. Such a result there may have been. Providence shapes our ends, rough hew them how we will; but the laity, when they claimed to be represented on the council which they were demanding had no thought of a re-formation of doctrine. The Church insisted that they were no judges of such high matters. Some of them were willing to believe it. All, with a few fanatic exceptions, would have thought it a crime to disturb the peace of Europe on questions of speculative belief. Their complaint was of definite material wrongs, for which they demanded redress. An overwhelming majority would have been content to leave the mysteries of the faith untouched and unchallenged if the clergy would have consented to enforce their own canons. Luther himself said that if the Pope had withdrawn his indulgences he would have gone no further. The toleration which had been conceded at Nuremberg was not valued as the triumph of a principle. So long as it was thought a duty to hold a right theological belief, so long as to be in error was regarded as a crime, it might be necessary to leave false opinion unpunished, as it is necessary to leave many sins unpunished; but it was welcomed rather as a possible mode of dealing with an immediate difficulty than as a point gained in the emancipation of the human conscience. The soundest human consciences did not then care to be emancipated; they were more anxious for truth than liberty. Heresy was still a crime, though it might be uncertain what particular opinions were heretical. It is among the commonest complaints against the Reformers that when in power they were as intolerant as their opponents. They had been bred up to be intolerant, and they could not cease to be so until their whole religion had virtually changed its character, until the points necessary to be held for salvation had been reduced to those common obligations of moral duty, which the conditions of human society require to be observed. In the early history of Christianity heresy had been only punished with excommunication. The Reformers professed to revert in all the changes which they made to earlier practice. The frightful massacres in the name of religion had roused pity and startled conscience, and it is possible that the penalty for heresy would have been softened even if there had been no Reformation. But there was no article in the old faith which died harder than the article ' De hæretico comburendo.'

I am tempted to add a few reflections. The laity were united as to the necessity of a Church reform of some sort. But in the best kinds of men there are two broad types, which in times of movement diverge. There are the ardent, the enthusiastic, the hoping, those who, when they see a thing which they consider evil, are for hurling it away; who rush boldly on, full of new ideas, half true, perhaps, but not always the whole truth; and there are those who know how little actual facts correspond to ardent expectations, how many difficulties are found in practice which had been unforeseen or unheeded: that, in fact, events never do answer to the anticipations even of the most gifted of prophets: that, as the proverb says, nothing is certain but the unforeseen.

To us with our modern ideas no right seems clearer than the right of men to think and speak as they please about religion; yet, to thoughtful persons who could look beyond the day that was passing over them, to such a man as Charles V., for instance, who was responsible for the administration of Europe, it might have seemed likely that toleration would be followed by one of two things—either that the people themselves would not bear it, and the different communities would fly on one another sword in hand, as they did in France, where the experiment was tried, or else that, as men and women professing different opinions came to live side by side, associating on friendly terms, intermarrying, discharging all the common duties equally satisfactorily, and disagreeing only on points of ceremony or speculation, the differences would gradually come to be looked on as unimportant. What men of character and ability doubted about would be held as doubtful. Dogmatic formulas would be disbelieved or disregarded. Religion, which had been the rule of life and the sanction of law and authority, would dwindle into an opinion, while practice would be determined by expediency, and mankind at last would be left without certainty about their nature or obligations. Far-seeing statesmen could not look forward without misgivings to either of these alternatives.

It cannot be denied that something of this sort has actually happened since toleration has been elevated into a principle. So long as religious truth was looked on as sacred and indispensable, the communities which adopted the Reformation were no less zealous than the Catholics; and their Christianity under the altered form produced as elevating an effect on character as mediæval Catholicism. English, Scotch, Germans, Dutch, Danes, Swedes, and Norsemen have shown no degeneracy. The history of the last three centuries has been a signal evidence that, in taking the Bible for their rule in the place of the Decretals, they had forfeited no privilege and lost no grace. But as long as they were deeply in earnest they were not tolerant. We only tolerate what we think unimportant, and the things which we are obliged to tolerate, we gradually come to think unimportant. There are indisputably symptoms at last that liberty of opinion has produced, and is producing, a general uncertainty, a gathering indifference; and ideas of duty and moral obligation, losing daily the positive sanction of authoritative religion, are living on upon inherited habits of action and conviction, which, under the present popular forms of thought, may in their turn be disintegrated.

Protestant nations are not worse off than Catholics in these respects. Judged by the coarse test of finance, the great defaulters, who repudiate their debts, have been the intensely orthodox Spaniards and Portuguese, with their kindred in South America. Those who rejected the Reformation three centuries ago show no moral superiority to those who accepted it. Their lives are not more pure, their social organisation is not more just, their literature is not more lofty, their educated intellect is not less penetrated with scepticism. If Charles V. could come back to life, he would see on the church walls in the remotest villages of Castile, pathetic warnings to the peasants to beware of the new ideas which are threatening society. But this comes from the variety of beliefs which now distract the world.

There were wise men even in the sixteenth century who could see dimly the possible far-off issues of the revolution which was then beginning, and were perplexed as to what they should do with it. It is better perhaps to observe what they actually did than to pass our glib censures upon conduct which we can hardly understand, ignorant as we are of the motives which then influenced alike both thought and action. Toleration may have all the virtues which we attribute to it; but we are judging men in whose inmost being lay the conviction that a right religious faith was the only basis of a right life.

But to go back to our story. The Pope had been brought at last to recognise that, whether he liked it or not, he might be forced to call a council. The Emperor was peremptory. The alternative was such a council as the Germans were asking for, called by the Emperor himself and meeting on the Rhine or the Danube. That a council of this kind might actually be brought together was more than a possibility, and the probable effect of it became curiously visible in the fall of papal securities in the European money market. One of the first acts of such a council, it was well understood, would be to deal promptly with the Roman courts of law, and their subsidiary branches in the rest of the Catholic world. The official posts in these courts had been so lucrative that they had been purchased at high premiums. Cardinal Pallavicino says that, with a council in view which might be independent of the Pope, the value of these situations fell at once *ad vilissimum pretium*. The money market is a sensitive barometer in the spiritual world as well as in the temporal.

If the English historians, who tell us that the Act of Parliament abolishing appeals to the Court of Rome was passed, merely to enable Henry VIII. to marry Anne Boleyn, had observed these words of Pallavicino,

they would have seen that the relief of his subjects
might also have had something to do with it.

The prospect of the council was dreadful to Clement.
But how was it to be averted ?   The Emperor had
promised Germany that it should meet.   He had also
promised to support the Papacy, but only on condition
that the Court of Rome should be reformed.   In such
a situation Clement, like Erasmus, might have asked
what he had done that he should fall in his old days
like a mouse into a pot of pitch ?

France was his best hope.   France and the Empire
were now at peace, but France had Pavia to revenge,
and was only watching for an opportunity.   Clement
had quarrelled with England to please Charles, and
now Charles was driving him to what he most
abhorred.   The French Court were always advising
him to make up his quarrel with Henry and offering
their own services as mediators.   Why might not the
old alliance be patched up again ?   If the Pope would
sanction Catherine's divorce, Henry and Francis might
then join and support the Pope and the Papacy against
the Emperor and the Germans.   Circumstances, and
Clement's terrors, seemed as if they might reproduce
the situation of 1528, when the Imperial army was in
occupation of Rome, and the kings of England and
France had declared themselves the Pope's champions.

Charles could have escaped his worst difficulties
could he have made up his mind to abandon Catherine;
and Catherine was not a little trying, for she and her
friends were urging him, in the midst of his other

perplexities, to send an army to England to back up an insurrection there. This he would not do. The Spanish Council of State would not hear of it. The peace of Europe was not to be broken for a family quarrel, even though it was a Spanish princess who was injured. But Charles was in the highest sense a gentleman. He felt that Catherine's treatment touched his honour, and he would never allow the Pope, if he could help it, to give judgment against her.

What was he to do then? It was very hard to say. Charles, like other conservative princes and statesmen, disliked Lutheranism, disbelieved in religious novelties, and wished to maintain the Church, if the Church would mend its ways. But if the Church would not mend its ways, what then? The German Protestants saw their way clearly. They had a faith of their own, and for their part were determined that, come what would, they would be ruled no longer by Pope or priests. It cost them a century of fighting, but it was they and the English martyrs, and Cromwell's Ironsides afterwards, who in fact saved the Reformation, or made it what we know. The Erasmian says it ought to have been left to the thinkers; that it could have been managed better by reason and moderation. But reason and moderation are for a world which is itself reasonable and moderate; they call out no enthusiasm and generate no vital force. The Church had at its back the superstition of a thousand years, and the practical strength which that superstition could still command. Reason is no match for such an antagonist.

' One nail drives out one nail.' Passion only can successfully encounter passion.

Charles still hoped. He went again to Italy to try
persuasion with Clement, but from Clement he heard
only complaints that laymen had been allowed to judge
upon mysteries of faith. Clement was negotiating
below the surface with France, and Francis had been
exhibiting his lately born zeal for orthodoxy by burning heretics in Paris, and massacring the Vaudois
peasantry—wretched masses of mankind, sacrificed
without scruple when a move required it in the political
game. Clement played skilfully with the Emperor's
demand for a council. He could trust France to support him in refusing to allow it to be held in Germany.
If a council met, he said, it must be an ecumenical
council, in which all the Powers, France among them,
must take part. This conceded, he professed himself
willing to consent to its meeting, and even to take the
lead in bringing it together. He drew up conditions,
and sent them by a Nuncio to the Elector of Saxony,
conditions which he knew that the Germans would
refuse. The failure could then be attributed to them.
He himself would stand excused. The terms were the
old ones. The council must be called in the Pope's
name, and the Pope must preside. It must be composed of bishops and abbots, as they alone must vote.
The Germans must promise to be bound by its decisions, as it was demanded by the Germans. It must
meet in Italy, at Bologna or Parma, or Mantua, if the
Germans preferred it. The several States of Europe

must be represented, either by their sovereign or their ambassador, and absence must not excuse disobedience. The Nuremberg toleration might last till the council's work was done, and not longer.

The Emperor was eager for peace—peace at any price. Any council he thought was better than none. If it could once meet, and if Germany were represented on it, it could be reshaped into some more convenient form. His own Spanish bishops he knew he could rely upon to enforce the reform of the Court of Rome, and he entreated the German princes to close with the Pope's offer.

In vain is the net spread in the sight of any bird. The Protestants of the League of Schmalkald replied that the chief object of the council was to impeach the conduct of the high ecclesiastics. To accept a council in which bishops only were to sit and vote was to twist a rope for their own necks. Bologna was in the papal territories. Parma was a papal dependency. Mantua was on the border, and was equally objection-able. If they went to either of these places, they would be walking into the lion's mouth. The Pope might offer them a safe-conduct; but, after the fate of John Huss, they could not rely on papal safe-conducts. The council which the Pope was proposing would be a mere synod of his own creatures. The original cause of the disturbance had been the papal indulgences. Leo X. had defended indulgences—had condemned Luther for crying out against them—had committed the See of Rome to the special scandal which most required redress. A council, therefore, over which the Pope was to preside would be a farce. It might be called free, but it would be only free in name. The questions which had been raised must be decided by Scripture, and by Scripture only, not by bishops and so-called Apostolic tradition. As to precedents, the situation itself was unprecedented, and Scripture had laid down no rule that only bishops were to have a voice in the Church's assemblies.

The Protestants appealed to the Emperor's word. He had promised that they should have a free council. They said that they looked to him as the head of Germany, and they threw themselves on his protection. The Pope, of course, could if he pleased summon such a council as he had offered. He might cite some of them to appear there, and if he did they would go and answer for themselves and their faith. But, as for promising submission, they would promise none, save to a council called by the Emperor on the lines of the Imperial Diet.

The answer was resolute. The Protestant leaders meant what they said, and were not to be moved. It was probably exactly such an answer as Clement expected and desired. He was able to say that he had offered a council composed as councils always had been composed since the time of the Apostles. It was not to be expected that he could change the ancient form to please the German heretics. If they would not have it, the fault was not his. The Emperor argued and threatened. But Clement and the cardinals were immovable. Their existence was at stake. In the present humour of Christendom a council really free would be their certain destruction. They had lost England by yielding to Charles. They did not mean, if they could help it, to lose Germany also.

Rome threw itself more and more upon France. The Pope married his niece to a French prince, and gave the Emperor to understand that, if he was pressed further, his whole influence in Italy would be thrown on the French side. About the council he had done his utmost, and would try no more till Europe was politically quiet.

So matters hung for the short remains of Clement's life. Fate had dealt hardly with him. For half his reign, as he said, he had been between the anvil and the hammer. But the Roman bishops are of unmalleable metal. He had yielded nothing. He had defended the spiritual citadel against the Emperor with better success than his troops had defended St. Angelo. It was the Roman See against the world. The wounds of Christendom might have been healed while they were still fresh by a few concessions. Clement had not to reproach himself with having conceded anything.

The cause perhaps lay more in the genius of the Papacy than in the character of Clement or of any individual Pope. Personal disposition seemed to make no difference. Whoever sat in the chair of St. Peter, the action continued the same.

Cardinal Farnese, who succeeded Clement, as Paul

III., was over seventy years old at the time of his accession. While a cardinal he had called himself a reformer. He had been on the side of Henry VIII. about the divorce, and had laboured hard and long to persuade Charles to yield the point. He was experienced in all forms of political intrigue. He had served under Alexander VI., Julius, Leo, Adrian, Clement. None knew better than he, and none had denounced more loudly than he, the degeneracy and profligacy of the Roman Court. He had seemed to wish to come to a peaceful arrangement with the Germans, and to think much as Erasmus thought about it all. After his elevation he continued to talk about the necessity of reform. In public he spoke of appointing a commission of enquiry. In private he was still more earnest. Father Paul doubts his sincerity. Father Paul thinks that he knew reform to be impossible, but that he believed the best way to silence the demand for it was to try and to fail. The great Venetian is less charitable than he might be in his interpretation of the actions of the Roman bishops.

One of the first acts of Paul's reign was to make advances to Henry VIII. for a reconciliation, and all appearances promised a vigorous, and perhaps honest, pontificate. Extraordinary or inconvenient virtue he soon showed was not to be expected from him. Like other great prelates, the new Pope had a family of illegitimate children, and was not the least ashamed of them. He had two grandsons, Alexander Farnese, and Ascanio Sforza, the son of his daughter. They were still boys, the elder fifteen, the younger fourteen. Paul, immediately on his accession, made these lads into cardinals, as props, he said, for his old age. Times were moving on. The world did seem slightly astonished. Pallavicino makes the best excuses for him that he can. Paul, he says, did no worse than other contemporary princes. He had been bred in an age of iniquities *quorum memoria non sine horrore et vituperatione repetitur*—' the memory of which cannot be recalled without horror and indignation.' He drowns the individual sin in the universal wickedness, and on the whole thinks that Paul did better than might have been expected considering the school in which he had been trained.

His reign opened quietly. The vexed question of the council was for the moment suspended. The Emperor was occupied elsewhere. In all the Empire, in all Europe, there was, perhaps, not a single man on whom Providence had laid so many burdens as it had flung on the heavy-laden Charles V. It was not enough that he had a jealous rival in Paris, always watching for a weak point to set upon. It was not enough that he had a religious revolution to compose and direct, which was changing the face of Europe, and shifty Popes and obstinate Diets to work with. It was not enough that he had the vast hosts of Solyman, hanging for ever like a thunder-cloud over the eastern provinces of Germany. Any one of these problems would have sufficed to occupy the whole energy of the ablest and most powerful of

sovereigns.   But a new enemy had now sprung up
who required to be immediately dealt with.

The Moorish corsairs, under the famous Barbarossa,
had developed into a force as formidable as the Cilician
pirates had been in Pompey's time. The capture of
Rhodes by the Turks had shocked and startled the
Christian world. Barbarossa, an irresponsible roving
chief, half ally, half subject to Solyman, had his head-
quarters at Tunis, which he had fortified and made
almost impregnable. From behind the Tunis fortresses
his flying squadrons sallied out across the Mediterranean, and descended on the coasts of Spain and Italy,
carrying off tens of thousands of captives. Delicate
ladies were sold for the seraglios of the Porte. Common men were held as slaves, or set to row in the
galleys. The better born were kept in the bagnios till
their friends could ransom them, while the ranks of the
pirates themselves were reinforced perpetually by renegade Greeks and Illyrians, desperate and reckless, who
cared only for plunder, and robbed and murdered with
equal indifference under Cross or Crescent. Barbarossa
himself was one of these renegades.

Christendom ought to have combined to root out
such a nest of villany. Christendom would do nothing
of the kind. It was all left to Charles. Henry VIII.,
who had been threatened with an invasion from
Flanders, was not displeased to see Charles with his
hands full elsewhere. The French, it was said, would
make an alliance with the Devil to be revenged on
the Emperor, and regarded the Moors rather as friends

than foes. The Germans were a land power, and could not help. Charles—loyal, chivalrous, ready always to go where duty called him—undertook to deal with the intolerable nuisance. He collected a fleet in Sicily at his own expense. He took the command in person, stormed the Tunis forts, liberated twenty thousand Christian slaves, burnt the corsair squadrons, and for the time cleared the seas. It was an exploit worthy of a knight of romance, to be sung of by poets. He returned, covered with honour, to take up again the other burdens, which had not grown lighter in his absence.

Paul, perhaps a little ashamed that all should be left to Charles, was now working apparently with good will to help him with the difficulties about the council. He affected to be earnestly anxious for it. He appointed his commission of cardinals to examine into the abuses at the Court of Rome. As the Germans had rejected the scheme offered by Clement, he proposed to make a cardinal of Erasmus, to prove to them that he meant reform in earnest. He sent a Nuncio to Wittenberg to consult the Elector—to see and, if possible, conciliate Luther himself. The Nuncio did see Luther, flattered him, blamed the violence of Leo X., assured him of Paul's esteem and admiration, and intimated that there was no reward which he might not expect if he would sanction the meeting of the council and assist in making it a success.

We have two accounts of this curious interview,

the Nuncio's and Luther's own. Luther, it seems,
had no belief in a Pope who made cardinals of his
bastards' children. He says that he told the Nuncio
he cared little for the Pope's opinion of him. He
would continue to do what he believed to be his duty
to the best of his ability; but his connexion with
Rome was ended. Leo's excommunication of him
had been a special act of Providence. Till then he
had seen only the wickedness of indulgences, and had
meant to go no further; but Leo had opened his eyes
to the tricks of the Roman Court. It did not lie in
him to make the council a success. It would succeed
if it was free and was guided by Scripture. Otherwise it would not succeed. For himself, he would
accept nothing from the Pope.

The Nuncio's account is different from this, but
not inconsistent with it. Luther, he says, was not
disrespectful, conversed with him bare-headed, and
spoke civilly of Paul, of whom he said he had heard a
good report at Rome. But the Nuncio's general impression was that, whether Luther was possessed by
a devil or not, he was full of arrogance and insolence.
The Nuncio asked him what he thought of the conduct of Henry VIII. He declined to give an opinion,
and would neither condemn nor approve. The interview was not pleasant. His last words were: 'I will
go to this council if it meets, and I will defend my
faith there, though it costs me my life. The cause is
not mine, but God's.'

Luther was wise in refusing to be entangled.

The Nuncio had brought a profusion of benevolent promises. But the definite proposals of Paul were, after all, the same as Clement's. The council was to sit at Bologna or Mantua. The Pope was still to preside, and the bishops alone were to vote. The Protestant deputies might appear under a safe-conduct, and should be heard, but might take no further part.

Fifteen Protestant dukes and princes, and thirty representatives of the free cities, replied for Germany. They said they were willing and eager to submit the question which divided them to a free and lawful council, but they would acknowledge none that met in the Papal States or at Mantua, and none over which the Pope presided. The Pope had condemned them already and was not an indifferent judge. The laity must sit in the council as well as the clergy, and on equal terms. The Pope must expect to be called to account, and the place of assembly must be determined by the secular princes.

The Nuncio had to return as he had come. He carried the answer of the German States to Charles, who was at Naples, just returned from his African victories. The Emperor had ventured much and sacrificed much for the rest of Europe. Others, he thought, must sacrifice something too. He hurried to Rome, and was for seven hours in secret conference with the Pope. Paul insisted that he was in earnest about Church reform; pointed to his commission, which was actively at work, and expressed his willingness to submit everything to an ecumenical council of a regular kind, even though outside the papal dominions. When the world is divided upon great questions, and the object is to settle them without fighting, neither side can have its own way entirely. Charles thought that the Pope's offer ought to be accepted. He agreed on Mantua as a place of meeting, and undertook that the Germans should attend there and submit to what should be decided. The Pope issued a Bull for an ecumenical council to be held at Mantua. Charles informed the German princes that submit they must. Germany could not give the law to the rest of Christendom. Mantua was a fief of the Empire, close to the border, and not under the Pope at all. But the princes of the League continued obstinate. They refused, as always, to acknowledge a council composed only of Pope, legates and bishops. Mantua was an Italian city, and all the Italian prelates were the Pope's creatures. They again referred to the dark perfidy of Constance and the burning of Huss.

The Emperor's honourable object was to prevent a civil war, envenomed, as he knew that it would be, by religious hate and fury. Yet it seemed impossible to move or reconcile the parties in the quarrel. Paul was privately as determined as Clement had been that if a council met he would be master of it himself. The Germans were equally resolute that they would have none where the Pope was master. At this particular moment the *Deus ex machinâ* appeared in the Duke of Mantua himself. The Duke had no wish for a congregation of holy fathers in his territory. He would have to increase his garrison, and he said the Pope must pay for it. The Pope answered that during the session the city must be passed over to the jurisdiction of the Holy See. The Duke of Mantua resisted. No other spot could be thought of which at the instant would answer. The project had to be abandoned, and the state of Europe immediately after made the meeting of a council impossible.

Amidst scheming Popes, recusant Germans, Anabaptists breaking out in Flanders, and the shattered remnants of the pirates threatening to collect again, the Emperor now found himself confronted once more with a French war. France had recovered from its defeats, and there was Pavia still to avenge. Lying in the centre of the Emperor's dominions, the French armies could strike where they pleased, either at Spain, or the Low Countries, or Italy. It had been long perceived that there must be another struggle. But Charles, when the declaration of war came to him at Rome, felt that he was hardly dealt with. There was something very human about the great Emperor. Indignant, with the spirit of Don Quixote himself, in a great speech in Spanish before Paul and the Conclave, he denounced Francis as the cause of all the misery of Christendom, and challenged him to fight out the quarrel single-handed, they two in their shirts, with sword and dagger, in the sight of both their armies.

The French Ambassador was present. Pleading that he understood Spanish imperfectly, he asked for the words in writing, and enquired if the Emperor was in earnest. Charles felt that what he had proposed was impossible ; but he did say that it would save their subjects' blood, and would be better than a general war.

There was nothing for it but to accept what fate had sent, and to prepare for a fresh campaign in Lombardy. The council project had once more to be suspended; the Germans to be again left to themselves. The fruit was not ripe; even Paul's reform commission was to prove barren. As this commission was remarkable, I must say a few words about it. The members of it were among the most distinguished men at Rome : Cardinals Contarini, Reginald Pole, Caraffa and Sadolet, three bishops, among whom was Aleander, an abbot, and the master of the palace. The worst enemies of the Church never spoke more hardly of it than did this distinguished body.

They found that there were abuses and corruptions in the bestowal of Church benefices and dignities, that no care was taken of fitness for office, that the Church revenues were misemployed, that simony and pluralism were everywhere. Cardinals absorbed the bishoprics, heaping see on see. Bishops and clergy generally had ceased to reside, and their flocks were neglected. Exemptions from duty were sold for money. Monasteries were disordered. There was notorious lewdness in the nunneries. Simony had grown to such a height that people had ceased to be ashamed of it. Religion was made contemptible, specially the Sacraments. Indulgences, which Leo had defended, the commission considered mischievous and demoralising. They found that among all the Churches, the Church of Rome, which ought to be an example to the rest, was the loosest and most slovenly. Shameless strumpets rode through the streets with cardinals' retinues to wait on them. Never in any town were such marks of dissoluteness and debauchery as in the home of the Papacy; and so on, and so on, with an accumulating list of iniquities.

The report was honestly drawn. It was debated in the Consistory with closed doors, and the Cardinal of Capua summed up the general sentiment of the College. This general sentiment was that the corruption was so inveterate that it was past mending. Custom had reconciled men to these practices, and it was better to leave them untouched; the more they were stirred, the worse the odour which would rise from them. To attempt reform would only give a triumph to the Lutherans, for it would amount to a confession of guilt. Cardinal Caraffa, afterwards Paul IV., observed that, if they did nothing with such evidence before them, they might fall under God's displeasure; but he was not supported, and it was decided that the enquiry and all connected with it should be suppressed. The Pope was, or professed to be, disappointed. A copy of the report was obtained—not, it was supposed, without the Pope's connivance—and was sent to Germany, as an evidence that Paul, at least, was in earnest. There it was printed, and was read by everyone with shouts of scorn.

Meanwhile the French had re-entered Lombardy. Charles, finding that he could have neither reform nor council, joined his army, and rolled the invaders back over the Alps. He was sore and angry. He resented this last attack upon him as gratuitous and unworthy; and, not contented with having repelled the invaders, resolved, if he could, to make an end with Francis, and followed him into Provence. He expected an easy victory. He had a magnificent army; he had the best generals in Europe; he was pursuing an enemy already defeated. But his fortune for once failed him. The French wasted their own country and entrenched themselves behind impregnable lines. He could not advance. Summer heat brought pestilence, and in a few weeks the Emperor had to retire along the sea road to Genoa, wrecked and ruined.

It was the worst reverse which he had yet met with. He was in no condition now to threaten the German princes or force reforms on Pope and cardinals. He had to patch up a truce with France, and go away to Spain to recover himself.

The council was still talked about. Vicenza was proposed; but there was no longer any earnestness, and the Pope was occupied with other matters, which for a time took entire possession of him.

I mentioned that on his accession he made advances to Henry VIII. These advances were received coldly, and Paul resented it. Eustace Chapuys, the Emperor's Ambassador in England, had been for several years intriguing with a disaffected party of English nobles and clergy. Vast and determined preparations had been made for a rebellion, which Catherine of Aragon was to lead, or of which Catherine's restoration was at least to be the object. The King was to be disposed of, and the Princess Mary was to take his place, at the head of the clerical reactionaries. The particulars of the conspiracy are to be read in great detail in Chapuys's despatches. Clement VII., in giving judgment against Catherine's divorce, had declared Henry VIII. excommunicated if he did not submit. The sentence of excommunication would only come into effect when followed by a Bull of deposition calling on the Catholic Powers to support the Pope by force. The party of insurrection in England, Catherine herself, and the Ambassador Chapuys, had urged the issue of such a Bull without delay. Clement had hesitated till he could be assured that the Emperor would act, and the Emperor had declined to commit himself; so the matter hung at pause at Paul's accession. But the conspirators were hot and eager as ever, and the most active of them, and the most dangerous, was Fisher, bishop of Rochester. There is no doubt about this; Chapuys's letters on the subject boast of Fisher's communications with himself as the highest evidence of the strength and importance of the revolutionary party, and the

communication between Chapuys and the Court of
Rome was so constant and intimate that it is impossible
to suppose Paul to have been ignorant of a fact of so
much consequence. He was harassed day and night
with the English problem. Reginald Pole was ever at
his ear, telling him that force was the only remedy,
and urging him to strike. He did not venture to issue
the Bull of deposition without Charles's consent, but
he did what was equally certain to bring on the crisis.
Many particulars of the English conspiracy had become
known to the Government. The discovery of the im-
posture of the Nun of Kent and her own confessions
had revealed how large a party of the nobles and clergy
were concerned in the plot. It was known that Fisher,
above all, had urged the landing of an Imperial army
to support the rebellion. Most of the persons whose
names had come out had made their submission, had
begged for pardon, and received it; Fisher had refused,
and was attainted for misprision of treason. A few
months later he was committed to the Tower for a
fresh offence. In the face of the Pope's sentence, Parliament passed an Act declaring the legitimacy of Elizabeth. An oath recognising her right of succession to
the crown was required of all the peers. Fisher declined
to take it. The Act of Supremacy was passed to meet
the Pope's pretensions to absolve English subjects from
their allegiance to the Crown. It was no more than a
reiteration of the old Acts of the Plantagenet kings
which declared England to be a self-governed country.
With invasion impending, all subjects were fairly

required, if demanded, to promise to stand to their allegiance under pain of high treason. Fisher had refused again, had been tried and received sentence : but the sentence had been suspended in the hope that he would submit, or that it would itself be a sufficient warning. Paul III. took this particular moment to call Fisher into the Sacred College. He professed to have nominated him only because he wished to have an Englishman on the intended council. He said that he had heard of Fisher as a holy and learned prelate, that this was all that he knew about him, and that his appointment had been meant as a compliment to the King. It is impossible to believe this. Every Court in Europe was watching the proceedings in England with peculiar intensity. The Court of Rome was the best informed of all. The sending a cardinal's hat to Fisher could only have been meant, and must have been meant, as a reward for his resistance to the Crown and Parliament, and as an encouragement to the English clergy in rebellion. Pallavicino himself partially admits this.

The effect was instantaneous. The reply to Fisher's promotion was his execution on Tower Hill. This has been denounced ever since as a wanton and wicked act of cruelty, the sacrifice of a pious and innocent old man by a sanguinary tyrant.

For myself, I think that, if high treason is a crime at all, if it is not permitted to subjects who are dissatisfied with their governments to invite foreign armies into the realm, and force upon the country other rulers

whom they and their friends prefer, then perhaps none
of the great sufferers on Tower Hill ever brought their
fate on themselves by their own act more entirely than
Fisher, bishop of Rochester. If piety, if generosity, if
loftiness of motive are to excuse treason, then treason
ceases to be a crime, and must be blotted out from the
Statute book. The higher the reputation of a con-
spirator, the greater the danger from him. Fisher had,
there is no denying it, passionately invited the Pope to
declare the King deposed. He had implored the
Emperor to interfere in England by force, to crush the
King, to crush the Parliament, to stamp out the fast
spreading revolt from popery. Suppose him to have
succeeded, England would have been inundated with
blood. The civil wars of the past century would have
been lighted up again, and the flames would have been
made fiercer by religious animosity. Surely, if history
has any use or meaning, the writers of it ought to pause
before they excuse such conduct as Fisher's, and execrate
his punishment.

That Rome should be startled at such an incident
was natural enough. Martyrs are the seed of the
Church, and Fisher's death on the scaffold served the
cause of Rome more than he could have served it in
his life. In the flesh he was an old man near his end.
In the spirit the axe of the executioner gave him the
immortality of a saint. It is not to be supposed that
Paul deliberately calculated on such a result. He
probably contemplated nothing more than an artful
move in an intricate game. The members of the

conclave were sacred persons. Far as apostacy had
gone, and much as it had dared, it had not yet been conceived possible that cardinals could be tried and executed
as common mortals. Pricked, like the dragon in the
'Faery Queen,' with the knight's lance, the Pope shook
with anger. Heedless of remonstrances, he prepared a
Bull in the haughtiest language of the old pontiffs,
declaring Henry deposed, and calling the Catholic
world to arms to punish him. He was pleased with his
composition. He called a meeting of the cardinals in
council to hear it read. He read aloud in the Consistory the story of the enormous doings of the new
Nebuchadnezzar. If the saints could not or would not
move to revenge their own injuries, the Church at least,
he said, must not be silent; and he produced the
thunders which he had prepared. The cardinals, more
wise than he, doubted whether France or the Empire
would approve so uncompromising an assertion of the
Pope's right to depose kings; and Paul was with difficulty persuaded to leave his Bull in a drawer till some
fresh provocation. He had not long to wait.

The rebellion in England broke out unsupported in
the Pilgrimage of Grace; blazed up and burnt down
ineffectually. Having disposed of the Church insurgents
in the field, Henry went on to attack the superstition
which was the secret of their power over the mind.
Archbishop Becket had been the great English champion
of the sovereignty of the Church over the State. His
bones had worked miracles for 400 years. They could
work none in their own defence. The Government

destroyed the shrine at Canterbury, seized the
treasures collected there, the offerings of the piety of
centuries, burnt the relics, and threw the dust to
the winds.

The cup was now full. Such a challenge could not
be passed over. The lightnings of the Vatican flashed
out. The wicked King of England was placed under
the ban of Christendom. The Catholic Powers were
invited and ordered to unfold Christ's banner, and
Reginald Pole was despatched to Charles and Francis
to urge them to forget their quarrels and join their
forces in a holy war.

To the astonishment of Pole, both the Emperor and
the King of France refused even to admit him to their
presence. The pretensions of the Popes to depose
princes had never been patiently acquiesced in. Now,
in this strange sixteenth century, these antiquated
ambitions were things to be rather smiled at than
obeyed. Not only could the Pope's Ambassador obtain
no hearing, but he had to learn that both the leading
Catholic Powers were actually competing for a renewal
of friendship with Henry, and that Charles especially
had chosen the moment of his excommunication to
enter into a close alliance with him.

Paul had been striking his best supporters. Not
only had he excommunicated Henry, but all those who
should uphold or favour him. His throne rested on
the belief that at least his curse was fatal. The frank
contempt with which the curse was treated was an open
intimation that such things were no longer to be taken

seriously, and that a new page had been turned in the history of mankind.

Less than ever could Paul now look with equanimity on the prospect of a council. Of all the reforming princes, the papal party most hated Henry of England. He had gone his own way. He had thrown himself on the laity and the commons. He had actually done what Charles was requiring the Pope to do. Others had talked about reform. Henry had carried it out. He had abolished the extortions and exemptions and scandals of which his people complained. Worst of all, he had maintained the orthodox Catholic faith when it was supposed that England would become a nest of heresy.

It was but too likely, after such a proof of the light regard in which the Papacy was held, that the council would only meet to be forced by the Emperor to imitate his uncle Henry's example.

LECTURE VI

THE DIET OF RATISBON

I SPOKE in my last lecture of the Commission of Reform which had sat at Rome, of its report and the resolution of the cardinals. If that report had been honourably acted on, it was not then too late to have saved the unity of Christendom. Germany had not yet cut herself off by any formal act from the communion of the Church. England had abolished the temporal jurisdiction of the Popes, but the reforms carried out in England had been what the Emperor desired to see in every Catholic country; and Germany so far had professed only to revert to the original model of the first Christian community. The primacy of the See of Rome, the three orders among the clergy, the necessity of ordination as a point of discipline, even as a point of belief, would have been easily acknowledged by the laity, if churchmen would have ceased in their own lives to turn into ridicule the doctrine which they taught. But the sand was running out. Each day that went by was bringing the Papacy itself into contempt. It had ceased to command respect by its holiness, but its supposed supernatural power had been feared after the respect had departed. If with the respect the fear departed also, if the terrors of interdict and excommunication were shown to be phantoms only formidable as long as they were believed in, contempt would follow and resentment at having been so long deceived. There is no object so certain to be despised as an idol which has lost its divinity. The clergy had rested their claims on the supernatural powers supposed to be conveyed in ordination. These powers, whatever they might be, had produced so little effect on their personal characters that they were no longer looked up to or obeyed. Ministers had taken the place of the priesthood in the reformed States and cities of Germany, men of pure and simple habits, who had come to be called pastors, shepherds of the people, who lived like the peasants, and worked like Luther, or St. Paul before him, with their own hands. The pastors were on their mettle not to discredit their calling. Their poverty contrasted with the avarice and ostentation of the higher clergy. They baptized the children, they administered the Communion. The Court of Rome and the bishops talked of unhallowed censers, of Dathan and Abiram, and the earth opening. But it was dangerous to appeal to miracles. If the earth did not open, the argument recoiled. The longer the new order of things lasted, the greater would be the difficulty of returning from it.

The Church still threatened fire and sword. Idolatries are forced to become cruel to escape ridicule. But fire and sword seemed to be passing out of the Church's hands, when France and the Empire alike treated its curses as a form, and allied themselves openly with excommunicated princes.

Nevertheless there was among the moderate part of the laity, even in Germany, a real desire for peace and unity, if peace and unity could be preserved in a rational way. The Pope had shown that he personally was ready for reform. He had offered a council, on terms which the Protestants of the League of Schmal-kald rejected, but terms which Austria and Bavaria, which Charles and Ferdinand, desired to see accepted. The Emperor had convinced himself that, if it could once be brought together, if the Germans on any terms could be persuaded to attend and could make their voices heard in it, the council could then easily remodel itself into a shape which would satisfy moderate opinion.

The difficulty on one side lay in the obstinacy of the Church of Rome, on the other in the resolution of the Protestants of the League and of Henry VIII. in England to recognise no council over which the Pope was to preside. The Emperor was irritated at what he regarded as an unnecessary scruple, and many of the German princes felt as he did. In the unsettled state of Europe, with war always blazing or smouldering between France and the Empire, there were inherent difficulties in the meeting without needless additions to them. If the council did not meet, Charles had promised that the settlement of religion should be referred to a German Diet. Paul, always dexterous, suggested to him that a counter-league should be formed among the princes who shared his feeling. The Emperor's chief dread was of a civil war in Germany, especially a religious war. He encouraged the proposal of a Catholic league, but it was to be a league which would act within the limits of the constitution. He felt himself bound by his promise to submit the question to the Diet. The Pope might send a legate. Perhaps France might be induced to help, and in some way or other terms of agreement might be found.

There was another alternative. Many of the cardinals believed that the seat of the mischief was England. If the movement against the Papacy could be crushed in England, it was thought that Germany would be easily managed. The Emperor would have no war in Germany. He might not equally object to a war with England. Both he and Francis had refused to receive Cardinal Pole. But might they not reconsider the matter? Might they not forget their quarrels and combine? Henry was excommunicated. The Pope had called on the Catholic Powers to execute the sentence. He again urged it on the Emperor. Henry, he said, had no army, and would fall at the first blow, or rather there need be no blow at all. Let the Emperor and Francis send a joint embassy to England requiring the King to return to his allegiance to the Church, and his own subjects would force him to submit.

Charles, then and always, was loyally anxious to

maintain the Papacy, if it would rouse itself to repent
and mend; but an armed crusade in its defence, after
it had declared itself incapable of reform, did not com-
mend itself to him. He replied to the Pope's letter
that, if he quarrelled with Henry, the English and the
Lutherans would instantly unite. Fourteen thousand
Germans would be thrown across the Channel from the
Baltic. The English people were warlike, and if the
King had no standing army, he was rich and could
easily provide one. He said England must wait till
Germany was settled. He must try once more what
could be done with a Diet. It was still to be compromise, only compromise. Paul had hoped for a better
resolution, and made one more effort. He despatched
Cardinal Farnese to press the usual objections. The
guidance of the Spirit, he said, was promised only to
the clergy. Questions affecting the Church ought not
to be submitted to congresses, where laymen sat and
voted. At the Diet there would be Lutheran representatives, who would attack dogmas which had been
held by the universal Church from immemorial ages.
If Catholics and Protestants came to an agreement, one
condition of it would probably be the sacrifice of the
Papacy. At best the Lutherans would insist on toleration, which would hardly be less dangerous.

The Emperor was not to be moved with the threats
of these dreadful consequences. Ferdinand, to whom
Farnese had been directed to apply next, was no less
impracticable. Ferdinand was a good Catholic, but half
his council were Lutherans, and he wanted Lutheran

help against the Turk. Farnese felt the danger of the situation. He wrote to Paul anxiously, and even passionately. If the Church was to be saved, there was not a moment to be lost. He advised the Pope not to depend upon the Emperor, but to make friends where he could among the Catholic Germans; above all, to set about reform in earnest, and begin with his own Court.

Meanwhile the arrangements for the Diet went forward. A preliminary congress was held at Hagenau, on the Rhine, near Strasburg. Paul's first impulse was to stand on privilege and take no part; but he thought better of it, and he sent Campegio, already favourably known in Germany, to represent him.

After a stormy debate, the congress adjourned to Ratisbon, and was there formally opened, on November 15, 1540. Granvelle, Charles's old experienced Chancellor, declared the purpose for which the Diet had been called. Campegio spoke mildly, as was expected of him. Disputes on doctrine he had always thought needless. He was all for peace, and ventured a few sentences for his Roman master. The Diet thanked him personally for his good will, but made no reference to the Pope in their acknowledgments. More time was needed for consideration, and there was another adjournment till the following spring. Campegio was thought at Rome to have been too ready with concessions. He was recalled, and Cardinal Contarini was sent in his place. Contarini was a reformer, but passionately papal. He was the friend of Pole, and

the friend of Ignatius Loyola, who was just then found-
ing his new order. The Pope professed himself still
unable to believe that the Emperor or his brother
would agree to anything against the dignity of the
Holy See. Should signs appear of dangerous measures,
Contarini was directed to protest and withdraw.

Contarini had to report, on his arrival at Ratisbon,
that he found the Protestants united and resolute, the
Catholic princes divided—their orthodoxy was qualified
with strong national feeling. Like the Emperor, they
all dreaded civil war, and meant to prevent it if
possible.

March came, 1541, and with it the reopening of the
Diet. The Legate found that, if he was to form a
party, he must be moderate in what he demanded.
He told the Emperor in a preliminary interview that
the Pope was prepared with concessions if the supremacy was untouched. The Emperor gave doubtful
answers. The Catholic leaders were lukewarm. Contarini feared they were too anxious for a share in the
plunder of the Church. He tried Granvelle. He
hoped, he said, that the Emperor would at least stand
by the Edict of Augsburg. The Chancellor shrugged
his shoulders. If you want to manage wild beasts, he
said, you must humour them. It was a special distress
to Contarini to find that the most popular man in
Germany was the Landgrave of Hesse, the inspiring
genius of the Schmalkaldic League.

April had arrived before business commenced. On
the 5th the Emperor in person addressed the Diet.

He said that he had called it together, as he had
promised, to compose the differences in religion. He
alluded to the Edict of Augsburg, but only briefly, as
if excusing it as the best which he could do. He said
he had hoped for a General Council, but so far the
difficulties had seemed insuperable. He had therefore
invited the representatives of the nation to come together and give him their opinions. The Empire, he
said, had enemies on all sides. He had spared neither
himself nor his treasury. He had fought the Turks,
and the Moors at Tunis. But the Turks were still
strong, and the pirates were again collecting. France,
instead of helping him to defend Christendom, was still
threatening to attack him. He appealed to his German
subjects to compose their own quarrels, and stand by
him in the common cause.

He spoke simply, truly, and like himself. He
suggested another conference of divines to review the
disputed doctrines. It had been tried before and failed.
It might now do better. If the divines could agree
upon a common set of articles, they could then be
submitted to the Diet.

The efforts of the Ratisbon conference survive in
the language of some of our own Thirty-nine Articles.
Three champions were selected from each side. The
Chancellor presided, and laid before them twenty-four
disputed questions on which they were to devise some
common form of expression, which would admit of an
elastic interpretation. They were on the old familiar
subjects—free will, justification, original sin, the Church,

the interpretation of Scripture, the marriage of the
clergy, the sacraments, baptism, the Eucharist, orders,
and the rest.   The metaphysical points were settled
without difficulty.   Clerical marriages might be permitted, though they were not to be encouraged.   The
first serious check was at the Eucharist.   The Catholics
maintained their own well-known view of it.   The
Lutherans admitted the Real Presence, but said that
it depended on the faith of the receiver, not on the
consecration by a priest; that it did not survive the
ceremony, and that the elements resumed their natural
condition; they argued that transubstantiation was a
phrase unknown to the early Church.   The distinction
was subtle and serious, but might not have been in-
surmountable, for it turned on the nature of substance
when detached from its sensible qualities; and what
substance was or is when so detached, or whether it
was or is anything at all, no one knew, and no one
knows now.

There was stumbling again at the power of the
keys, and at the splendour and assumptions of the
hierarchy.   Pallavicino admits that the lives of the
pastors contrasted favourably with those of the Catholic
clergy.   On this point he allows they had the clear
advantage; on others he complains that they were
hopelessly obstinate.

Complete agreement could not be arrived at, but
progress had been made.   The Emperor presented the
formulas which had been commented upon to the Diet.
He expressed his extreme gratification with what had

been done. He hoped that the rest would be settled
equally well. He promised emphatically a complete
and immediate reform in clerical manners and discipline. The bishops in the Diet took alarm. In reform
they would be the first victims. They took their stand
on the plausible ground of doctrine. They protested
against all that the conference had done. But the lay
majority were satisfied and pleased. Contarini himself
made no objection to the formulas to which the two
parties had agreed, and consented to send them to the
Pope. Disputes on subjects which had no practical
bearing he regarded as a harmless form of heresy. He
reprimanded the bishops for their opposition. He told
them that if they wished to escape being reformed by
the Emperor, they must mend their own manners,
reside on their sees and do their duty. He even
complained to the Pope of their general hopeless
negligence. He mentioned that when their conduct
had been before the conference, the Protestants had
denied their title to be called bishops at all. Bishops
meant inspectors, and these German prelates had
inspected nothing.

For the moment no more could be done; but, so
far as Germany was concerned, the Diet had given
satisfaction to all except the bishops. A beginning
had been actually made of a peaceful solution of a
problem which had threatened universal chaos. It
was the more gratifying as the competency of the laity
to share in the settlement of religious disputes seemed
to have been so successfully established. No one

doubted that after so much had been accomplished the rest would soon follow.

The Pope perhaps thought so too, though with less gratification. The Reformation really and truly turned on one point, whether the laity were or were not to have a voice in spiritual questions; anything like a successful assertion of this principle seemed to threaten Rome with destruction. Contarini might have been acquiescent. The Pope entirely disagreed with him. He approved of the opposition of the German bishops. He disallowed every one of the formulas. He protested that he would take no articles of faith from a secular Diet till they had been revised and approved by himself. The Emperor did not appear to care. His one honourable determination was to prevent a civil war. Completely and finally to settle a great religious quarrel without the assistance of the Pope was an extreme measure which was to be avoided if possible. The moderate part of Germany which still wished for unity desired at least that the Church should co-operate in some sort of council. Charles undertook to go immediately to Rome and once more to discuss the matter with the Pope, and urge the meeting of the council, and he promised that, if nothing was done within eighteen months, he would again call the Estates together and make a final end. Meanwhile he reminded Catholics and Protestants alike of the duty of forbearance. He required the Protestants to define no more doctrines, and suppress no more religious houses. He ordered the bishops and the superiors of such monasteries as were left to reform their manners, and lead a more Christian life. Church property in general he allowed to be applied equally to the support of priests and pastors. Voluntary converts might follow their conscience, but he recommended both sides not to be too eager to make proselytes.

With these wise words he dismissed the Diet.

The future of Western Christendom now turned on whether the long talked of council could or could not be immediately held. If it was again a failure, and the Reformation was left to be disposed of by diets and parliaments, things would go as they had gone in England. The German Church would be a national Church; the German clergy would be under the control of the German laity. The separation would be carried out with the consent of the Emperor. Other countries would follow the example; and the Pope might weep by the Tiber for a lost empire. Contarini pleaded with the Catholic princes of Germany. The council should meet, must meet, that was certain; but let it still be a Catholic council, a council of the universal Church. He implored them to bring their countrymen to agree to take part in it. He had an interview with the seven Electors; they were all of one opinion. The council, if council there was, must meet on German territory, where the Protestants might be present without danger. The Elector of Saxony was stubborn in his old demand that laymen should sit and vote, and that the Emperor and not the Pope should preside. Contarini argued that a council so composed would be only a German synod. The faith of the world could not be settled by the representatives of a single nation. A German synod would be followed by a French synod and a Spanish synod. In Germany they would be hopelessly divided; some would be for Luther and some for the Pope. However that might be, the Elector told him it was vain to hope that the Schmalkaldic League would ever acknowledge a council summoned by the Pope.

Charles went to Italy as he had said. He saw the Pope at Lucca. Pallavicino endeavours to save Charles's orthodoxy at the expense of his good faith. The Emperor, he says, assured the Pope that the threat of a national synod had been mere talk, never seriously meant, and mentioned only to keep the Protestants in good humour; the Pope should call the council, and the Protestants should be forced to acknowledge it. Something of the kind may have passed, but there is no occasion to charge Charles with insincerity. He was confident that if the council could once be brought together, the rest would go well. Having to conciliate two angry opponents, and himself better inclined to the old faith than the new, he did perhaps endeavour to sweeten the pill which the Pope was to be compelled to swallow. He did consent that the Pope should be left with the presidency, but he was resolute as ever that the council which was to meet should be a real council, a council of reform, a council at which the Papal Court itself would be brought to account. The Pope or a papal legate might preside, but the Protestants were to attend and to have free speech. Papal control there should be none, and the meeting must be outside Italy, in a place which would satisfy the demands of Germany without wounding too deeply the interests and sensibilities of Rome.

In the Austrian Tyrol, on the river Adige, a few miles above the Lago di Garda, was the small episcopal town of Trent. It was near the Italian frontier. It was easier of access to Italians than to Germans, while in the letter, if not in the spirit, it met the requisition of the German Diet. It lay within Ferdinand's dominions, and here it was that Charles and his brother had arranged that this memorable congress should be held. To Paul, Trent was tolerably satisfactory for many reasons. In the unsettled state of Europe it would be difficult, if not impossible, for the German or French bishops to attend in any numbers; the Italians would necessarily predominate. The distance from Rome was not too great for couriers to pass to and fro. He could direct the legates what to do and what to leave alone, and in the winter the climate was so trying that he could hope that the session would be short. Everyone present would be eager to be done with it.

Trent therefore was resolved on, and it remained to collect the prelates there with as much haste as possible. Unfortunately there was another interruption. Charles meant to be master of the council himself, and to be present in person at the opening. In his vast empire difficulties were always breaking out at one point or another. The council might be urgent, but immediate duties had first to be attended to; and Charles perhaps hoped that his position would be strengthened by another brilliant military expedition. Barbarossa's squadrons, which had been scattered from Tunis, had been reinforced by swarms of renegades, and had again combined at Algiers. They throve in the distractions of the period, and were tolerated, if not encouraged, by the French. A secret and scandalous correspondence had grown up between France and Constantinople. To be revenged on the Emperor was the fixed passion of Francis I., and any alliance was welcome to him, however foul the hand that offered it. The Algerian pirates became a nuisance and a danger, and once more the Emperor had to put his hand to the work. The capture of Tunis had been the glory of his reign. Another final victory over the enemy of the faith would lend a fresh splendour to the council by which the Church was to be purified and restored.

While Paul, therefore, was preparing for the meeting at Trent, Charles once more collected a magnificent fleet, and 200 transports carried an army so powerful and so well provided that victory was counted on as a certainty. It was late in the season, November in the year 1541. The Genoese pilots and the Spanish admirals did venture an opinion that the weather in the winter months was uncertain and might be dangerous. But Charles was impatient. He had much to do, and he believed himself irresistible. He sailed, and landed with his troops just outside the city of Algiers. The fleet and transports with the stores on board anchored at a gunshot distance. So far, all went well with him; but he was no sooner on shore than he was overtaken by a north-west hurricane. The roadstead was open; provisions, tents, and military stores had been left in the ships, as it was thought that the work would be short and they would not be needed. The transports were driven from their moorings, and were dashed to pieces in the breakers. The sands were littered with drowned bodies, stoven casks, and shattered boxes. Eight thousand seamen and soldiers were said to have perished. The Imperial ships which escaped wreck were forced to slip their anchors, and make for shelter in a bay fifty miles away; and the Emperor and all who had landed with him were left desolate and helpless, without food, without tents, without the commonest necessities, on an enemy's soil, beneath the walls of a fortified city. No preparations had been made for a land campaign. Guns, military engines, sappers and sappers' tools were left on board. To attempt to storm a fortress defended by desperate men, without ladders or siege material, was to invite destruction. There was nothing for it but to follow the fleet along the shore, and there was not a moment to be lost. Foodless, and harassed by swarms of mounted Arabs, the army had to struggle through the sands. The Emperor shared every suffering, went up and down the ranks encouraging, helping,

setting the fallen on their feet again, beating off the
attacks of the pursuing cavalry, never nobler, never
brighter than in misfortunes which he had the sorrow
of knowing to have been caused by his own sanguine
rashness. The march was accomplished at last. The
army was saved and carried back to Sardinia, but the
least part of the disaster was the material loss which
crippled his strength and exhausted his finances. His
reputation was clouded. His enemies all round him
exulted in his failure. One noticeable point deserves
to be remembered in the general calamity. Among
the Spanish cavaliers who had volunteered in the
expedition was Fernando Cortez, home for a time from
Mexico, who was so little accustomed to turn his back
on coloured foes that he offered to stay behind with
anyone who would remain with him, and take Algiers
single-handed.

Cortez would have found the red-beard renegade
a more dangerous enemy than Montezuma. He was
not allowed to try the perilous experiment. No fresh
Imperial success was to help Charles to impose his
will on the opening council. He returned to Europe
to find France in open alliance with the Turks, and
certain to use the moment of his misfortune to set
upon him again. He condescended to remonstrate.
He said it was ill done of the most Christian king to
bring the Moslems to attack him in Europe when he
had been risking his own life to check them in Africa.

Francis retorted by reminding his rival of the
storm of Rome and the Pope's imprisonment. He

by his league with the Turk had secured access for Christian pilgrims to the Holy Sepulchre. What had Charles ever done for the Church comparable to that? Mortified, harassed, and in real danger, the Emperor had to entreat the help of his excommunicated uncle of England, and appeal to his German subjects.

With another French war in view it had become necessary to recall the Diet. Charles could not attend himself. The congress met at Speyer, and Ferdinand presided in place of him. All Germany, Protestant and Catholic, was united and enthusiastic. The theological exasperations had lost their edge. The Emperor's action at Ratisbon had convinced the most suspicious that now they had nothing to fear. They at least had no alarm that he was playing with their confidence about the council. Trent had satisfied the great majority as a place of meeting. It was within the German border, and Charles had kept his promise, and in the general improved humour even the Pope was more gently thought of. Cardinal Moroni had been sent as legate this time to attend the Diet. Conciliation was the order of the day. The Cardinal said that if Trent was not satisfactory, the Pope would agree to Cambray. The larger part of the Diet preferred to do as the Emperor had desired. They would not add to his troubles by fresh contradictions. Satisfied that a real honest effort was now to be made to reform the Church and settle peaceably the questions which divided them, they were willing to meet the Emperor half way. They voted all the supplies which Ferdinand asked for, and were not precise in insisting upon conditions.

There were still dissenters who protested against a Pope-called council, the Elector of Saxony and the Landgrave of Hesse among them. In them there was a fixed conviction that from Rome and its bishop no honest dealing could be looked for; but this time neither the high character of John Frederick nor the personal popularity of the landgrave could carry the Diet with them. Powerful religious prejudices are often politically clear-sighted. Germany had to regret its credulity and to suffer for it, but in the prevailing good humour distrust was not allowed a hearing. Peaceful means were to be tried first, and the peaceful means were, in fact, to lead to the first civil war and the elector's and the landgrave's imprisonment.

But this was in the future. The Diet over, and the consent to Trent obtained, Paul, on May 22, 1542, issued his Bull convening the council there for the ensuing August. Doubtful points were evaded or touched lightly. Patriarchs, archbishops, bishops, abbots, and all persons privileged by custom to vote on such occasions were required to appear in person or by proctor. Secular princes were requested to attend or send ambassadors, and a special invitation was addressed to the princes of Germany. The purpose of the council was declared to be the determination of certain doctrines of the Christian religion which had been insufficiently defined, the reform of the discipline of the Church, the composition of the disputes between Christian nations, and the defence of Europe against the infidel.

As a practical comment on the last of these objects, France a month later again formally declared war against the Emperor, 100,000 Turks entered Hungary, and French armies were once more poured into Lombardy. The rival sovereigns each appealed to the Pope to condemn the other. The Pope sent a legate to Paris to advise peace, but probably Paul did not altogether regret the confusion into which Europe was plunged. With the world at strife again, few French or German bishops would be likely to make their way to Trent. Prelates were not valiant. His own Italians would have the field to themselves, and a body so composed could be managed as a domestic conclave.

Accordingly, in August 1542, the grapes ripe and summer not yet over, distinguished ecclesiastics and their retinues began to gather into the quiet city. Cardinal Moroni came, and our Reginald Pole and a few besides. In October Don Diego de Mendoza, the Imperial ambassador at Venice, made his appearance. The Emperor was too busy to be present himself, but he sent to represent him the chancellor Granvelle, with his son the Bishop of Arras, and a few prelates followed from the Emperor's Neapolitan dominions. The numbers were still too thin to allow an opening for despatch of business. But Granvelle had little time to spare. The Emperor intended Pope and bishops to understand from the outset the position in

which they stood, and the Chancellor desired to say a
few preliminary words in the cathedral to explain the
Emperor's absence and to declare his wishes.

Granvelle was a secular statesman. To permit the
secular representative of the Emperor to assume an
attitude of command in the cathedral pulpit, would be
an acknowledgment that the council was really summoned, as the Germans had demanded, in the Emperor's name. The intrusion of the lay element was
to be resisted at once, and Granvelle, who might have
done what he pleased if the African campaign had been
less unfortunate, was unable to insist. The cathedral
was refused. But the legates consented to hear him in
a secular hall; and on January 9, 1543, the Chancellor
delivered his master's wishes to the scanty gathering
of Italian bishops, who were all that as yet had arrived.
The Emperor had foreseen what was likely to happen.
He intended the council to reform the Church. He
knew perfectly well that the Italians whom the Pope
had sent up meant, if possible, to push reform into the
background. If left to themselves, they would probably define a few metaphysical doctrines, declare the
business completed, and go their way.

Granvelle had been sent to defeat and forbid the
convenient evasion. He complained in violent terms
of the action of France, glanced obliquely at the Pope
as too favourable to the French, and then informed his
hearers of the Emperor's object in having promoted
their assembly. Their real business was the reformation of the morals and manners of the clergy, so often

promised and so long neglected. The Emperor had hoped to impress their duties on them in person. The breaking out of the war had made this impossible, and he, Granvelle, had been sent to declare his master's resolution. He had made his way there with difficulty. A Turkish squadron had been lying in wait for him in the Adriatic. The roads were unsafe. The German and Spanish bishops were still absent, and weeks or months might pass before they could arrive. He was directed by the Emperor to inform the council that, in their absence, all action on important subjects was to be absolutely suspended.

The Chancellor was heard in angry silence. Trent, no pleasant place in summer, in winter was detestable. The lodgings were inconvenient, the climate bitter to soft southern constitutions. The bishops had been already waiting impatiently for three months. They were now threatened with further indefinite delay in the worst season of the year. The Emperor, it was said, was false to the Church after all. Did he want merely to frighten the Pope? Did he mean to hold his German synod, while they had themselves been drawn together to be made a mock of? The news from Germany looked like it. In his eagerness for the council, Charles had left untouched the critical question of the terms on which the Protestant divines were to be present. He had promised that they should take part. The council was now actually sitting, and so far only the bishops and princes had been invited. The Diet met again in haste at Nuremberg to have their doubts set at rest, and Granvelle, having delivered his admonition at Trent, had to hurry away to it to explain, leaving Mendoza as a watchdog to prevent mischief after he was gone.

Affairs were now critical, and Paul, sitting in the centre at Rome, had to keep his eyes everywhere. He despatched a Nuncio to Nuremberg to quiet the Protestant alarms. The Nuncio was plausible. He said that the Pope earnestly hoped to see German representatives at Trent; he did not say who, or in what capacity. The Diet answered that he had only invited the bishops. The bishops were sworn to the Pope at their induction, and were therefore nothing but his servants. The Nuncio assured them they need not be afraid. The princes' ambassadors would be there to see that they suffered no injustice. In the composition of the council the Pope had followed the universal custom. The Pope was to summon. The bishops were to deliberate and vote; this was the invariable rule, and could not be departed from.

The mystery was out then. It was as the Protestants had feared. They were not to be consulted after all. They were to be handed over to their enemies, and the Emperor had been taken in. The Emperor had *not* been taken in. He understood the men with whom he had to deal, and did not mean to be played with. Mendoza kept guard at Trent. Legates and bishops were eager to get upon the doctrines, settle these, and wind up their work. But Mendoza kept his hand upon their throats. At last, when nothing else would do, he was obliged to order them in peremptory terms to sit still till they had leave to begin. To give emphasis to his command, which he knew that they would not dare directly to disobey, he withdrew to his own post at Venice, and the Pope's band had to stay shivering in helpless inactivity through the frost and winds of a Tyrolese winter.

Paul had missed his first stroke. The position of things was exasperating and humiliating, and when May came, and there was still no sign of the Spaniards, he called a meeting of the cardinals at Bologna to consider what was to be done. Were the bishops of Italy to linger on indefinitely in a Tyrolese town waiting for the Emperor's pleasure, or should they be content with having made a beginning, and leave the seed to ripen into harvest at a more propitious time?

The cardinals answered unanimously that it was not for the dignity of the Church that legates, and nuncios, and holy fathers should remain longer under political enchantment. They recommended that the council should be immediately suspended. The Pope issued a Bull proroguing it. The unhappy victims were released from their purgatory, and the first act of the Trent drama came to a helpless end.

Meantime the war thickened, and the great Powers of Europe played their game as they could. The partners were curiously distributed. A French Admiral took command of the Turkish fleet in the Adriatic.

The coasts of Naples and Sicily were ravaged. The papal territories were spared, and there were suspicions that the Pope himself was a secret confederate in the Turko-French alliance. Charles, to the no less scandal of pious Catholics, entered into a league offensive and defensive with his uncle, Henry of England, whom the Church had consigned to eternal damnation.

In such an action Paul might well think that he saw completed at last the ruin of Catholic Christendom. He protested, but his protests brought only the cold answer that England, though separated from the Papacy, was still a Christian country, while Francis, to whom the Pope was now attaching himself, was hand in hand with the infidel.

Cardinal Pallavicino mourns over the fatal blindness of the Emperor at this crisis, and attributes to it all the woes which subsequently afflicted the Church. The Emperor had spared the Protestants in Germany when he ought to have destroyed them. He had bought the support of heretics by granting them liberty to profess a false religion. He had sought the friendship of the wicked apostate of England, and part of the compact had been that the heretic English were to make war on the Catholics of France. It was dangerous to play with serpents. Happier far, Pallavicino thought, it would have been for the world if the Emperor could have resigned his claims on Milan, and taken Francis for an ally instead of Henry. They two with the Pope's blessing might then have driven heresy out of Germany, have invaded England, and brought the insolent islanders to sue for pardon at the Pope's feet. Unhappily for himself, unhappily for mankind, the Emperor chose the other course, and the effect was that England was lost to the Church and the United Provinces to Spain, and the Devil, in Pallavicino's opinion, was universally triumphant.

The opinion of others will differ from that of the Great Jesuit Cardinal.

LECTURE VII

THE DEMANDS OF GERMANY

SIR ARTHUR HELPS, the author of 'Friends in Council,' makes a wise observation that the understanding of history is spoilt by our knowledge of the event. We see what has come of particular actions or incidents, and we see how it came. We assume that what is so plain to us must have been, or ought to have been, equally plain to the actors themselves, and when we see things turn out differently from what they professed to expect, we moralise over their want of foresight, or their insincerity. We ought to remind ourselves that this is the condition of all human action at all times. We act in the present, the future is dark. Wise men may hope, cunning men may calculate, but the future when it comes is always different from what anyone expects. Any man who has lived long, who has observed the course of his own life, or the course of public history, will have seen how reason has been baffled, prophecies have been proved foolish, and hopes visionary. The intelligent and the ignorant are alike incapable of seeing beyond the day which is passing over them. Lord Melbourne used to illustrate this from Catholic Emancipation. All the clever men were for it, he said, and all the fools were against it, and the fools were right. Knowledge of the event, of course, has an instructiveness of its own; but it does not help us, it only misleads us, when we are judging the conduct of human beings. Men act from interest, from passion, from habit, conviction, or prejudice. Nothing considerable ever came from looking too precisely to the event. To understand men, to form any just conclusion about them, we must know what they were in themselves, we must put ourselves in their position with the future all uncertain, think as they did, feel as they did. The great men in history who have accomplished anything worth remembering have been those who have gone forward upon the duties which lay nearest them, in the faith that good would result; if not the good which they expected, then something else greater and better than what they expected.

The Reformers of the sixteenth century have been accused of breaking the unity of Christendom, and rebelling against the Church's authority. When Luther's movement began there was nothing further from the minds of any of them. Religion was the basis of all their convictions on all subjects in heaven or earth. It was the sanction of civil government. It was the bond of society. It was the sole interpreter to all serious men of their existence and condition in the world.

Three centuries of change have accustomed us to

a variety of views about it. We have discovered that human beings can live together, discharging their common obligations, while on this particular subject they can agree to differ. When the sixteenth century opened over western Europe there was as little notion that there could be two religions, as that there could be two suns, or two multiplication tables. The Turks were infidels. The Greek Church was far off, and no one thought about it. The faith of Western Christendom was the faith of the Catholic Church, of which the Pope was primate. Unbelief in its doctrines was treason to God and man. The feeling attaching to heresy survives in the word *miscreant*—misbeliever. The storm which had risen had no connexion with doctrine. It had been merely a boiling over of indignation against the tyranny of the ecclesiastical administration, the impurity of the lives of the clergy, and their cynical disregard of the practical duties prescribed by the creed which they taught. The disease had spread through all ranks. At the Court of Rome the corruption was at its worst. The encroachments of the Papacy had absorbed all subordinate authority, and from the Papacy the poison of simony and profligacy had gone through every vein and artery of the Catholic communion.

This was the meaning, and at the outset the single meaning, of the Lutheran insurrection. Tetzel and the indulgences had only lighted the flame. I suppose no Catholic now defends the open sale of indulgences as a source of papal revenue. If Leo X. had admitted that in this instance he had abused his privilege, Luther would have gone no further, and have kept the rest of his thoughts to himself. But the Court of Rome had treated Luther as a rebel. He had been stamped with the hateful name of heretic. The secular power had been called in, to put him down and kill him, him and all his supporters. The secular power could not or would not do it; and the consequence was that the minds of men turned from the persons of the hierarchy to their teaching, teaching which was to be defended with weapons so ferocious; and all Europe came to be agitated with discussions on the mysteries of the faith.

We are now at the year 1544. Twenty-seven years had passed since Luther's theses had been nailed on the church-door at Wittenberg. England had broken away from the See of Rome. France was shaking, on the verge of following England's example. Norway, Sweden, Denmark, and two-thirds of Germany had reformed the Church, each in their own way, protesting, however, that they were setting up no new religion, but were willing and eager to submit all questions to a free general council in which the laity could sit and vote with the clergy.

Had the quarrel remained within the original limits of the Centum Gravamina, the Roman Court would have been brought rapidly to judgment. The laity, even the most orthodox, had been unanimous in their demand for a reform of morals and discipline in the Church. The bishops threw the blame on Rome for the disorders in their dioceses. The Popes had robbed them of their authority and stolen their money from them. Could a council have met for nothing save reform, it would have been Constance over again, and quick work would have been made with papal vanities and usurpations.

Unfortunately new elements had been thrown into the caldron. The Popes had thundered. The mendicant friars, the janissaries of the Vatican, had raved from every pulpit in Europe. Violence had provoked violence. The fire spread. It was no longer simony and immorality that were attacked, but the spiritual prerogatives of the clergy, and the mystical powers in virtue of which they claimed their authority. The air became full of new creeds and new opinions. One side cried heresy, the other cried that the Pope was Antichrist and his doctrines were idolatrous. The belief of centuries will not change in a day or a year. Popes and bishops might be wicked men, but the Pope's curse was still feared, and heresy was a dreadful possibility. The unanimity was gone. Many a man who had been loud enough in demanding reform of morals was frightened by the denial of the smallest article of the received creed. In vain Diets met and theologians argued. Authority was in suspense, and enthusiasm ran into even wilder speculation. Zwingli denied the sacraments, Carlstadt preached communism, and Anabaptism acted on it and broke into incendiarism and plunder. Behind Anabaptism was rising the stern uncompromising form of Calvin, denouncing death to the idolater.

Germany was divided into more than a hundred States, free cities, dukedoms, principalities, each with home rule and full power over its own affairs. In all of these the old principle was left—that, as in one State there could be but one law, so there could be but one religion. And each now made its own. Two-thirds of them had shaken off Rome. They had suspended their bishops, dissolved the religious houses, sequestrated the Church property for their own schools and pastors, and substituted a Communion service for the Mass. But there were twenty different varieties of Protestant doctrine, one in one State, another in another; and in each State there was a minority who held to the traditionary beliefs and resented the alteration. As long as the change touched only the outside of things, the minority might submit. The forcing upon them articles of faith which they considered heretical was more intolerable than the old tyranny.

Thus all was confusion, dispute, and anger. The German laity, the intelligent part of it, had not meant all this. They had their grievance against Rome, and they could not allow the Pope to be brought in again, till there had been some real improvement; but they were an order-loving people, and hated anarchy; they had revolted against clerical fraud and cheating, but they had never wished to splinter the Church into fragments. Chaos would come back unless something was done, and even the wildest religious enthusiasts professed themselves willing to conform to some general regulations if the common voice of Germany could get itself distinctly expressed. Synods, diets, conferences led to nothing, and there was a general cry, growing louder and louder, for a national German council.

Charles had not refused, yet he had not consented. A national German council was a resource to be tried at last, but only if other means failed irretrievably. He was not Emperor of Germany only. He was King of Spain and Naples, sovereign of the Low Countries, sovereign of a new world across the Atlantic. The diseases which had led to the confusion of Germany affected his whole dominions. He could not easily settle one part and leave the rest. He did not wish, the opinion, perhaps, of his Spanish and Flemish subjects would not permit him, to break completely with the Pope. His hope was rather for an ecumenical council of the whole Church, Germans, English, Italians, Spaniards, Flemings, French if they would consent, all to meet together, laity as well as clergy, and effect a universal reformation. The Pope was at the heart of the mischief, but Charles did not wish to lay rough hands on the Pope himself. The Church must deal with the Pope, and reduce the Apostles' successor to the model of the Apostles themselves.

Doubtless there were difficulties. According to precedent, an ecumenical council could be called only by the Pope himself. It was hard to require him to call an assembly together for his own condemnation. Even if the Pope could be forced to consent, a council of the established sort would consist only of bishops and abbots ; and the German princes and Henry VIII. also, when Charles consulted him, replied naturally that, next to the Pope, the bishops and abbots were the chief delinquents. They were ready to submit to a council, but it must be a free council, where the laity were on equal terms with the clergy. They would never agree to a council where the principal offender presided, and his assessors were his servants or accomplices. Charles could only answer once more, ' Let a council meet—meet on any terms—send your representatives on any conditions. I will see that you have fair play, and when we are once collected, we can remodel it as we please.' The Germans were shy. Henry said he had no wish to separate from the Church or to set up a God of his own. He would be satisfied with such a council as the Germans asked for, but he would not trust the interests of England to what he called ' the prestraille.'

So the question had hung fire through Diet after Diet. The Pope would have far preferred, if he could manage it, to escape a council of any kind. If a council there must be, it must be on the established lines, with himself as president. The Pope said, naturally, that, if he was to call a council, he would have no laymen sitting on it. Laymen had nothing to do with religion. He had prayed the Emperor, as a much more satisfactory plan, to put the mutinous heretics down, and he still thought that, with skilful handling, the Emperor might be brought to try it. Charles was honestly convinced, on the other hand, that, if the Germans and English would yield the first point, and take part in the council on any terms, he could himself undertake that they should be allowed their due weight in the discussions, with the help of the bishops from his own dominions.

The objections at last had been evaded rather than overcome. We saw in the last lecture how the council was set moving. A legate or two and half a dozen Italian prelates were collected at Trent —Trent having been chosen as a place of meeting, because it was in the Austrian Tyrol, inside the German frontier.

The Pope had made up his mind to the inevitable, when fate came to his help for the moment in the shape of a renewal of the war between France and the Empire, and nothing could be done while the war lasted. The fathers waited at Trent for six months, and then went their way. Paul III. had no objection. The council was no object of his. His chief fear was from the Emperor, and war with France, or civil war in Germany was the best security for the Court of Rome, as keeping Charles employed. Unhappily for Paul, the respite was brief, and the manner in which the war was conducted and brought to an end promised worse for him than anything which had yet happened.

The Emperor bought the support of Germany by fresh edicts of toleration; by promises, distinct and lavish, that, if nothing could be done with a General Council, they should have the synod which they had asked for. The smoke of Paul's curses was still hanging over Henry VIII. The Emperor, as if in studious contempt of papal excommunications, made a formal alliance with him. They took the field together, the most Catholic Charles, and the prince whom, above all others, Roman churchmen most abhorred and feared.

France was forced to sue for peace at Crépy, and the Emperor, victorious by the help of his Protestant subjects and heretic ally, summoned the Diet to meet again at Speyer. He felt his obligations, and acknowledged them; and he now besought the Diet once more to assist him freely and earnestly in bringing the religious discords to an end. He said nothing of the council, save making a brief allusion to it, as having been tried and having failed. He gave no more views of his own; he asked the Estates for their advice as to what they desired him to do.

The Diet, being German, thought only of German interests. They saw the Emperor in active alliance with the Pope's worst enemy. If the Emperor was not afraid to take Henry for a friend, he might be prepared to take him for an example also. What an English Parliament had done a German Diet could do. Let the experiment be made. Let it be announced that at a fixed date a synod of both orders would meet and take up the question. All quarrels might be suspended meanwhile. Protestants should not injure Catholics, or Catholics Protestants. Each State and each free city might send in at once a sketch of the form of Christianity established within its limits. These, when the synod met, could be compared, and a common constitution be arrived at under which they could all live at peace till better times, when a General Council could be held which would be free indeed.

The English example was encouraging. The Parliament, in passing the Six Articles Bill, had shown its ability to correct Protestant extravagance, as well as to abolish Romish abuses. Charles promised that a synod should meet, and it seemed now as if the end was really come, and that there was nothing left for Paul but to gather his pontifical robe about him, and fall, if fall he must, with becoming dignity. Evidently he thought so himself, but he determined to try the effect of one last appeal. He wrote a letter to Charles, and despatched Cardinal Moroni with it to the Imperial Court. He was himself a far from immaculate son of Adam, with many sins about him, but when he spoke as Pope he could rise to the majesty of his office.

He told the Emperor that he remembered the sin of Eli, and feared that if he was silent longer he might fall into the same condemnation. The resolutions of the German Diet, to which Charles had consented, would destroy the Church, and with the Church the Emperor's own soul. 'You propose,' he said, 'to regulate religion in Germany; you pass over without mention the Apostolic See, which you are bound to consult. You allow laymen, even laymen who have maintained damnable heresies, to be judges of spiritual things; you have received to trust and honour men whom you once condemned. It is not you that have done it; you are led astray by ill advice; but the fact is the fact, to all our sorrows, and woe is before the Church, and before yourself, unless you repent. Who are the allies with whom you are associated? Evil communications corrupt good manners. Ask of the wise, and they will tell you that those who rob the Almighty of His due will not be unpunished. You fight with Providence; remember Uzzah. Uzzah thought he did God service when he held up the ark of the Lord, but the Lord slew him. He had usurped the office of a priest. Listen not to those who tell you that you must reform the Church. To reform the Church is for priests alone. Think on Dathan and Abiram—a lesson they for all the ages. The root of the offence is pride. It is right to offer incense to the Lord, but none may offer save the priests. You are piercing the body of Christ.

'Nay, you will say, it is only for a time, till a council shall otherwise decide. The thing you seek may be good, but in you it is impiety; you intrude into a province which is not yours. Those princes have been honoured who have held up the Apostolic See. Such was Theodosius, such was Charlemagne; but, mind you this, princes who have turned *against* that Holy See have gone from crime to crime, till they have received the reward of their iniquities. There may be some (like Henry of England) who seem to triumph in their wickedness. All crimes are not punished in this world, lest men might doubt of a judgment to come; but every sin is found out at last, and the worst penalty is to seem to escape and to have the eyes of the soul blinded. The crime of crimes, the guilt of guilt, is to injure St. Peter's See. This bad age has seen too much of it. That you, dear son, can so act I cannot yet believe, but your edict compels me to admonish you. None desire concord more than I desire it; but I, not you, must find out the way. You would have the discipline of the Church restored. The object is good. For you to meddle with it is evil. You take advice from those whom the Church has condemned. I do not desire the destruction of such men, ill as may be their deserts. I would rather have them recovered as sheep that have strayed. But why should you join with them while they are outcasts from the Church,—men whom gentle treatment has hardened into insolence?

'We have done our part: we sent our legates to Trent; we called, but there was none to hear. They went, but found no man. We still invite you to a true council, a council where angels will be assessors with us. We pray that Christendom may be joined together again in faith and charity. Lead you in this campaign, and you will be at your proper work. While the council sits give peace to Europe. Return, return, I beseech you, to the right road. Return at the rebuke of your father. Meddle not with sacred things in worldly Diets, from which those are absent who alone may handle them. Leave religion for the council, and recall the toleration which you have allowed to rebels. Have pity on your own soul. Reflect on the hurt you do to the Church. If you will not, if you will persist in disobedience, we must then use our power, and be more severe with you than we desire to be. Eli was punished because he forgot his duty in weak affection for his sons. I may not neglect that signal example. Two courses are now open to you. Either to support your father with the strength of the Empire in maintaining the unity of the Church, or to support those who have broken it down and desire now to finish their evil work. The God of peace deliver you from the counsels of the ungodly. Amen.'

Cardinal Pallavicino saw the original draft of this remarkable composition. The language as it came fresh from the Pope's alarmed or wounded feelings was even more vehement than in the form in which it was sent, and Paul was very unwilling to allow it to be modified. The Emperor, in kindness to him, would have kept it secret; but it had been written for the world, and the Pope himself published it. Calvin observed that it was no wonder the Pope thought so much of the sin of Eli when he had been so indulgent to his own bastard children. But Paul knew well what he was doing. Unwelcome as a council had ever been to him, he saw that his best chance was to summon one himself on the established lines and without a moment's delay. There was now peace.

The Emperor was at leisure; the synod in Germany was impending. If the Pope delayed till the synod had met, and had settled its scheme of reform, the council would probably assemble only to register what the synod had decided, or to have laymen forced into the middle of it. He resolved, therefore, at once to take possession of the ground. The synod would take time, and the interval would be his own. Without consulting Charles, he issued a Bull commanding the bishops to collect again instantly at Trent. At the outset they would be in manageable numbers, and would consist chiefly of Italians, whom he could control. Resolutions could be passed rapidly, defining the Church's doctrine on the points which Luther had raised. Decrees once completed could be declared irrevocable, and thus the synod would be anticipated. The Germans would either refuse to recognise the council at all, and in their absence he would have nothing to fear; or else they would appear as already condemned, to receive sentence and be dismissed.

It was an ingenious move. It put the Emperor in a position in which he must either break with the Papacy, which his Catholic subjects would resent, or break the promise which he had just renewed to the princes of the Schmalkaldic League. Germany opened astonished eyes. The Emperor had engaged distinctly at Speyer that when a council met again, it should be the free council which they had always asked for. They had relied on him, given him their money, fought for him in the war. What did it mean? Was it all treachery?

Charles had to recall the Diet to Worms and try to make the best of it. He was himself ill with the gout, to which he was already beginning to be a martyr. His brother Ferdinand presided, and had to tell the Protestant deputies and princes that the council was reassembling. Catholic Europe had agreed to recognise it. The settlement of religion could not be postponed. The Emperor trusted that they would not refuse to take part.

Had reform of the abuses of the Church been the only object for which the council was to meet, sooner than quarrel with the Emperor the Diet would probably have submitted. On the ground of reform they would have felt safe in Charles's hands. Unfortunately, as I said, passion and acrimony had been stirred on both sides by theological controversy. Special articles of faith had been adopted by the Lutheran divines, which had been as fiercely condemned by the Catholics. Erasmus had foreseen what would happen. Erasmus, when Charles consulted him, had entreated that there should be no fresh definitions of doctrine. Free will, original sin, predestination, justification, faith and works, the Real Presence, and sacramental grace, were serious and interesting problems; but, in Erasmus's opinion, they were mysteries incapable of precise explanation, and no matters to divide the Church upon. Christians who accepted the Apostles' Creed and the Nicene Creed and the

authority of Scripture might be left on such abstruse
questions to think for themselves.   Remaining as
mysteries they would be regarded with silent reverence.   Set out in dogmas they would be cries of battle.
So thought Charles himself, and had done his best
in his own Netherlands to silence disputatious tongues
—so thought most wise laymen.

A distinguished Huguenot once spoke to our Elizabeth about the abomination of the Mass.   Elizabeth
said she would rather hear a hundred thousand masses
than have on her conscience a millionth part of the
miseries which had risen out of the quarrels about
it.   But dogmas have a fascination for theologians,
and Catholic and Protestant were equally embittered.
The princes of the League had a majority in the
Diet.   Herman, the Elector Archbishop of Cologne,
had just joined them, and the Pope had excommunicated him.   This had added fresh fuel to the
flame.   In vain Ferdinand entreated.   They stood
to their old ground.   They must have a free council.
They would promise no obedience to the decrees of a
handful of Italian prelates nominated by the Pope
and sworn to the Pope's allegiance.   For three weeks
the discussion raged.   Charles had to rise from his
sick bed and hurry to Worms to take part in it.   He
wanted money.   The Diet would grant none without
a renewal of the toleration edict which the Pope had
required him to revoke.   He reminded them that
they had themselves asked for a council.   It had
been got together on German soil and for German

interests. Their deputies, if they would send deputies, should be fully heard. He would himself undertake for their fair treatment. He begged them to pause before they threw away their opportunity, at least till they had seen what the bishops at Trent would do. It was to no purpose. The princes of the League were stubborn. The council now meeting was not the council which had been promised them. If they sent deputies, they might be bound by its decrees, and bound they would not be.

The Emperor was an honourable man. Friars might rave and Popes might lecture their dear son, but civil war was worse than the anger of priests, and he began to think that he could do no more. Cardinal Farnese came to him from Rome while the Diet was still sitting to watch how things would go. Charles told him that, called as it had been by Paul's separate action, the council was obviously meant to be a tool in the Pope's hands. The Germans could not be compelled to take part in it. He gave no opinion. The Pope must now act on his own responsibility, continue the council or let it drop as he pleased. It was his own affair. Farnese appealed to Chancellor Granvelle, Charles's confidential minister. Granvelle told him gravely that the Protestants knew that they would be condemned by such a council as was now meeting. Their next step would, perhaps, be to do as Frondsberg had done—collect an army and march on Rome. 'How can you stop them if they do?' he said. 'The German Catholics

are weak and few. The Emperor will give you his
pity. He will give you nothing more.'

The sack of Rome by a German army was fresh
in memory—what had happened once might happen
again. Farnese was pathetic. ' Surely,' he said,
' his master might count on the Emperor's protection. The Pope wished only to extirpate heresy and
reform abuses, if there were abuses which needed
looking to.'

The ' if' would not do at all after the report of the
Pope's own commissioner. If Paul, instead of writing
letters on the sins of Eli, had taken that report up and
acted boldly on it; if he would have promised that
this should be the council's first business, and that
nothing else should be touched until the Tiber had
been turned in upon his own court, and had washed it
clean, then with a clear conscience the Emperor could
have required the Diet's obedience, and all European
history would have been different. But Paul had
taken another line. Granvelle said he must now do
what he liked ; the Emperor would not be answerable
for the consequences.

Farnese was perplexed. Was the Emperor serious,
or was he only manœuvring to bring the Diet to give
him a subsidy ? He could not tell. He tried Charles
again. He said it was unworthy of him to be afraid
of his subjects. Coercion would be easy enough if
he tried. The Pope would help. He would give him
half the revenues of the Church of Spain; a very
generous offer on the part of the Pope. The Pope

would provide an auxiliary army at his own cost. He would excommunicate; he would do anything in reason. But sooner than allow religion in Germany to be ordered by a lay Diet, he would abdicate and give St. Peter back his keys.

Pallavicino could but pity the unfortunate pilot who had to steer St. Peter's bark among such reefs and shoals. Farnese could extract no answer, good or bad. Paul decided that, having gone so far, he must now let the council proceed.

Since so it was to be, the Emperor advised that the consideration of doctrine should be at least postponed till it was seen what the Germans would finally resolve upon. He recommended the Pope to take up morals in earnest. The fathers would be in a better condition to deal with spiritual mysteries when their hands were cleaner.

This was precisely what the Pope did not intend to do. Never did he mean to allow the council to meddle with him or his court. He did not wish the Germans to attend, because he knew that they would insist upon reform; but the onus of refusal was to be thrown upon the Diet, and by hurrying forward with the doctrines he hoped to make the refusal a certainty. He understood the difficulties of the Emperor's position; he believed that he might safely do as he pleased, and he had the most orthodox of reasons to allege for persisting. 'The council must go on,' he said. 'The Church would be disgraced by a further failure.' He undertook that there should be no rash decrees; but it was

well known that right action could only proceed from a
right faith. Faith must come first. Doctrines must
be purified before morals could be touched. The
Church had always acted on that principle, and always
must.

So now we will turn for a few minutes to the scene
of the conflict itself. March 15th, 1545, had been the
day named in the Bull for the council to assemble.
At the beginning of April the little Tyrolese town was
filling again. Three cardinal legates came with their
suites of theologians and canon lawyers—Cardinal de
Monte, afterwards Julius III., the Cardinal of St. Cross,
and Reginald Pole. Many strangers had been attracted
by curiosity; there might be Lutherans among them,
and, for fear of accidents, the Pope had supplied a
garrison. By May 1st, ten bishops had arrived, and
Mendoza, the Spanish Ambassador, had come up from
Venice. Paul's orders had been to lose no time, and de
Monte wished to begin business. The Emperor had
instructed Mendoza to keep up some kind of authority.
Mendoza commenced by claiming to sit in the council
above the bishops, and next to the presiding Legate.
Outside of it, he said, he would give place to the
meanest priest. In the council itself the Emperor was
the next person to the Pope. The Legate yielded for
the moment, but referred to Rome. The Mass of the
Holy Ghost was said in the cathedral. By the end of
May ten more bishops had arrived, all Italian and
papal. Twenty, the Legate thought, would be sufficient to reconstruct the creed of the Universal Church.

Mendoza, however, insisted that he must wait for the Spaniards. June went by, and it was the same story. The fathers murmured and complained of the expense, and asked to be paid for their time. De Monte quieted them with a few presents, but could not have it said that they were taking the Pope's wages. The additions dropped in slowly. The machinery was in order, but the council could not move, and the Pope, who had hated Trent from the first, and had wished to have the meeting in his own dominions, began to hint that the fault was in the place which had been selected. The climate was bad, the situation was exposed; the surrounding population were heretics. The bishops could not attend at such a spot. Why not move down to Italy, or, for that matter, what need of a council at all? There were books enough to settle doctrine, and he and the Emperor could arrange Church reform between them.

Charles remained inscrutable, contenting himself with forbidding the remove to Italy. Couriers went twice a week between Trent and Rome, Pope and Legate exchanged their perplexities, and Paul complained that no one but himself appeared to care for the glory of God. The summer wore on, the fathers chafed and fretted, but nothing was done. The Emperor was still trying to persuade the Diet. It rested with them, he said, to make the council a success. If they objected to the papal presidency, let them send their deputies to Trent and say so. He significantly added they would not be unsupported. The Diet was still suspicious. They said Trent was an Italian city. The Pope was master there, and the bishops were his sworn servants. Thus all was again at a standstill. The unfortunate fathers declared that they were being played with, and would bear it no longer. Some asked leave to go home, some went without leave. When September came the problem was likely to settle itself, as no one would be left.

The Pope might, of course, have ordered the opening if he dared, but he did not dare with the German national synod hanging over him. He had taken one bold step in summoning the council as he did, and another in insisting that he would proceed at once upon doctrines. But if Charles chose to desert him in earnest, it was too possible that he might see a German army at his gates again. He appealed to Charles. The bishops, he said, could not be kept together any longer. They had waited on his pleasure for six months. What did the Emperor wish him to do?

Charles himself could not tell. He was personally a devout believer in the Catholic faith. He disliked novelties. He regarded the Protestant formulas as a doctrine of yesterday, and distrusted the capacity of enthusiastic individuals to discover a truer religion than that which had descended through the usage of a thousand years. But the creed was one thing, and loose and scandalous Popes and cardinals were another. He answered at last that the council might open, but he warned the Pope once more that doctrinal questions must wait till the Lutheran theologians had been heard upon them. He entreated, he commanded, that the fathers should confine themselves to purifying morals and discipline, and go to work upon these in earnest.

The Pope would have been better pleased had Charles advised him to let the council drop. If Paul had been a great man, he would have followed the Emperor's advice, and he might have made himself another St. Gregory. But far were any such aspiration from the present occupant of the Holy See. If the council was once launched seriously upon reform, he well knew what would follow. The Church might be regenerated, and Catholic unity preserved; but the splendour of the Papacy, the pride, the wealth, the world-wide dominion would be at an end for ever. A genuine searching enquiry into the disorders of the Church could have no other result. All that Luther had said would be proved true. The German Diet would send their representatives. The Catholic Germans would go with the rest. The Romans would be overwhelmed. The one escape was to appeal to the dread of heresy, and to stand before Christendom as the champion of the orthodox faith.

It was a bold course, but the boldest is often the safest. The bishops who had left Trent were ordered back. De Monte was directed to open the council at once, take up the articles of the Confession of Augsburg, whether the Emperor liked it or not, examine and condemn them, and do his work swiftly, that no questions might be raised about hearing opponents.

As to morals, the Legate was not to seem as if he wished to avoid the subject. He might tell the bishops that, if any of them had complaints against the See of Rome, the Pope would consider what they might say. He must not let them think that they were in any sense judges of St. Peter's successor; but merely that, if there was anything which they were dissatisfied about, the Pope wished to know its nature, that he might find a remedy.

Such were the orders for the opening. Mendoza might protest, the Emperor might regret; but if the Pope was obstinate, the only alternative was to drop the council altogether—a last resource, not to be resorted to till all else had been tried.

LECTURE VIII

THE COUNCIL IN SESSION

THE council so long talked of which was to determine the faith of the world was now to become alive.
Popes and princes had intrigued and skirmished, each
struggling to control its action. In theory ecumenical
councils were controlled by the Holy Spirit, but neither
Charles nor Paul seemed practically to expect such high
assistance. A profane father at the council itself said
that the Holy Spirit would come to them from Rome
in the courier's bag.

The Bull for the opening arrived on December 11,
1545. The attendance was scanty for so large an
enterprise. Some of the prelates who had been at
Trent all the summer had gone home weary of waiting.
Of these a part had been recovered; thirty bishops
and abbots, with three cardinals—de Monte, St. Cross,
and Reginald Pole—had been at last brought together,
and the 13th, being the third Sunday in Advent, was
chosen for the initiatory ceremony.

At Rome the occasion was celebrated by a jubilee,
and the prayers of the faithful were asked for the

council's success.   The troubles in Germany had risen
out of indulgences; with pointed meaning, a plenary
indulgence was granted to all Catholics who would fast
three days, join the procession to St. Peter's, confess
and communicate.   The fathers at Trent went in state
to the cathedral between files of soldiers, followed by
the divines and canonists.   De Monte said Mass.   A
bishop preached the sermon, in which he promised his
brother prelates that the Holy Spirit would come upon
them like water on a dry land.   The Holy Ghost might
not, he said candidly, improve their characters or touch
their hearts, but He would direct their judgments and
forbid them to err.   The president, Cardinal de Monte,
then explained the causes for which the council had
been assembled.   The first was the growth of heresy,
the second the question of reform.   About the second, in
spite of Paul's directions, he allowed himself to yield to
some extent to the Emperor's and Mendoza's insistence.
The decayed discipline of the Church was to be restored.
The corruption of morals among the clergy de Monte
admitted to be notorious.   Both the immorality and
the spread of heresy he attributed to the negligence of
the bishops.   He invited the bishops present to confess
and beg for pardon, remembering in whose presence
they were.   All knelt and prayed.   De Monte read a
collect and the gospel for the day.   The choir sang the
Veni Creator and the *Te Deum*, and the Council of
Trent was declared to have begun.

The bishops during their long waiting had doubtless
talked over many things among themselves, and

perhaps were not pleased to be so early made responsible for what had gone wrong. There was a feud of
old standing between them and the regular orders.
The first question raised was, who were to vote? The
bishops claimed the exclusive right. The abbots said
they had as good a right as the bishops. It was
decided that only the generals of the orders and mitred
abbots should vote, and only those abbots should be
admitted who had been specially sent by the Pope.
The Regulars were the Pope's special guard. The
animus of the council had already shown itself, and
became more evident at the second step. The fathers
enquired next in what relation they stood to the Pope;
did they meet immediately under Christ, or under
Christ through the Pope? Were their acts to run in
the name of the council only, or in the names of Pope
and council? These and other similar questions were
asked.

The ship was scarcely under way when she seemed
driving on the rocks. De Monte, who had to watch
the symptoms, sent off a courier to Rome. The bishops,
he said, were in mutiny already. They had raised the
most dangerous points. They had enquired into the
Pope's powers. They had asked whether they could be
dissolved without their own consent. He begged the
Pope to send him money. Nothing could be done
without money, and he recommended that the tenths
of the bishops' incomes usually paid to the Holy See
should be remitted while the council continued.

Paul had expected trouble, but this was worse than

he had looked for, and worse still was to follow. He had encouraged the bishops to produce their grievances. A provincial of simple habits had taken him at his word, and complained of the palaces and fine clothes of the cardinals. Serious scandals were hinted at in their establishments. It was said loudly that, if the high officials of the Church were to edify the world with their example, they had work before them in their own households.

The Pope was prudent. He showed no irritation. He sent the money which the Legate asked for; he remitted the tenths, getting small thanks for his liberality. A few bishops expressed gratitude, but the majority accepted the concession ungraciously. They seemed to think that to allow themselves to be excused from paying tenths to the Pope might imply a recognition of the Pope's right to demand them.

The form in which the acts of the council were to run continued to be a subject of debate. The evident wish was that decrees should be in the council's name alone, the Pope not being mentioned. It seemed as if at the very outset they wanted to declare themselves independent of the Pope, or, as at Constance, superior to him. Paul tried to meet the difficulty by proposing that the decrees should be issued in the name of the Holy Ecumenical and General Council of Trent, presided over by a Legate of the Apostolic See. But this would not do. The bishops required to be 'representatives.' As 'representatives' they would have a position of their own. The bishops at Constance had claimed to represent the Church universal. They too, they said, represented the Church universal, and so it must be acknowledged.

De Monte ingeniously replied that the Church was composed of clergy and laity. If the bishops sate as representatives of the clergy, the laity would claim to be represented also. The bishops magnified their office. They said that, by taking the title of representatives, they would teach the laity to know their places. Servants were not to be masters. The laity were the servants of the clergy. The real object was to repudiate subordination to the Pope. De Monte saw the dangerous spirit growing. He was obliged to tell the Pope that the bishops were almost unanimous. In all ways they were taking state upon themselves. They required a guard of 300 soldiers to attend them to Mass, and to fire salutes when they entered or left the cathedral. The Legate checked these ebullitions of self-consequence as well as he could, but they burst out on all occasions, and it was the more provoking as the bishops present were almost all Italians, and individually insignificant.

Mendoza, too, was a thorn in de Monte's side. He had claimed in the Emperor's name to sit in council next to the presiding Legate. De Monte had yielded, but the Pope had disapproved. Mendoza was imperious and insolent. Twelve Spanish bishops were on the road, and were soon to arrive with Don Francis, the Archbishop of Toledo, at their head, all, it was reported, men of conspicuous character and ability. It was to be feared that they would support their Ambassador, support perhaps the Emperor's views on all subjects. Already a Neapolitan prelate, a subject of Charles, had ventured to urge that they should leave doctrine alone, as Mendoza had required, and address themselves exclusively to reform. He had dared in a sermon in the cathedral to tell the fathers to weep for their sins. They well knew there was occasion for it. De Monte advised the Pope to send up the ablest men that he had, to encounter these people.

Things were looking serious. The monster whom Paul had created was slipping out of control. All his schemes, all his hopes would be defeated if the council were to fling itself upon reform; and if doctrinal questions were to be suspended, till the German heretics could be present to help in discussing them, fatal consequences would follow. He wrote passionately that in all councils the rule had been to take doctrine first. A sound faith was more important than morality, because it was the root of morality; and that was not a fit time to weaken the defenders' arms by proclaiming their faults to the world when the enemy was beating at their gates. The bishops might talk about sins and immoralities. Paul said he saw what all that meant. They were aiming at him and the Court of Rome. They must be brought to their senses. Inferiors were not to judge their superiors. Popes were to be venerated, not accused. It was easy to talk of reform; men were willing surgeons upon their neighbours' limbs.

As to the princes (meaning of course the Emperor), they were enemies also. They might talk of restoring the Papacy. They intended only to take its power away and intercept the sap of the mystic vine. If, through ignorance, or with sinister objects of their own, the bishops played into the princes' hands, the Church might be ruined; but for himself, Paul said, he would never consent to impair the dignity of St. Peter's chair. A council convened against heresy would be introducing heresy. The army would be turning its back to the enemy and fighting with its own generals. It would be Constance over again. Reform, he said, must and should be kept in the second place. It would bring nothing but schism and confusion. The council must occupy itself usefully with the Lutheran heresies. He and the cardinals meanwhile might agree on moderate alterations of discipline which the council could afterwards adopt.

So Paul would have arranged it. But the Spaniards were on the way, and the Imperialist prelates already at the council stood to their ground. They said, as the Emperor had said, that the heresies which the Pope talked of had grown out of the immoralities of the Church, that never in Christian history had the moral character of the higher clergy been more depraved than it then was, and that for them to talk of purifying the Church's creed, with their own sins so rank, was to make themselves the jest of mankind.

A few faithful voices echoed Paul's phrases: ' Belief was the foundation of Christian life'; 'Good conduct could grow only out of a right creed'; 'Errors of opinion were more dangerous than sins,' and so forth. But the cry was too loud to be so disposed of. The Legate saw that the opposition really rose from the eagerness of the provincial bishops to recover the rights which they thought Rome had stolen from them. But it was evident that a good many did actually believe that the Church was in a bad way and needed mending, and this party, when the Spanish bishops arrived, would be irresistible. The Pope had ordered him to shelve reform. It could not be shelved. An eloquent father said openly that the Holy Spirit would never inhabit vessels so impure as some of his colleagues on the council. They must mend their faults before they could approach the mysteries of the faith. The Cardinal of St. Cross answered that, if that was all, they might begin on the spot. Each member of the council might repent at once of his sins, and in a day or two all would be done. That might suffice for the members of the council themselves, but the whole Church needed cleansing. De Monte was obliged to agree at last that doctrine, and reform of morals and discipline should proceed on parallel lines, alternate sessions to be given to each. De Monte had to trust to his ingenuity to prevent mischief. Separate Congregations were to meet, composed of bishops, theologians, and canonists, who were to examine the subjects and prepare resolutions to be afterwards submitted to the vote of the council; and active business was at last upon its way.

Paul had thus lost the first battle. The legates had done their best to please him, but the pressure was too strong. There was consolation. Doctrine had still

the first place, and, with good management, the articles
of the Augsburg Confession might still be condemned
before a synod could meet in Germany, or German
deputies arrive at Trent. When the thing was done
the council might refuse to reopen a closed discussion.
The Emperor would hesitate to submit to a lay assembly
decrees once passed by the Church. Germany, it was
hoped, would then be divided. The Protestant part of
it would finally decline to recognise the council in any
form. The League of Schmalkald and the Emperor
would quarrel, the Catholic States would come back to
their allegiance to Rome, and the wars would begin, in
which, as Paul shrewdly saw, his best hope of safety
lay.

The Imperialists at Trent still protested that thirty
or forty bishops were too small a body to define the
Church's creed. They were expecting the Spaniards.
They demanded delay. They urged that circulars
should be sent to Spain and France, to hurry up the
laggards and fill the benches. But de Monte had now
his majority in hand. A scornful voice suggested that
perhaps the Imperialists would like to send a circular
to Prester John's country.

The two Congregations were set about their work.
Time had still to pass before the first reports could be
prepared, and business had to be found for the fathers
meanwhile, to keep them out of mischief. The great
Powers who were represented by ambassadors would
have to be mentioned in the council's documents. A
debate was got up on the order in which they were to

be named. Was France to come before Austria, or
Austria before France? The subject was found too
dangerous to go on with. Someone proposed a general
resolution on the interpretation of Scripture as a useful
step. This was premature. The courier from Rome
brought no instructions, and Pole then suggested that,
as a beginning, and as a general declaration against
heresy, the council could do no better than affirm the
Apostles' Creed. The use of this was not obvious. It
was observed justly that the Lutherans received the
Apostles' Creed as devoutly as Catholics did. Pole's
proposal, however, it was thought, could do no harm,
and the Apostles' Creed was affirmed accordingly.
This being done, a loyal follower of the Pope asked
leave to move that the affirmation should not stand
alone. Engaged as they were in a great work, and
having to wrestle with flesh and blood, as well as with
spiritual wickedness in high places, he thought it would
be well if the council would proceed next with a
declaration of allegiance to the Apostolic See. The
proposer of this resolution could not have been ignorant
of the general feeling. The bishops were all sworn to
the Pope when they received their pallium, and most
of them notoriously resented the obligation. Ingenuity
could not have invented a proposal more likely to create
disturbance. So much passion showed itself that the
Legate was afraid how the votes might go. Happily
for the peace of the council, news arrived which changed
anger to delight. Luther was dead. The arch-heretic
was gone to his account. No one could doubt that it

was a miracle sent for the council's special encouragement. God was manifesting Himself at last.

This was cheering intelligence indeed; all hearts were thankful, and all differences forgotten. Other good news came too. The Diet had met at Ratisbon, a rift had actually shown itself in the Protestant party, and a moderate section was forming and was going with the Emperor against the League. To Paul this was the confirmation of his warmest hopes. He had always believed that it would be so. Luther's influence while he lived might have prevented any open rupture; but Luther was gone, and Germany was now divided. There would be war, and the Emperor would think no more of compromise. His hands would be full, and there would be an end of serious reform. The Pope could not contain his satisfaction. Cardinal Contarini was obliged to tell him that his delight was premature. Paul thought that the whole disorder in Germany had risen out of innovations in religion. Contarini, who knew Germany well, had to inform him that it lay immeasurably deeper. The revolt was not religious, but secular and political. If Luther and all the Protestant divines had been converted and received back, the reconciliation of Germany with Rome would be as far off as ever. Contarini was perfectly right. The laity of Germany, the laity of England, had risen against ecclesiastical supremacy in all its forms. The Church's doctrines had only been offensive so far as they symbolised the usurpation of an overbearing and self-indulgent hierarchy.

The Pope, however, was confident in his own judgment. He believed the worst danger was past. The council might go on, and even touch on reform of discipline, if it was done with a light hand. The bishops wished it. It would please the Emperor, and no harm need now be feared.

Meantime the doctrinal congregation had selected four propositions out of the writings of Luther which the council was to be asked to anathematise.

'That Holy Scripture contained all things necessary for salvation, and that it was impious to place Apostolic tradition on a level with Scripture.

'That certain books accepted as canonical in the Vulgate were apocryphal and not canonical.

'That Scripture must be studied in the original languages, and that there were errors in the Vulgate.

'That the meaning of Scripture is plain, and that it can be understood without commentary with the help of Christ's Spirit.'

In the Congregation canonists and theologians sat and debated with the bishops. The points were taken one by one, and as the discussions were only beginning, every one was eager to give his opinion. Some wished, like the Emperor, to stop arguments on doctrine altogether. Others, like Erasmus, deprecated precise definitions. A Carmelite friar said that no doubt the Church was complete before any book of the New Testament was written. The Apostles themselves had taught by word of mouth, and much of what they had said was only known by tradition.

Tradition, therefore, had always been held in respect. But the fathers of the Church generally in their writings had appealed to Scripture rather than tradition, and it might be wise to follow their example. On the whole, he thought the first proposition might be left alone. To condemn it would make divisions and raise new questions.

Reginald Pole, with his keen scent for heresy, detected poison in the Carmelite's argument. He said the speech to which they had just listened was fitter for a German Diet than a Catholic council. Tenderness to Lutherans was folly. They must be broken down, driven upon their knees, every one of their errors dragged to light and condemned. Agreement with heretics was impossible, and the world must be made to see that it was impossible.

If agreement was impossible, why were the Lutherans invited to attend? The debate went on. Were all the books of both Testaments to be declared of equal value, or were the claims to be examined separately? Were Apostolic traditions to be limited, or were the decrees of Popes and councils to rank along with them? Was Scripture to be translated into the vulgar tongues of Europe? What was to be done when manuscripts were at variance? When scholars disagreed on the meaning of a word or paragraph, who was to decide? Pole's summary methods were rejected. Specialist divines were selected to make further enquiry on these points.

Great things and small jostle each other on all

occasions, even in the debating halls of councils. The discussion on Scripture was interrupted by a bishop who produced a personal grievance against the Court of Rome. That Court had an exasperating practice of granting pensions to favoured individuals, and instead of paying them out of the papal treasury, charging them on the income of some episcopal victim. A member of the council had been charged in this way with an annual payment of two hundred ducats. The see was poor. The whole proceeds from it sufficed barely for the bishop's support. Residence at Trent had increased his expenses. The pension had been left unpaid, and the bishop produced a letter which he had just received from the auditor of the Rota, informing him that, unless the money was sent immediately, he would be excommunicated. He appealed to his brother prelates whether it was fit that the Roman officials should handle a member of their body so cruelly when engaged in the Church's service. Every bishop present caught at the chance of denouncing the detested Roman Curia. Doctrine, tradition, Vulgate, all were let drop while they flew to the defence of their injured brother. The storm was hardly appeased by abject apologies, and promises of instant redress.

Calm was restored at last, and the fathers returned to Scripture. The position of the Vulgate in the Church had never been defined. It had been declared to be of authority but, after the criticisms of Erasmus, no one knew of how much authority. It could no longer be said to be free from errors, yet if private individuals were allowed to translate for themselves, no authority would be left. It was observed that the primacy of Rome rested on the single text, 'Thou art Peter'—a different construction might be given to the words, and what was to happen then? Another important objection was raised. How were the inquisitors to deal with heresy? If they were to refer to the original they would have to learn Greek and Hebrew—an intolerable addition to their labours. The longer the fathers considered the less they could see their way, and they concluded naturally that the Vulgate must stand as it was. There was reasonable likelihood that the Spirit which had dictated the original had also dictated the translation. Nay, it was ingeniously argued that the council then sitting was confessedly inspired. The council therefore had but to approve the Vulgate, and the Vulgate itself would be inspired. This reasoning had the merit of dispensing with further enquiry. A Benedictine abbot, indeed, was still unsatisfied. He pointed out that St. Jerome, who had made the translation, distinctly said he was not inspired. One language could not be completely rendered into another. The Vulgate was excellent, and the council might safely sanction the use of it; but perfect it was not, and it ought to be revised.

But the abbot found no supporters. The fathers generally thought it enough to be assured that the Vulgate contained no errors in faith or morals, and

must be accepted as the rule of the Church. No
ordinary readers could be led into heresy by it. The
learned might study the originals if they pleased.

The canon of Scripture being thus made co-exten-
sive with the Vulgate, and the errors disallowed, three
of Luther's four propositions were disposed of. There
remained the fourth, on the meaning of Scripture.
Luther was made to say that it was plain and could be
understood by any ordinary intelligence. The bishops
generally were of opinion that the reading of the
Scriptures, on the contrary, was the principal cause of
heresy. All heretics quoted Scripture, and nothing
could be more dangerous than for private persons to
try to form their own opinions out of it. One or two
voices were heard saying that the primitive fathers had
enjoined Scripture reading, and had allowed even a
latitude of interpretation; but the overwhelming sentiment was that Scripture had been already studied
sufficiently by competent persons. The real meaning
of it was well known, and novelties ought to be dis-
couraged. The vulgar had no occasion to read it, and
would do better to leave it alone. In the early centuries Church doctrine had not been defined; but
everything necessary to be believed had been since
drawn out completely by the scholastic divines. The
sacred writings, therefore, were no longer required,
and might be even extremely injurious to minds not
properly trained. Instances were mentioned of the
abuses of Scripture, which are some of them curious.
It was observed that preachers habitually applied

Scripture texts to contemporary events. The early fathers themselves did it, as if the texts had no proper historical meaning at all. The bishops admitted the paradox, but declined to forbid a practice so wide and ancient. They could censure more freely superstition like the *Sortes Evangelicæ* or the use of magical formulas constructed out of parodies of Scripture language. The discussion strayed into sorceries, love philtres, necromancy, witchcraft, astrology, and trials by ordeal. On such points the fathers at Trent were more enlightened than the Puritan witchfinders; some of them were for branding every one of these pretensions as fraudulent impostures, not believing them supernatural at all. The council declined to lay down a general rule, and left each offence to be tried on its own merits.

Any way, however, Luther's propositions were duly condemned. The Vulgate was canonized, tradition and Church authority were declared to rank with Scripture as the rule of faith, and the vulgar were forbidden to think that they could understand Scripture for themselves. The emphatic anathema of one at least of Luther's positions was accomplished, and Paul saw everything going as he wished.

The outer world was not so well satisfied. The outer world had been told that the council had been called to reconcile differences. They found it breathing nothing but censures and curses. Three cardinals and forty bishops, mostly persons of no consideration, had laid down the law upon questions which had been agitating the ablest minds in Europe. They had

engaged that along with doctrines they would take up
the reforms which were so much looked for; yet, beyond appointing a Congregation, not a step had yet
been taken.

The Emperor sent a mild message of surprise and
disappointment. Two score of Italian bishops, without
a single man of learning among them, taking upon
themselves to regulate the creed of all Christendom was,
he said, an extraordinary spectacle. The theologians
whom they had with them he understood to be below
mediocrity. Their canonists might know law, but
knew nothing of divinity. The council as it stood did
not represent the thousandth part of the Christian
world, yet it had canonised the Vulgate. It had ruled
what was Scripture and what was not. It had declared
tradition equal to Scripture, but had not explained the
nature of tradition, nor the limits within which it was
confined.

Whether Charles was pleased or displeased was
now comparatively of little moment to Paul. He believed that he had the control of the situation. He
thanked and applauded Cardinal de Monte, and urged
him to go on as he had begun. The more points he
could decide, the greater would be the difficulty in
reconsidering them. The one thing de Monte was to
be careful about was to allow no question to be raised
on the authority of the Roman See. He must use his
skill, parry, evade, in extremity he must absolutely
forbid, such questions. As to the council's title, which
the bishops had been anxious about, they might, if

they liked, call themselves representatives, but they must add 'Mediante summo Pontifice,' and no harm would be done. He had gained an advantage, or he thought he had, and could venture bolder language. He had excommunicated Herman of Cologne. He now dared not only to deprive him of his see, but to depose him from his rank as one of the seven Electors. It was late in the day for the Pope to interfere in the secular government of Germany. The object was of course to put the Emperor in a difficulty, and force him on into open quarrel with the Protestants.

Charles's position as a pious Catholic was every day growing more difficult. The Pope saw how it was with him, and pressed his advantage. The resources of moderation, however, were not yet exhausted. Scripture being disposed of, the next article on which the legates were instructed to proceed was original sin. The promise that the alternate session should be given to reform was not to be construed literally, perhaps might be escaped altogether. Original sin would interest the fathers, divert their attention from the papal court, and more than anything else exasperate Protestant sensitiveness. Original sin was thus announced for consideration. Divines and canonists were set to work preparing resolutions, the bishops all forgetting their other grievances in the excitement of the expected discussion, when the peace of the council was disturbed by the arrival of Don Francis of Toledo, and his dreaded phalanx of Spanish representative bishops. The Spanish prelates were the purest in Europe. In the

long fight with the Moors they had retained the stern-
ness and severity of the era of the Crusades.   Cardinal
Ximenez, the great minister of Ferdinand, wore a hair
shirt, and used the discipline of the scourge.   Such
men as these despised the effeminacy and vice of the
Italian metropolis, and were as eager as the Emperor
to apply the surgeon's knife.   They appeared at Trent.
It was necessary to receive them into the council, and
Don Francis at once demanded that the doctrinal discussions should be suspended, and that the fathers
should now address themselves in earnest to the serious
business for which the council had been assembled.

Cardinal de Monte was the adroitest of presidents.
He expected to follow Paul in the pontificate, and did
not mean, if he could help it, to succeed to a diminished
inheritance.   Fortunately, original sin had been already
launched before the Spaniards came.   He replied to
Don Francis, that, of all theological questions, original
sin was the most important.   The council had begun
upon it, and ought not to be called away from an occupation so interesting, till they had reached a definition
of its nature.   Reform, no doubt, was most important.
The committee was busy upon it, but the council had
met rather to condemn heresy than to censure churchmen, and a special error, once taken into consideration,
must not be left unrefuted.   Don Francis declined to
be convinced.   He produced an order from the Emperor
that reform must and should be seriously undertaken,
and undertaken without delay.   De Monte, entrenched
in precedents, replied that it was impossible.   Original

sin could not be withdrawn without the Pope's permission. A courier flew to Rome, and came back with an answer that the Emperor did not understand Divine mysteries. The one thing needful to the Church was a correct dogmatic system. Original sin was the keystone of heresy, and must be removed before anything else was done. The Pope having given the note, the Italian bishops assented in chorus. They would rather the council should be dissolved, they said, than that original sin should be left an open question. Don Francis was plain-spoken. He said he understood what it all meant; but the position was serious, and it would be dangerous to trifle. The Pope wished to drive the Emperor into war with the Protestants. The Emperor did not mean to be driven, and the Catholic princes of Germany were as anxious to avoid war as he. The council must meet their wishes at least in some degree, or the Emperor would cease to interest himself in anything which the council might do.

Mendoza supported his countrymen, and in such haughty terms that the Legate was driven to yield so far as that the formal arrangement should be adhered to, and reform and doctrine be taken alternately. The Italian bishops did not wish it. Still less did they like to be dictated to by the Emperor and the Castilian new comers. They hated Trent. They, like the Pope, wanted to hurry through the doctrinal business and go back to their soft skies and vineyards. Was the Emperor in earnest? That was still the question. The Legate could not tell. The Pope could not tell. The

Spaniards were pious Catholics, but they had helped the Germans to sack Rome only twenty years before. It would be too dangerous to disregard them altogether, and a reluctant consent was extorted to make the reform committee a reality.

The bishops had not forgiven de Monte's opening speech, in which the blame of the German revolt had been laid upon them. If enquiry there was to be, they declined to be the only sufferers. If they were to be put on their trial, the Court of Rome, which was the chief offender, should not escape. With his tenths and his annates, his dispensations and his licences, the Pope had picked their pockets, stolen their authority, and made them into his minions. If the sewer of corruption was to be opened, so let it be. They had not the most cause to be afraid. De Monte had said that the spread of heresy was owing to them and their negligence. They flung the charge back. The Popes had made it impossible for them to do their duty. Itinerant monks wandered about with papal licences, preaching where they pleased and what they pleased. Monks, and even their own secular clergy, had thrown off their habits, dressed and lived as laymen—all with indulgences from Rome. What was Luther but a vagabond friar, let loose from his convent because the bishops had no power to restrain him ? Let the Pope and cardinals look at home before they accused others.

Again it was a pretty quarrel. The generals of the religious orders retorted that the bishops had neglected their duties for centuries. Their schools were empty, their pulpits silent. The friars whom they so abused had done their work for them for three hundred years. Without the friars no Christianity would have been left in Europe.

The time had been when the friars deserved what the generals said of them, but they had fallen away like the rest; and when Erasmus formed his estimate of them they were the worst hated by the laity of all the instruments of papal despotism. Again the courier went for instructions to Rome. Paul did not mean to sacrifice the orders. They were far too precious to him. The bishops, he said, appeared to wish to be Popes, each of them in his own diocese. Place the orders under them, and the Pope's power would be gone. De Monte was directed to pacify the bishops with a promise that they might visit the monasteries occasionally as papal delegates. The generals were to be told privately that it meant nothing, and that they need not be alarmed; but so inflammable were the materials lying about that the least spark threatened a conflagration. The peril of enquiry into ecclesiastical disorder might be measured by the storm which had burst out when it was perceived to be seriously intended.

LECTURE IX

DEFINITIONS OF DOCTRINE

THE first step towards reform had been like the opening of Pandora's box. In consenting that the question should be raised, the Legate had stipulated that the doctrine of original sin must first be brought into a condition in which it could be decently left; that it must be followed at least as far as a definition. A session, therefore, was still to be devoted to it. A good many bishops besides the Spaniards would have preferred that it should be let alone, and one of them, when the debate opened, flung on the table a bone of contention by which, perhaps, he hoped to stop it altogether.

Original sin had been understood generally to be a corruption inherited from Adam's fall by all his descendants. There had been a dispute of old standing between the Franciscans and Dominicans whether the Virgin Mary was to be included among the descendants so corrupted. The Franciscans maintained the immaculate conception; the Dominicans said that, although Our Lady had never actually sinned, her nature had shared in the general calamity. The bishop argued that this point must be decided before original sin could be defined. The champions on both sides at once stripped for the fight, and it seemed as if a desperate and unnecessary discussion was not to be avoided. The Legate, however, for the moment interposed. He said that the truth about the conception of the Virgin had not yet been revealed to the Church. Original sin was a feature in the Lutheran heresy, and could be defined by itself.

A second bishop said he thought a definition unnecessary. The Lutherans believed that original sin remained after baptism, but was not imputed. Catholics said it did not remain at all. It was a dispute of words, and was not worth contending about. A third, impatient for reform, repeated what had been said before, that while they had so many sins about them, they were not fit to discuss Divine mysteries. De Monte answered impatiently, as the Cardinal of St. Cross had done, that if the fathers were not good enough, they must make themselves so—repent on the spot, wear hair shirts, and lie in ashes. That could be done easily and quickly, and meanwhile they must get on with their business. The heresy to be condemned was that original sin remained after baptism. Anathemas were passed, as before, on those who maintained in any form so monstrous a proposition. The victory was celebrated by a solemn Mass, a special prayer, and the invocation of the Spirit. The Legate was so well satisfied that he resolved to pursue the subject at once into its subordinate branches, and go on to grace and justification.

The Spanish Ambassador again objected. The Legate said these last were part of the same matter, and formed the heart and root of all Luther's errors. Luther began with denying indulgences, then penance; from that he passed to justification by faith alone and the denial of good works. Thence followed his heresies on purgatory, the authority of priests, the sacrifice of the Mass, and other remedies for sin. Luther had marked out the road, and the council must go step and step with him.

So then it was the old story. There was to be nothing but doctrine after all. Years might pass before all these questions could be disposed of. The promised reforms were still to be shirked. The Ambassador would not have it, and with a sigh of foreboding the Legate consented to fix a session for the consideration of Church discipline. Morals might still wait. Individuals whose consciences were uneasy might wear the hair shirt.

The bishops were to open their various grievances, and the difficulty was where to begin. Some wanted larger incomes, some wanted schools and colleges. Others objected to the Inquisition, others brought fresh complaints against the religious orders. The chief cries of all were against the Pope, and the standing injury of annates, tenths, and pensions, the enormous fees demanded for the Bulls of investment, and the dispensations from episcopal authority. With the many voices clamouring to be heard, there was no hearing for any. Vainly the Legate ordered silence. 'Silence?' cried one. 'What am I to do, then, when I have a thought in me?' 'Woe is me,' cried another, 'if I preach not the Gospel!' The Legate said that he did not object to discussion, but there must be a limit, or work could not be got through. An audacious member of the council, speaking for the rest, asked whether, when they had been brought to Trent at a heavy cost to themselves, they were to be forbidden to utter their opinions? Were their resolutions to be formed for them by committees? Was it not enough to steal their money from them? Must their authority be stolen from them too? Were they to be treated as puppets? Were they to be bishops in nothing but the name? They had been called careless and idle. If their duty had been left undone, the fault was not theirs. They were 'Christ's vicars.' In Christ's name he exhorted his brethren to insist on their rights. The legates were bishops themselves, and ought to stand by their order.

'Christ's vicars' was flat mutiny. The Roman Church knew but one Vicar of Christ. Such a spirit must be checked at the first utterance, or all would be lost. De Monte called on the bishop to explain himself. The bishop was bold, but he was not bold enough. He hesitated. He said he had spoken only to relieve his conscience. He had supposed bishops to be vicars of Christ. The Pope was of course Vicar-general. He had meant nothing against the Pope's primacy.

This was not enough. The question which lay in every bishop's heart was, whether he held his see direct from Christ or whether he was a papal official. All secretly believed the first, or wished to believe it. The temper was dangerous. Pole had to rise to support the president. 'Would to God,' he said, 'the bishops would do their duties without needing to be reminded of them! The Church would be in a happier condition.' He implored the council not to forget their loyalty. He could not stop the excitement, and de Monte had to adjourn the session. The wound festered. Night did not bring reflection. The president the next morning read the bishops a lecture on their insubordination, but he was met with indignant cries. They asked if they were never to differ from the Legate? The Legate said they must not attack the chair, or the Holy See, or the Sacred College. If they had anything to say, they must first consult him privately. A scornful Spaniard answered that he thanked God he could maintain his own opinion without leave from any legate.

De Monte had ascertained that the Italian majority were still faithful, and would do what he ordered. It was life or death to stop these displays of liberty. He found a member to propose that the speech of the bishop who had called himself vicar of Christ should be taken down and sent to Rome. Though unloved, the name of the Pope had not lost its terrors. The offender said, with tears, that he had meant no reflection on the Apostolic See. He hoped his words would not be misconstrued against him. He broke down. He threw himself on the Legate's mercy, and was forgiven. The ruffled plumes were smoothed, and this particular incident was ended.

But the discontent, though checked in its first outburst, was too deep to be easily silenced. The bishops had been blamed for neglect of their dioceses. They insisted on explaining the reason for it. The Pope's action had made their residence useless. Itinerant titular bishops *in partibus*, whom the Pope had consecrated, went about where they pleased, ordaining any vagabond who would pay them for it. Travelling friars carried about indulgences, heard confessions, distributed pardons, and they could not control them. Even their own secular clergy could buy dispensations from obedience at Rome. Every cathedral chapter had its privileges, and every parish priest some exemption which made him independent of his bishop. They could do no good in their dioceses, and they lived elsewhere to avoid quarrels. If they were to be forced to reside, their authority must be given back to them.

All this was bitterly true, and there were other wrongs behind which could not fail to be heard of. The president had to promise that the committee of canonists should look into the matter and find a remedy.

Preaching was another sore subject. The bishops never preached, and it was said that they must be forced to do so. One of them answered that if bishops were ordered to preach, archbishops must be included,

or they would plead that they were not bound *odiosis
legibus.* What was to be done, another asked, if they
did not preach, or if they only read old sermons?
Were they to be punished, or were they to be left to
God? On one point they were unanimous. If there
was to be any change, they would have no monks
preaching in their parish churches without their leave.
The generals of the orders said the monks should cease
to preach when the bishops ceased to strut about in
fine clothes, and had learnt to preach themselves. De
Monte took the side of the generals. It was inexpedient,
he said, to inhibit the preaching friars when so many
bishops were absent at the council. On broader grounds
it would be unfair to deprive them of a privilege which
they had held so long when they were fighting so bravely
against heresy. The bishops insisted on putting the
matter to the vote, and a resolution was carried that
monks should not preach outside their convents without
special licence, nor even in their own chapels without a
bishop's leave.

It was not without reason that Pope and Legate
had dreaded the stirring of reform. De Monte recalled
the council to the particular question of the bishops'
residence. He only fell from one pitfall into another.
The bishops, it was said, were obliged by the canons to
reside. They desired to know whether the obligation
was '*jure divino*' or '*lege ecclesiastica.*' This meant much.
It meant the old question in another form, whether
they held their offices directly under Christ or under
the Pope. If it was '*jure divino,*' they were not under

the Pope. The Spanish bishops were all loudly in favour of the '*jure divino,*' and even claimed to hold their own provincial synods. The Italians and the canonists were for the '*lege ecclesiastica.*' Timothy was bishop of Ephesus, they argued, yet he travelled with St. Paul. The Apostles were all bishops, yet they had no special dioceses. Peter was universal bishop, and he could not be everywhere. Residence could not, therefore, be essentially connected with a bishop's office. The Decretals were examined. It was found to have been ruled that bishops absent at a council or absent anywhere on the Pope's business were to be counted as resident. The old blind Archbishop of Armagh, who had never set foot in Ireland, observed that it would have been a bad thing for the Church if the Apostles had been forced to reside. The bishops said that, if they were to be driven into residence, cardinals should be made to reside as well as they, and as cardinals often held five or six bishoprics, they would be in an uneasy position.

All turned on the '*jure divino.*' If the bishops were attached to their dioceses by Divine institution, there they must remain. The Pope could not dispense, and cardinals, as they could not divide themselves, would be reduced to single sees. De Monte had to sum up the discussion. He said he was sorry to see a disposition in the members of the council to treat the Pope as an equal and limit his prerogatives. He thought it would be enough to declare that bishops were bound to residence unless the Pope gave them

leave of absence. As to cardinals, many of them were
not bishops at all, and those who were bishops were
such superior persons that they could rule their flocks
better in absence than others could do when on the
spot. De Monte breathed more freely when the session
could be adjourned, and the fathers could return to
their original sin. When engaged with heresy their
personal complaints were forgotten. The Franciscans
could not lose the chance of having their favourite
theory confirmed ; they raised it again, and desired the
council to attach as a rider to their resolution, that it
was a pious opinion that the Virgin Mary had been
born without original sin. Of course the Dominicans
contradicted ; they objected that to call one opinion
pious was to call the opposite opinion impious. The
council would be deciding a dispute which was not
legitimately before them. The Franciscans retorted
that the council, in declaring all men and women to
have been born in original sin, had included the Virgin,
and had decided the other way. De Monte disliked
the discussion, but inclined to the Franciscans. Pole
said nothing. The council prudently refused to enter-
tain the subject, and left the monks to fight over it.

Of original sin itself the general principle had been
affirmed in contradiction of Luther. His special errors
remained to be separately anathematised. There were
five of them :—On the nature of original sin, the
propagation of original sin, the injury resulting from
original sin, the remedy for original sin, and the effect
of the remedy.

In such an element the bishops forgot their grievances and were happy in enquiries which seemed to
have peculiar attractions. There were no quarrels and
few disagreements. It was found that before the fall
the free will of man had been in harmony with the will
of God. After the fall it became subject to the Devil.
The condition was inherited, and the children could not
lawfully complain. Adam at his creation received a
right habit of mind. Whether he received at the same
time a knowledge of outward nature, of the movements
of the stars, for instance, was uncertain; but he did
receive moral goodness; and this he lost for himself
and his descendants. The remedy was baptism, on
which grace followed as *forma sanitatis*. A single
member of council wished to add faith, but faith had a
suspicious sound. Baptism operated before faith was
possible. In baptism was conveyed the power of leading a good life. It was true that what Luther called
concupiscence remained after baptism. This Luther
said was the same as original sin, but he was wrong.
Concupiscence, unfollowed by action, was not sin.

De Monte proposed a resolution declaring that the
fall so completely depraved man's nature that no part
of it remained uninjured. It was objected that the
five senses were part of man's nature, and that they
were not injured; also that baptism took away the
nature of sin as well as the penalty of it. Pole thought
evil was transmitted even to the baptized. Concupiscence was transmitted. Intellect was less bright than
it had been when originally given. We were taught

to pray 'Forgive us our sins'; therefore sin was in us
all. The council came to the conclusion that concupiscence did not damage those who did not consent to it,
that the material part of original sin did remain after
baptism, but not penally or fatally. It was agreed
finally: That Adam by sin incurred death, and fell
under the power of the Devil. That Adam's posterity
were under the same condition. That sin was transmitted by propagation, not by imitation, and the
remedy was through baptism, and baptism only. That
infants were to be baptized to escape the sin contracted
in their birth, and that in baptism all was taken away
which had the nature of sin. What remained in the
baptized was concupiscence, which was not sin, though
it was inclination to sin.

Theological eyes might distinguish speculative
differences between these opinions and Luther's. In
practice and bearing upon life there was no difference
at all. Yet on such points as these the Council of
Trent thought it wise and right to curse all who
expressed the same thing in other language; to split
Christendom asunder, teach good and godly men to hate
each other, and stain Europe red with blood.

In the doctrinal intervals the council was at peace;
and when the bishops differed, they could differ without quarrelling. Even reform, it was hoped, could
now be pursued with less acrimony. The bishops
had relieved their feelings by speaking out their
wrongs. So long as Rome was not touched, the
Legate saw the prudence of conciliating them. It

was agreed that some general supervision of the religious houses might be allowed them, subject to the Pope's final authority. The '*jure divino*' was left undetermined. Bishops and archbishops were to reside. Schools were to be provided and Scripture-readers. The bishops were to preach on Sundays and holy days, or, if unable, were to provide substitutes. On the other hand, the unlimited liberty of the friars was to be restricted. They were to preach only when licensed by their own superiors, and with the bishops' consent. De Monte had to yield even further. Papal officials were spread over the Catholic world; some collecting revenues, some, like Tetzel, selling pardons and indulgences. They had used the pulpits freely to exhort the faithful to contribute. The bishops insisted that this practice should be discontinued. These collectors were odious everywhere. It was proposed even to describe them in the clause of prohibition as *quæstorum pravum genus*. But, as they were the Pope's servants, they were spared so ignominious a designation.

Things seemed now to be going on better. Reform was actually begun. Something had been done, if not much. The Emperor was gratified. He could now press the German Diet with a clearer conscience to send their deputies; and the Legate was able to go back to the doctrines, about which the Pope was urgent as ever. To have the Lutheran theology condemned throughout before the Lutherans themselves could come to argue it, was the key of his position. The central citadel was now to be stormed, Luther's canon

stantis aut cadentis ecclesiæ,—'justification by faith.'
To hasten the process the Legate proposed a summary
anathema on Luther's doctrines as a whole. It would
save trouble, and expedite the despatch of business.
The bishops, however, preferred going into particulars,
and sifting the false from the true. Many of the
questions were new and intricate. Much was to be
said for the Legate's method of wholesale condemnation; but the subject was seductive and the majority
decided to plunge into it.

The Lutheran theory of justification is a passionate
expression of truths undeniable in themselves, yet it
is a stumbling-block to reason, and only apprehensible
by emotion. It is true that the best works of so poor
a creature as man cannot endure the scrutiny of omni-
science. If we look into our own deservings, the best
of us are the first to acknowledge that we have none at
all. In man there is no merit, he is an unprofitable
servant. All he can do is to devote himself with complete self-abandonment to what is higher and nobler
than himself. He will be always falling, but he can
rise and stagger on, be loyal and faithful to Christ
through and in spite of natural infirmity. All generous
minds acknowledge this: yet when reduced to formulas
by theological pedantry, technicalised into imputed
righteousness, grace resistible and grace irresistible,
grace of congruity, grace of condignity, it becomes
dead, dry, unfertile, even incredible and deniable.
Reason does not understand emotion; what is true
to conscience and imaginative feeling becomes a

stone of stumbling when it is made into a scheme of salvation.

When the fathers at Trent went to work upon Luther's metaphors, they were like surgeons anatomising the human body and trying to discover the soul. No soul can be found in any such way. It was in the recoil from the extravagant theories of the merits of the saints that justification by faith took the place which it has held in theological history.

The secret of the strength of Protestantism lies in its name. Luther, Calvin, the Reformers everywhere, protested against the imposition upon them, in the name of religion, of things which were not true. They protested against papal indulgences, pretensions of priests to pardon sin, lying miracles, conscious falsehoods, and childish superstitions. Against these they fought, and died as martyrs, as the early Christians died for refusing to acknowledge the divinity of the Emperor. They were required to say that they believed what they knew they did not believe, and they gave their lives rather than lie against their own souls. This was a great and noble thing. But the positive theology of the Protestant Confessions, though it may be beautiful, is only intelligible to mystical self-abnegation. The best part of it might be held by Catholics, if religious hatred had not turned the language into a war cry.

The fathers found Luther saying that faith justified without works. They distinguished three kinds of works: works done before grace, works done at the infusion of grace, works done after grace. St. Paul did say that faith alone justified; but what was faith? The Dominicans said that if they allowed in any sense that faith was sufficient, they gave up the field. Faith meant either assurance of the veracity of a person promising a thing, or the assent of the believer. In neither sense could faith alone justify. What, then, did St. Paul mean? He meant—he could only have meant—that faith was the assent to revealed truth which the Church ordered to be believed. It might justify when animated by charity, but it might also be the dead faith of sinners. Was a man just before his faith had begun to operate, or did he become just through the works which his faith produced? A perilous question. God justified. The sacraments justified. The preparation of the soul to receive grace justified. Justification was a word with many meanings.

As to works done before grace, works done by heathens, it was doubtful whether they were good at all. Some had held that there was sin in every one of them. Man without grace could no more produce good works than a wild vine could produce good grapes. But, on the other hand, if this was so, what became of free will? Luther said it did not exist. The Catholic principle was that every man, heathen or Christian, had strength to obey the law substantially, if only he would. But then, again, could he will? Of course grace might be necessary; and grace to receive grace. It seemed as if in a certain sense Luther might be right—a dreadful hypothesis, which was dismissed by a unanimous repudiation of the theory of imputed righteousness.

The fathers would have been wise if they had followed de Monte's advice, and been content with a universal censure. They were now in a worse than Cretan labyrinth. Everything that was said and done was reported in Germany, and Charles, who had begun to hope, was again in despair. To allow Christ's Church to split into factions, each armed in a panoply of doctrinal formulas, could lead, as he well knew, to nothing but hatred and war; nay, in the end perhaps, might shake the credibility of religion itself. The wounds which he was labouring to heal, the council was envenoming. Protestants and Catholics accepted the three creeds; why could not the creeds be a sufficient basis of union? One might believe in justification by faith, the other in justification by works; one might think the Real Presence at the Eucharist depended on the faith of the receiver, another on the consecration by a priest. Let them believe as they would, Christendom need not tear itself to pieces about such things.

Laymen are instinctively more tolerant than clergy. The Pope insisted always that laymen did not understand theology. Perhaps they are better without it. Henry VIII. had succeeded in England by making the laity supreme. Parliament had taken the control, checked doctrinal extravagances on both sides, reformed abuses with the help of a lay Vicar-general, and brought

Convocation under the Crown.   England, however, was
a single country under a single head.   The Emperor's
position was infinitely more difficult.   He probably
thought much as Henry did, but if he had gone to
work with the German Diet as his uncle did with
Parliament, he would have offended Spain and Flanders
and Italy.   Toleration was not understood.   Toleration,
if it meant the free permission to establish different
sects with different creeds and rituals, was certain, as
the minds of men were then constituted, to lead to war.
Catholics could be brought to toleration of differences
only on one condition, that the points at issue should
be treated as indifferent by a General Council.   To a
council they were ready to bow, but to nothing else.
Terms had to be kept with the Pope, and terms with
the Diet.   Anabaptist extravagances had to be held in
check in the Low Countries.   Protestants, as well as
the fathers at Trent, had to be kept from imposing new
doctrines.   This was called persecution, as Henry's Six
Articles Bill was called persecution, but it was to
prevent the Protestants from provoking explosions of
Catholic hatred.   The Emperor had appeared at last
to be succeeding, when the council had begun upon
reform, but the Schmalkaldic League was in arms again
now, when the council was heaping anathemas on their
cherished beliefs.   Passion was getting the mastery
over judgment, and it was too likely that his efforts
would be thrown away, and that a religious war might
be forced upon him after all.   The princes of the
Schmalkaldic League were powerful.   If they chose,

they could bring half Germany under arms. It might easily come to that, as Granvelle had told Farnese. Luther had always warned the Protestant States not to take arms against the Emperor, even in their own defence. Truth, he said, did not require the sword to protect it. But Luther was gone, and had left no one behind him with equal influence. The Emperor had promised that till the Lutherans could be present and take a share in the debates, the council should leave doctrines alone. They saw it passing decree upon decree which they believed were to be forced upon them by arms. Local quarrels broke out. The Imperial Chamber interfered. It was thought too partial to the Catholics. The Elector of Saxony and the Landgrave of Hesse, as the natural protectors of the Protestants, set themselves in readiness for the worst, and all was anger, fear, and suspicion.

War was a bad alternative, and as yet there was no fair ground for it. The Emperor still protested that he would never force conscience. He would never injure German liberty. All he asked was that Germany should at least try whether anything could be made of the council. There were still some moderate men who understood and trusted him. Their numbers increased as the war party grew louder. The princes of the League had bound themselves to stand by each other in defence of freedom, but the obligation held only if freedom was really in danger. The Elector called on them to arm. More than one of them replied that the occasion had not arisen and might not arise.

Even Saxony itself, Luther's own land, was divided. Duke Maurice, a younger member of the electoral family, was a Protestant of the Protestants. He had married the daughter of the Landgrave of Hesse. He was young, but he was wise beyond his years, and he, and half the State along with him, inclined to stand by the Emperor, and give his policy a chance. Beloved though the Elector was, the prudent part of his subjects looked to Maurice as a safer guide.

In complex situations posterity cannot judge men fairly. Posterity sees what actually happened, explains history by its own imperfect knowledge, and is lavish of its censures. Protestant tradition has said hard things of Maurice, and knows quite well that he had no motive but personal ambition, and was base and ungrateful. Perhaps he was only trying to be reasonable and moderate; but reason and moderation are no match for such forces as were let loose in the sixteenth century. Religious passion is a whirlwind which sweeps all before it, yet those are not the worst who are for giving reason a chance, even if they fail.

It was impossible to stand still. The council was at work. The sand was running. If things were left to take their course at the rate at which the council was going, it would soon have closed every avenue for peace. The only check that could be placed on it would be the presence of Protestant delegates, and Charles was more than ever urgent that they should go to Trent and speak their thoughts. Threatened as he was by the arming of the League, he was forced to raise an army of his own. He sent for troops from Spain and the Netherlands. He sent for Alva, the ablest soldier that he had. He was still emphatic as ever, however, that he would make no war for religion. The Pope, whose hope from the beginning had been that it should come to war, believed now that, with a little help from himself, the war could be given the character which he desired. Again and again he had urged the Emperor to put heresy down by force. He had offered men and money to assist in this holy enterprise. Hitherto Charles had turned a deaf ear, but the Pope now came forward with proposals still more liberal, which could not be absolutely rejected.

Charles was really in difficulty. The force which the League could bring into the field far exceeded any which he could himself gather together out of his own resources. The Pope, after all, was one of the parties in the dispute. He had never wished to crush the Pope, ill as he thought the Pope had behaved. He wished to reconcile the antagonism of the contending factions. If the Protestants began the appeal to violence, it may have been imprudent, but it was not unnatural in Charles, to accept the Pope's offer.

A papal force of 15,000 men was despatched under the Pope's grandson, Octavio Farnese, and his brother the Cardinal Alexander. Their appearance on the scene with priests carrying crucifixes, and a cardinal carrying his cross, completed the conviction of the mass of the people that the Emperor had betrayed them. The war broke out—begun by the Protestants themselves. Charles replied with a proclamation, again insisting that religion was not the cause of the quarrel. The Elector and the Landgrave had renounced their obedience, conspired against his authority, seized and confiscated the property of the Catholic Church. He was compelled to take the field against them to uphold the law of the Empire. That was all.

The Pope was determined that it should not be all. He would force Charles's hand, and a religious war it should be, in spite of him. He held a jubilee at Rome. He issued a Bull in his own fervid style, declaring that a religious war it was. In his zeal for the faith, in his tenderness for the flock of Christ, in his grief for perishing souls and his horror of the rebellious heretics, he announced that he had made a league with the Emperor to reduce the Protestant States. He called on the faithful to fast and pray, confess and communicate, for the success of the adventure.

The papal contingent proved useless in the field, but the Pope's announcement answered its purpose of ingenious mischief. Protests were of no avail in the face of so positive a demonstration. The confidence of the moderate Germans in the Emperor's honesty was seriously shaken. Even the Catholic States were alarmed by it for their constitutional liberty. The doctrinal campaign at Trent, the decrees on justification and original sin, were now set down to treacherous collusion. A decisive act of some kind could alone clear Charles from a suspicion of bad faith. He wrote publicly to the Pope that many of the Protestants had been willing to take part in the council and accept its resolutions, but submit they would not if they were condemned before they were heard. He desired, he insisted, that no· further offence should be given to them. He directed Mendoza once more to convey a strong opinion to the Legate that doctrinal questions must be left untouched, and the order was executed with a hearty good-will. Mendoza knew the treacherous nature of the ground. He thought it not unlikely that the Pope might suddenly dissolve the council if he found that he could not have his own way with it; and he calmly told the Cardinal of St. Cross that, if any trick was played of that kind, he would fling him into the Adige. The contempt of the Spaniards for Popes and cardinals is one of the most extraordinary features of the time. When the Spanish army occupied Rome, a member of the Sacred College having spoken disrespectfully of Charles, the Spanish Ambassador wrote thus to the Emperor: 'I did not call on his Holiness, but I sent him a message that if it ever came to my notice that the same cardinal or any other dared to speak so indecently of your majesty, I took my most solemn oath I would have him beheaded or burnt alive in his own apartment. I had refrained this time out of respect for his Holiness, but if the insult was repeated,

I would not hesitate. They might do as they would with their Bulls and other rogueries, but they should not speak evil of princes or make themselves judges of the affairs of kingdoms.' The original Spanish is even more emphatically scornful.

LECTURE X

DEFINITIONS OF DOCTRINE—(*continued*)

FROM the day on which Luther burnt the Pope's Decretals at Wittenberg, the Roman Conclave had been persuaded that force was the only remedy. Rebellion against the Pope was as the sin of witchcraft. Fire and sword could alone extirpate it. The day so long hoped for seemed to have arrived at last. The Emperor was at war with the Protestants. A division of the papal army was in the Imperial camp. It was commanded by the Pope's grandson, and a cardinal with a train of clergy accompanied the troops. The Emperor had announced that the war was political and was not for religion. The Roman Court was determined that it should be for religion. To force the Emperor into the attitude which the Pope desired him to adopt, Cardinal Farnese carried his Legate's cross in front of the army, and published an indulgence in the form only used in a crusade against infidels.

The ardent believers in the Papacy were to be once more disappointed. Maurice of Saxony and many others of the moderate German leaders had disapproved

of the violence of the Protestant League. They believed
the Emperor to be honest, and at his request they had
resolved to give the council at Trent a chance, and try
what could be made of it. They had brought a large
force to the Emperor's support. If they were to remain
with him, Farnese and his crusade must be disowned.
The Legate's cross was ordered away, the Legate
vanished along with it; the papal contingent remained
for a few months, but had no opportunity of showing
its zeal for destroying heretics. The campaign opened
in July, 1546, but on neither side was there any heart
in the war. The Emperor and the Elector were both
unwilling to begin a fratricidal conflict. All the summer
and autumn the armies manœuvred. There was
skirmishing and distant cannonading, but no battle
and no wish for battle. In December, the papal troops,
which had arrived in such fine enthusiasm, went home
without having fired a shot, and the Emperor and the
German princes were left to settle their differences
among themselves.

The Council of Trent, which had been made happy
by the prospect of a holy war, was in dismay and con-
sternation. If the war was not for religion, the success
of either side might be equally dangerous. The
Emperor's Ambassador had threatened to fling the
Legate into the Adige. If Charles was victorious, he
might himself descend on them and force them to go
to work with their reforms. If the Protestants got the
better of him, the dreaded Landgrave of Hesse might
swoop down on them with his Lanzknechts. The

Tyrol itself was strongly Lutheran, the neighbourhood dangerous. An archbishop declared that he did not wish to be crucified. Half the council represented to the Legate that, under such circumstances, they could not remain at Trent. The Legate was equally uneasy, and had to tell the Pope that the fathers could not be kept together. An addition to the garrison had been suggested, but the fathers were afraid of soldiers of any kind. Catholics and Protestants were equally rough and dissolute; a few poor priests, they said, ought not to be left to be devoured by wild beasts.

The Pope would have been delighted to call them down to Italy. He had wished for nothing else. But since his troops had been so rudely treated, he, too, knew not what to think. Each day brought him news that the Emperor s army was becoming more Protestant. The Duke of Wurtemberg had joined, the Count Palatine had joined, and no promises had been demanded from them to restore the Mass, or even to recognise the council. Charles's attitude was so ambiguous and so dangerous, that Paul dared not exasperate him by any further steps of a marked kind. With much reluctance he had to tell the Legate that the fathers must stay where they were.

De Monte thought Paul mistaken. In de Monte's opinion the safest way was still the boldest. He would have had him call the council to Rome itself. He had to do as the Pope ordered, however, and he had no easy task before him. Mendoza and the Spanish bishops, confident now in the Emperor's success, began to ask when the question of 'morals' was to be opened. There had been a session on Church discipline, of which the fringe had been just touched, but not a word yet of 'morals,' which ought to be their chief business. The easiest escape would be for the fathers who were so frightened, to slip away of themselves. This they were willing enough to do. They consulted de Monte, and the Legate, though he could not consent, yet answered that fear was not a sin, and if they did go away they could not be punished. The Spaniards found out what was going on. They said the Legate was playing false. The Legate charged the Spaniards with mutiny, and words ran so high, and the fathers so forgot themselves in their panic and anger, that the Archbishop of Panormo had to go on his knees in the hall and beseech them not to disgrace their office.

They agreed at last to send a protest to the Emperor. Trent, they said, was a barren spot; the climate hateful; the peasants round heretical, violent and insolent; unless they were allowed to go elsewhere there would be no council left. The Pope, to whom they also wrote, was so eager to have them near him that he almost made up his mind to sanction their departure. He told the Legate that, if there was a clear majority for removal, they might go. Lucca was an Imperial town. The Emperor would perhaps allow them to adjourn to Lucca. They might finish up the work they had on hand. There must be no nonsense about 'morals. The subject was too large to be then begun upon.

They might despatch justification and bishops' residence, and so take leave.

The Sacred College had a special reason for wishing to have the council closer at hand. Paul III. was old and had been ill. If he died while the council was sitting far away at Trent, the Emperor might make use of it to nominate a Pope of his own, who would be a mere instrument in his hands.

If the cardinals thought, however, that the Emperor would let the council go, either to Lucca or any other place out of Germany, they were to find they were mistaken. Without phrase or circumlocution, he ordered the fathers to remain in their places. He said he would hold the Pope answerable, and if they moved he would make terms with the Lutherans. All the pains which he had taken to bring the Diet to recognise the council would be thrown away if they were to leave Trent now. It was not to be. There was nothing for it but to submit, the Pope begging the fathers to understand that the Emperor, and not he, was keeping them at Trent. If they were to stay, they could at least occupy themselves in their own way, and make the Emperor sorry for keeping them. Mendoza might threaten to fling them into the river. The Spanish bishops might talk of enquiries into moral misdoings. They had their justification canon incomplete, and they determined to finish with it, as the Pope suggested, before they would touch anything else.

Justification had been discussed to weariness; it seemed as if there was nothing to be done but draft

the decree and attach the anathema; but the subject
was fascinating, and the fathers, once launched into it,
forgot their terrors and their grievances. The Legate
blew the fire to annoy Charles, and force him to let
them go. Father Paul says that no one who has not
read the debates can imagine the heat with which the
different views were maintained. A certain bishop
showed a Lutheran leaning. ' What say you ? ' cried
one. ' Silence with that impertinence ! ' cried another.
The bishop thus insulted seized one of his revilers by
the beard and tore out a handful of it. The fathers
' *incredibile turbati* ' adjourned. The Archbishop of
Toledo moved next day that the offender should be
chastised. De Monte lamented over human infirmity.
The sinner himself was an Imperialist. Mendoza inter-
ceded for him, and the affair was passed over. But
the storm raged on. Certitude of grace occupied
three days, and was left undefined after all. De Monte
drew the chase off after works preparatory, and thence
to the doctrine of works generally. Luther's passionate
rhetoric was caricatured into propositions for anathema.

He was made to say that God was the author of
all that men did, whether it was good or bad, of the
treason of Judas, of the conversion of St. Paul ; that free
will was a chimera ; that by Adam's fall man had lost
the liberty to do good, and retained the liberty to do
evil ; that the elect were converted without efforts of
theirs, and the reprobate consigned to damnation by
eternal decree. By means of judicious extracts, St.
Paul, as Erasmus observed, might be made to say the

same thing. The canonists easily proved that this contradicted common sense—that every one knew that he was free, let philosophy say what it pleased. Yet voices were still heard affirming that man could not do good without the grace of God, and so far therefore was not free. The Church had always held grace to be necessary for the works of the Spirit.

Again, unbelief was called a sin, and therefore belief must be an act of will; but could a man believe or disbelieve by any act of will? The Franciscans and Dominicans disagreed. The Franciscans said a man could only believe what appeared to him to be true. The Dominicans thought he could believe anything that he liked, evidence or no evidence. For instance, he could believe that the stars were an even number. Again, what was liberty? It was two-sided. If a man was free to do evil, he was free to do good; yet, on the other hand, saints and angels were free to do good, but were not free to do evil.

Prevenient grace followed, grace sufficient, grace efficacious, predestination and foreknowledge. From predestination the immediate step was to Calvinism. The bishops called it inhuman, monstrous, horrible to teach that God had created millions of souls only to torture them eternally. They insisted that God desired all men to be saved, and had given them the means if they chose to use them. But they were in the old dilemma. *Aut nequit aut non vult,* and they could not say *nequit.* They had their purgatory, and their inferno too, as bad as Calvin's, and they had to allow that God had foreseen who would use the means and who would not. Therefore predestination there must be, and they were involved in the same contradiction as Calvin.

So they went on through the winter months from enigma to enigma. Their formulas, and their decrees on discipline and residence, were at last drawn and forwarded for revision to Rome, where they gave general satisfaction. The decrees on residence had been expected with some alarm, as it was scarcely possible that they should not touch the cardinals, but they proved to be no more than a repetition of the old canons which had been easily evaded. A bishop was to reside on his see, but he might be absent for a just cause, of which the Pope was to judge. The doctrinal decrees condemned Luther, and that was enough. They were published at once. The Emperor was exasperated, but could do nothing till the war was over. In Germany they were received with amused contempt. The soul passive and the soul active, the will operated on by the object, the object operated on by the will, man doing everything and man doing nothing—such were the subjects of the decrees. The fathers at Trent in dealing with them were compared to astronomers trying to explain the motion of the planets by excentrics and epicycles. The soberest of the German thinkers represented that fifty bishops at a small town in the Tyrol could not lay down the law for the world. Their decisions would have to be reconsidered if the council was to be recognised in Germany.

The Emperor reported their opinions to Rome, adding his own displeasure that the reforms, the necessity of which he had pressed upon the Pope, were still persistently neglected. The Pope smoothly answered that truth did not depend on numbers. The council, no doubt, would be better attended and would carry more weight if it was removed to Rome, while at Rome the moral questions about which the Emperor was so anxious could be examined into more satisfactorily.

Doubtless such an arrangement would have pleased the Pope and cardinals. At Rome they would have been judges in their own cause.

Pallavicino, their great advocate, allows that the Court of Rome as it then stood was a surprising phenomenon, but he skilfully and elaborately defends it. The splendour of the Vatican he admits to have been maintained by the accumulation on the cardinals of Church benefices, to the duties of which they never attended. But a Church reduced to poverty would be a Church without power. Men of rank and ability would no longer be attracted into its service. There were good and bad among the clergy, as there were in all professions. The undeserving might be sometimes promoted and the meritorious neglected. But the Roman Court had produced a series of splendid men who had been ornaments to religion, and had played their parts in the history of mankind. All this would end if the reforms were carried out which the Emperor required. The clergy, high and low, would then be scattered in remote towns and villages, employed in hearing confessions and singing hymns away from all the centres of energy and intellect. They might be excellent pastors, but the Papacy would fall, and the influence of the Church along with it.

It was precisely with this object, it was precisely to restore the clergy to their proper place, that the laity of Europe were demanding the change. The decrees on residence, while a power was left to the Pope to dispense, they naturally regarded as a mockery.

More than ever distrusting the Emperor, the Pope turned for help to France. The Emperor observed to the Papal Nuncio that the *morbus gallicus* was usually a disorder of youth. The Pope seemed to have caught it in his old age. The Nuncio pleaded that the See of Rome must be neutral in the quarrels between France and the Empire. Charles said such neutrality as the Pope's was destroying Christendom. He had gone to war with the Schmalkaldic League in the Pope's own interest, and the Pope was going over to the French King.

Paul however got little out of France. Francis, if he interfered, was inclining to take the side of the Elector and the Landgrave. Had the Pope dared he would have called the council to Rome. But he could not risk it. The winter of 1546-7 was bitterly cold. The Adige was frozen, the Alps were deep in snow. The houses in Trent were ill-built and ill-furnished. The bishops in spite of their exertions were miserable, yet leave they might not; and the master whom they served was treating them with less consideration than they deserved. It was found at Rome that the decrees on discipline had not, after all, sufficiently guarded the cardinals; while the '*jure divino*,' about which the bishops were specially sensitive, though not affirmed in them, had not been denied. The Pope sent the decrees back to be revised. The cardinals were the worst pluralists in the Church. The Pope said they must be excepted, and reserved to his own special jurisdiction. The '*jure divino*' must not be allowed at all. If granted, it would teach insubordination.

The Italians were wretched, and had no spirit. The Spaniards, trained in the iron climate of Castile, were hardy and resolute. There were now twenty of them, and they intended to make their presence felt. The '*jure divino*' they had always insisted on. They did not care if it did make the bishops insubordinate. They had been steady for reform. They desired to see the Popes more like the Apostles, the Church more like what it had been before dispensations and exemptions were ever heard of. De Monte remodelled the decrees as the Pope directed. To prevent alarm he admitted, in the preamble, the degeneracy of the Church. He condemned the practice, which had become so common, of bishops haunting courts and following secular occupations. He proposed that bishops habitually absent from their sees should forfeit their preferments, and be reported to the Pope as contumacious. Nothing apparently could be more severe, but the cardinals were not comprehended. The '*jure divino*' was implicitly denied and the fatal power of dispensation still reserved to the Holy See.

The Spaniards were not to be caught with specious words. In a compact body they denounced the fine-sounding decree as fraud and illusion.

The Legate was bound by Paul's orders. Yield he could not. But he was adroit and smooth. He said the Spaniards were right in principle, but the time was inopportune. They were now excited. If they would reflect coolly, the Holy Spirit would, no doubt, help them to a more temperate conclusion. He promised to consult the Pope again, but his Holiness at that particular moment was specially anxious that the '*jure divino*' and the question of cardinals' residence should not be agitated. The Pope's hands must not be tied. The cardinals would reside on their sees whenever it was necessary, but such great persons ought not to be spoken of as criminals.

The Spaniards insisted that at least no bishop should hold more sees than one, since in that case he must be non-resident at one or the other. The Legate answered calmly that pluralities had been permitted *ad majorem Dei gloriam*. The Spaniards said that scandalous persons had been nominated by the Pope to bishoprics. The Legate replied that there were scandalous bishops in France, and Spain and Germany, where the nomination did not rest with the Pope. The Pope's bishops, in fact, were the best in Europe.

The argument was so hot and had run into such

dangerous regions that Father Paul takes the occasion
to describe how pluralism had grown to such a height,
and a very curious story it is. Small benefices were
first united where the income of one was insufficient
for an incumbent's support. Next came the opinion
that the incumbent of a benefice ought to have a
competency, a competency meaning an income large
enough to keep three servants and a horse. The higher
clergy required more. Bishops especially having a
state to maintain, expected a decent revenue, and
decency was an elastic expression. Cardinals ranked
with princes, and their establishments had to be on a
princely scale. The gradation of expenditure being
thus admitted, there was nothing for it but pluralism,
which meant, virtually, that every priest was to be
allowed to hold as many benefices as he could get.
The canon forbade it, but the Pope could dispense;
and as no one else could dispense, the clergy had
become his humble servants. Convenient pretexts
were made or found. The system came in by degrees.
At first when a see was vacant and could not be
immediately filled up, some eminent or favoured person
would be appointed *in commendam* for six months to
do the duty. An appointment of this kind was itself
harmless. But a papal dispensation would remove the
six months limit, and a commendam could be held for
life. Cardinal Wolsey, for instance, held St. Albans,
York, Durham, and Winchester, enjoying the whole
revenues after the Pope's share of the plunder had
been first duly deducted.

If Father Paul can be believed, Wolsey was by no means one of the chief sinners in such matters. Father Paul says that in 1534 Clement VII. granted *in commendam* for six months to his cousin, the Cardinal de' Medici, all the vacant benefices in Christendom, secular and regular. Father Paul may have been credulous of evil, but beyond doubt the practice had risen to a scandalous height, and the Spanish bishops at the council refused to let the matter drop. The legates did their best to check the discussion of inconvenient subjects. A few well-meaning members thought it would be enough to represent to the Pope that commendams had been abused, and to ask that the system might be modified. In the course of the debate it came out that Cardinal Ridolfi had held the see of Vicenza in addition to other benefices; not only having never been near one of them, but having never been so much as consecrated a bishop.

The Castilians, going to the root of the disease, demanded that dispensations for pluralities should be finally and unconditionally abolished. Less austere reformers would be contented if the council resolved that dispensations should not be granted without lawful cause; that to grant a dispensation without such cause, and to profit by it, should be held mortal sin.

To this the answer was that, though to grant a dispensation might be declared a sin, the dispensation would itself be valid, and might be used with a safe conscience. The question turned on the nature of the dispensing power. Some thought it was inherent in the Papacy. They said that all laws originated in Christ, and that, as the Pope was Christ's Vicar, he could suspend them as he pleased. Others said that only such laws could be suspended as had been established *lege ecclesiasticâ*. The Pope's authority could not make wrong into right.

The legates let the arguments roll on, not sorry to see the bishops disagreeing. The bishops were only dangerous when they showed signs of acting together. The Castilians were but twenty. They were outvoted on divisions by a docile Italian majority. Diego d'Alon, bishop of Astorga, said that, although they differed on the limits of dispensations, they might at least forbid commendams and life union of benefices. Both were scandals, invented only to gratify the avarice of great men. It was an open disgrace that such practices should have continued so long and so undisguised. Finding they could not carry their point, the Spanish phalanx drew out a list of their demands, which they required the president to forward to Rome. They were as follows :—Bishops to be bound to residence, '*jure divino.*' Plurality of bishoprics to be disallowed even to cardinals, and plurality of smaller benefices to be also disallowed, all dispensations notwithstanding. Every holder of a benefice on which he did not reside to be deprived. Candidates for orders to be rejected if found to be incompetent or to be vicious livers. On the nomination of a priest to a bishopric, an examination to be held on the spot into his birth, life and manners. No bishop to ordain in another bishop's diocese without permission from the holder of the see.

Such demands cut to the quick. De Monte was embarrassed and even alarmed. Behind the Spanish prelates stood the Emperor. The cardinals, whom the Pope had ordered him to protect, were specially aimed at, and through them the Pope himself. Bold speakers said openly that, if discipline was really to be restored, the cardinals should not escape. The Pope, it was said, was not sincere. He had called the council only to amuse the world, and did not mean to have any reform at all. If the bishops were to be forced to remain at Trent against their will, they showed an evident inclination to assert independent authority.

De Monte thought that the Pope had made a mistake in yielding to the Emperor and keeping them there when they wished to go. In reporting their disposition, he recommended the Pope to make a few improvements in the Court of Rome, as if of his own accord. He warned him, however, to concede nothing to the council itself. If he did, it would be all over with him. Charles and Ferdinand were at the bottom of the Spanish bishops' violence, and he must not let himself be bullied. He begged for a fresh batch of Italians who could be depended on to keep up his majority.

The Italians came, and de Monte, reinforced by their presence, brought the Spanish demands before the full assembly. They were found to be revolutionary ;

a direct attack on the Holy See; but there were still signs of a dangerous humour. Some concessions had to be made or the Spanish Church might revolt together.

Benefices, it appeared, had been largely held by persons not in orders. Here was a clear abuse which had risen out of the commendams. The Pope had allowed bishoprics to be held *in commendam* by sub-deacons, and worse still by laymen. The fathers were open-mouthed, even the most docile of them, in insisting that this practice should be abolished or qualified.

Paul had hesitated what to do or say. Instructions came from him at last. He stood out stoutly for the cardinals. Cardinal bishops, he said, were engaged in the service of the Church Universal. They were in residence while they were at Rome, and could not be absent in their dioceses. Nor would he make any absolute rule about pluralities of bishoprics. He was willing to limit bishops' dispensations for non-residence to half a year. In this concession he gained more than he lost, for it implicitly negatived the '*jure divino*.' As to minor benefices, he pleaded the rights of patrons as an objection to too narrow a regulation. A scrutiny on the spot into the character of an intended bishop, he said, would lead to slander and false witness, and was generally undesirable.

This was all which he could allow. If on these terms de Monte could come to an agreement with the Spaniards, he might do so. For himself, the Pope said he would prefer to reject the demands altogether.   But the Legate was on the spot and must judge.

De Monte, alarmed at the probable effects of such an answer, kept it for the present in his desk.   The turn for doctrine had come round again.   The reform agitation was suspended, and there was momentary relief.

Justification having been brought into form, the next heresy to be condemned referred to the sacraments.   Luther said there were three; the Church said there were seven.   There were seven virtues, seven mortal sins, seven consequences of original sin, six days of creation with Sunday making a seventh, seven plagues, seven planets.   Therefore there must be seven sacraments.

How did sacraments operate?   Luther said through the faith of the recipient.   The Church had not as yet declared an authoritative opinion.   Dominicans and Franciscans differed as usual.   The Dominican fathers said that, although grace was a spiritual quality conferred immediately by the Spirit, the sacraments had nevertheless an instrumental virtue, producing a disposition in the soul to receive grace.   The sacraments contained grace not as a vessel contains water, but as a cause contains the effect.

The Franciscans said that God being a spiritual cause could not use a material instrument to produce a spiritual effect.   They denied that the sacraments had any constraining or disposing operation.   Grace had been promised on the use of the sacraments; but only because they were efficacious signs to which an effect had been attached by decree, just as good works had a recompense attached to them, though without value in themselves, or as a bishop's ring was a sign of his authority.

The Dominicans called the Franciscans Lutherans. The Franciscans retorted that the Church must not teach what was impossible. More than one wise father urged that, as they were all agreed that the sacraments were accompanied by grace, to argue about the manner of it was needless; but Wisdom as usual cried in the streets, and few regarded her.

As a reason for denying the mysterious efficacy of the sacraments, Luther had argued that they could not be seen to produce an effect upon character. Here was a fresh and attractive subject, with infinite possibilities of difference. The Council went off upon character. What was character in its theological sense? Some called it a spiritual quality, others a disposition, others a figure of speech, others a metaphor, others a relation, others a fiction. Where did character reside? In the soul? In the spirit? In the will? In the hands? In the tongue? A philosophic Dominican was of opinion that, antecedent to infusing grace, the sacraments produced spiritual qualities of two kinds. The first of these was character. It was conveyed in the sacrament of baptism. The effect was permanent, and baptism was therefore not to be repeated. The other kind was capable of being lost and recovered, and, being supplemental, was not permanent, and a sacrament conveying it therefore might be repeated.

The theory was a subtle one, perhaps heretical, and was not adopted. The council contented itself with affirming that baptism, the Eucharist, and penance did impress character, whatever character might be.

Luther had denied the difference between a priest and a layman. According to Luther, the sacraments might be administered by any Christian of either sex. This was condemned without discussion; but a question arose whether intention was necessary for sacramental efficacy, and here a wide field was opened. The Bishop of Minorca put a case. Suppose a priest, he said, with four or five thousand souls under him to be an infidel or a heretic. Suppose that when he baptizes or consecrates, he has no right intention. It will follow, if intention is required, that all the infants are lost, all penitents unabsolved, all communicants without their spiritual food. To say that faith would compensate was Lutheranism. Again the Bishop proposed another case. Suppose a bad priest without right intention baptizes a child, and the child becomes a bishop, and ordains other bishops. The consequences would be too frightful to think of. There could be no Church without a bishop, and no true bishop who was not baptized. The speaker urged the council to declare that, if the form was rightly observed, intention made no difference.

The argument was interrupted by a suggestion of more immediate importance from the reforming canonists. The subjects ran one into the other and could not be kept separate. Among the abuses of the time, a very general one had been the taking money for the sacraments. Sometimes a fee was directly demanded. If not demanded, it was suggested by basin or bag. The laity had long complained, but the practice had been universal, and the Pope had instructed the Legate that it was not to be interfered with. The poor priests and mendicant friars had nothing else to live on. The discussion on the sacraments brought the question to the surface, with the Pope's defence of the custom. The irrepressible Spaniards saw another opportunity for striking at Rome. They said the Church was rich enough to support all its ministers if its wealth was properly distributed. The canons absolutely prohibited the taking of money for the sacraments. It was a scandal, and must be abolished. The answer of the Legate was fully characteristic. He admitted that a priest was not allowed by the canon to ask for money on such occasions, but he was not forbidden to receive money if it was offered. The sacraments were not to be paid for, but the priest might be paid for his trouble in administering them. To forbid voluntary offerings was to deprive the laity of opportunities of charity.

This was an interlude. The fathers returned with fresh zeal to the great subject which was occupying them, and which, perhaps, the last suggestion had been introduced to interrupt. Although the doctrinal party were in the vast majority, there were still a few members who felt as the Emperor felt. The council had been called to reconcile discordant parties. Precise definition, instead of being a road to reconciliation, was the way to ensure perpetual quarrels. On the sacraments, opinion was peculiarly sensitive, and when the doctrinalists, encouraged by the Legate, required an exact interpretation, a leading Roman ecclesiastic ventured a few reasonable words. He said truly that heresy could never be silenced by hurling anathemas at it. The way to get rid of heresy was to tolerate differences of opinion. Thus, and in no other way, could men come to understand each other. If the council went on defining, the difference of a vowel might a second time divide the Christian world. Luther had been violent and insolent, and was so far to blame, but no one ought to be troubled for opinions which he maintained with modesty.

Even at Trent, it seems, there was at least one wise man. But, as Gibbon observes, in theological councils the opinion most remote from what we call reason invariably prevails. The council, already in full cry, were not to be called off the scent. Thirty propositions were drawn with anathemas attached. Those who did not acknowledge that the sacraments were seven in number, and that all the seven had been instituted by Christ, or who denied that one was more efficacious than another, were declared heretics and accursed.

In the same condemnation were included those who said that men could be saved by faith without the sacraments, or that the sacraments were signs only, and did not convey grace by inherent virtue, or that grace was not imparted through them *ex opere operato*, or that all Christians had a right to administer them, or that priests in mortal sin could not administer them, or that the pastors of the Church could omit any part of the form or alter it if they saw occasion.

All those, again, were condemned who said that water was not needed in baptism, or that Christ's words were metaphorical, or that the Roman doctrine of baptism was not true, or that it was not necessary to salvation; or that sin after baptism could be remitted by repentance and faith, or that baptism ought to be deferred to mature age; or that infants were not made Christians by baptism; or that confirmation was not a sacrament, or that a priest could confirm as well as a bishop.

The lightnings flew. The Legate smiled. All was going well. As if for a special blessing came the news in the midst of their work that Henry VIII. was dead. He must have died some time. His dying at the moment when so many errors were receiving the curse of the Church was a clear miracle, and a thanksgiving service was held at Trent to commemorate so great a deliverance.

If the halcyon days would but last! But behind the doctrines came the alternate reform session, and this brought with it the Spanish bishops, who demanded the Pope's answer to their requests. The Legate had kept it back. He would gladly still have let it lie. But they would not be put off, and insisted on hearing what the Pope had written. Timidly, reluctantly, softening every harsh expression and making the most of the few limited concessions, the Legate communicated the reply.   Even when he seemed to have given way the Pope had added the exasperating reservation, *salvâ semper Auctoritate Apostolicâ*.   The cardinals were still to be exempted from the rules imposed on ordinary bishops, with them there was to be no constraining law.   They were said to be of such notorious virtue that they might be left safely to their consciences.

The Italians voted the answer sufficient, but so did not Don Francis of Toledo and the twenty Spaniards. The deliverance of the Church from the English tyrant was ungratefully forgotten.   Indignation left them no room for other thoughts.   The cardinals, the worst sinners of the whole, to be trusted to conscience!   It was too much.   The council became a mob.   The Castilians persisted that they would have their '*jure divino.*'   The rest caught the same spirit.   De Monte had to report that the council was in mutiny.   There was a visible determination to put down the Holy See and increase the powers of the bishops.   To himself the Spaniards paid no respect.   The Emperor was encouraging them, and the Emperor was courting the Lutherans again, and in speaking to the Nuncio had described the Pope as his enemy.   In de Monte's opinion the chances were that, when he had settled Germany, he would use the council to weaken the Papacy, and would find the bishops too willing to help him.

So thought the Cardinal President, and so thought

the Pope also. The continuance of the council at Trent, in such a temper, was too dangerous. It should and must be removed to a place where the Pope would be master. Rome was impossible, but Bologna was in the papal territory—it would be safe there. De Monte was directed to use his ingenuity and discover a means of conducting the council to Bologna without directly committing the Holy See.

How he managed it will be seen in the next Lecture.

LECTURE XI

THE FLIGHT TO BOLOGNA

AFRAID of what might happen if the council remained at Trent while Germany was still under arms, the Pope and the Legate had agreed that it must be moved into Italy. The removal, however, must be made to appear as the council's own act, and though the Italian bishops were willing and even eager, it was quite certain that the Spaniards would fiercely oppose.

It was the spring of 1547. The Imperial and Protestant armies were still keeping the field, but without decisive results. There were now sixty bishops at Trent, and thirty theologians and canonists. The Carnival was over. On the first Sunday in Lent, Mass was said as usual in the cathedral, but it was observed that there was no sermon. The legates were pre-occupied and anxious. The courier from Rome had arrived that morning, and had brought the Pope's final order that the council was to be taken down to Bologna. The Cardinal of St. Cross was afraid of the Emperor's displeasure. De Monte was afraid of nothing. He said that the life of the Holy See depended on their leaving Trent, and that he now saw more clearly than ever that the Pope was a wise man.

There had been the usual feasting at the Carnival. Trent being so miserable a place, the bishops' attendants and servants made the most of their rare opportunities of enjoyment. A good many had over-eaten themselves, some were sick: one bishop had actually died, presumably from some other cause, and the fathers had all been at his funeral. A rumour spread, no one could trace how, that the plague was in the town. De Monte seemed not to believe it, and prepared for ordinary business as usual. But two physicians were desired to see what was the matter, and send him a report.

The physicians, if Father Paul speaks true, had been instructed in the answer which was expected of them. They said that whatever the disease might be, it was certainly dangerous and of a contagious kind. De Monte called the fathers together and read to them the physicians' opinion. He said he had power to adjourn the council, should unforeseen circumstances require it, and he desired them to say if they wished him to use that power. Their answer was a matter of course; the Italians were wild to be gone, and some even of the Spaniards hesitated. Don Francis of Toledo alone, with the majority of the Spanish party, stood firm, and, danger or no danger, announced that they meant to stay. De Monte waited a few days. On the Sunday following it was found that thirteen Italians had stolen off in the night. Again the fathers

were consulted; they were all terrified, or pretended
to be so, and it was suggested that the council might
be prorogued for an indefinite time. De Monte, however, said that a prorogation would be fatal. The
national synod would be held in Germany, and they
would never meet again. They must keep together
and adjourn. If they adjourned, where were they to
go ? To move into the dominions of any secular prince
was impossible without leave asked and obtained. For
this there was no time. Their place of meeting must
therefore be in the States of the Church. Don Francis
said that before venturing on a step of so much importance, it would at least be necessary to consult the Pope.
De Monte replied that he could himself answer for the
Pope. Trent had been selected only to please the
Germans. No Germans had attended, and there was
no longer a reason for remaining there. However, he
said he was at the council's disposition. He would go
or stay as they pleased.

Again the physicians were brought in. One had
detected certain alarming red spots about his patients;
the other said he would not remain in the town for a
hundred ducats a day. De Monte then proposed that,
as their lives were in danger, they should adjourn to
the papal territory. They might promise to return
to Trent at a future time if the Pope and the Catholic
powers desired it. Thirty-eight bishops were in favour
of this resolution; fourteen only, all Spaniards, were
against it; and it was therefore declared to be carried.
Don Francis saw through the manœuvre and protested.

De Monte reproached him with ingratitude to the Pope. 'Deus non irridetur' was his stern and significant answer.

But De Monte had done his work, and done it admirably well. The responsibility had been thrown on the fathers, and he and his thirty-eight moved off to Bologna. The Spaniards stood fast at Trent, and each party now called itself 'the council.' As in the fairy tale, the magician's staff had been cut in two, and each segment had a separate life of its own.

The farce was well kept up. The Pope affected nothing but regret. Could the fathers have remained two months longer, he said, the doctrinal decrees would have been completed, and they could have been dissolved; but he acknowledged it to have been impossible. He consulted the College of Cardinals. The College of Cardinals decided that all had been for the best. Many bishops would attend at Bologna who would never have gone to Trent. At Bologna, if necessary, the Pope could preside in person.

The Emperor was at Ulm. The courier who brought him the news had ridden fast, and had been but four days on the road. Charles was, of course, extremely angry. In a brief note to the Pope, he required the bishops to return to Trent instantly. Already, he said, infinite injury had been done. The Pope politely repeated his regrets, but protested that the removal was by no order of his. The council had decided to go by a majority of three to one. They could not be sent back without violence. Bologna was an excellent situation, as the Emperor could not fail to see if he reflected. The College of Cardinals had recognised in the change a visible work of God.

Paul and his cardinals knew very well that it was no work of God, but a clever stroke of diplomatic cunning. The Emperor had been overreached. The Nuncio who brought the Pope's answer tried to soothe him. The Emperor would not even listen to the Nuncio. Hope of concord was now gone, he said. The Protestants had a fair reason for refusing to have anything to do with the council. The Nuncio repeated that the fathers had themselves chosen to go, and that the Pope could not stop them. The Emperor answered that the Pope could be arbitrary enough when he pleased. The Germans had been brought with extreme difficulty to promise to send deputies to Trent. To Bologna they would never send, nor would he try to force them. The Pope was an obstinate old man, and was destroying the Church. He would now himself call the national synod and make an end of the business. 'Away with you!' he cried, as the Nuncio persisted; 'I will not dispute with you. If the council sits at Bologna, I will take my army there and preside over it myself.' The Pope, when the Nuncio returned with the account of Charles's anger, fell back upon St. Peter. The Church was built on Peter, not on secular princes. He knew his danger, but he knew his strength also, and counted not unjustly on Charles's unwillingness to lay rough hands on the Ark. He was playing a bold game for all or nothing.

The war in Germany had gone against the Elector and the Landgrave. The heart even of the Protestants was not with them. There had been little or no fighting. The Elector's army was melting away, and the principal Protestant leaders were in Charles's camp. The Emperor had renewed his promise that no violence should be done to conscience. They trusted his word, and on the faith of it they had undertaken to try what could be done with the council. The flight to Bologna had come just at the moment when he had won their consent.

Before he could decide what to do, the war had to be wound up. The event was certain before the last blow was struck. In April, 1547, the Emperor, the Duke of Alva, and Duke Maurice forced the passage of the Elbe at Mühlberg. The scanty force which the Elector had with him was easily scattered, and he and soon after the Landgrave were taken prisoners. It was no victory over Protestantism; it was a victory only over an extreme and irreconcilable faction. The Emperor was as far as ever from a conquest of the Reformation, neither had he sought or desired such a conquest. He gave a signal and immediate evidence of his sincerity. Wittenberg capitulated after the battle of Mühlberg, and Charles entered the city at the head of his army. There at Wittenberg, the mighty revolution had begun. In the great church where Luther had preached, and on the door of which he had nailed his theses, lay now buried all that remained of the Apostle of the Reformation. The Emperor stood gazing on the tomb of the miner's son who had shaken Europe. He said nothing, and an over-zealous priest, misconstruing his silence, urged that the grave should be torn open and the body thrown to the flames.   Charles calmly answered, 'I war not with the dead.' I do not know that human history contains any more memorable incident.

At Rome and at Bologna they were pleased to call Mühlberg a Catholic victory, and held much rejoicing over it. But Paul knew better what it meant. The Emperor had won; but he had won with heretic help, and was himself now the leader of the warlike part of Protestant Germany. If he pleased, he could march into Italy, and take the fathers at Bologna into his own charge, as he had threatened to do. There was nothing to stop him, and a council presided over by Charles was more formidable than even a German synod.

The bishops at Bologna hastened to propitiate Charles with a thanksgiving service. They were as frightened as the Pope, and could not tell what to expect. They and the Court of Rome were perhaps slightly relieved when they learnt that, instead of coming to Italy, Charles had called the Diet together again at Augsburg. At his wits' end, and supposing that the Emperor might be worked on through his ambition, Paul devised a notable scheme for which Cardinal Pallavicino himself is the authority. Saying no more about the council, he wrote to Charles suggesting that, Henry VIII. being dead, Edward VI. a child, and the Protestant faction being in possession of the government, the Emperor might now conveniently take his victorious army across the English Channel, restore the Church, and, if he pleased, annex England to his dominions.

Happy would Paul have been to see Charles entangled in such an enterprise. Charles would not indulge him. He said that he had work enough before him at home, and would make no wars for religion. He returned to his old point. The fathers at Bologna must go back to Trent, where the Protestant deputies would be ready to join them. The Pope could order it if he pleased. The Pope, or a Legate whom he had sent to Charles, had an answer ready. The bishops, he said, might consent to go back and receive the deputies on certain conditions. The Protestant States must promise to submit to the doctrinal decrees which the council had already passed, and to be bound generally by the resolutions at which the council should arrive. If they would engage for this, something might be done, otherwise the council in returning would suffer too great an indignity.

The Emperor did not care much what the council suffered. He would hear of no conditions at all. Back the fathers must go, he said, and go at once. He would do his duty, others must do theirs. If that was the Emperor's resolution, the Legate answered, there was no more to be said. His mission was ended. He must go home. The Emperor told him that he might go if he pleased, but advised him to reflect.

The Legate did reflect. He informed Paul that, if he persisted in keeping the council at Bologna, it was probable either that the whole of the Emperor's dominions would revolt from the Holy See, or that the Emperor would do as he threatened, go with his army to Bologna, and dictate the council's decrees. Spaniards and Germans were of one mind; even the Duke of Alva himself had cautioned him against the danger of obstinacy. The Emperor was inflexible, and was sufficiently angry already at the doctrinal decrees having been pressed through so precipitately.

The flight to Bologna had released the Germans from the promises which they had made. The Diet had been called again to Augsburg to reconsider their resolution. The Emperor opened the session in person. He said that from the beginning of his reign he had been striving to restore peace in Germany. Diet had followed Diet without success. A council had met at Trent, but that seemed to have failed also. He appealed for advice to the Electors. The three bishop Electors—Mentz, Cologne and Trèves—said that, if the council returned to Trent, they were willing to join it without making any further stipulation. The lay Electors—Maurice of Saxony, the Elector of Brandenburgh, and the Count Palatine—went back to their old position. They had seen that the Pope could not be trusted. They would recognise no council where the Protestants were not admitted to speak and vote. The decrees already passed must also be re-examined. The Catholic princes—Austria, Bavaria, and the rest—

agreed with the bishop Electors to accept the council as it stood, provided it returned to Trent. The Protestant divines, however, must be heard in defence of their opinions, and must have a safe-conduct to go and return. To the Pope the German Catholics sent a separate remonstrance. It was for Germany, again they said, that the council was most needed. It ought to have been held on the Rhine or the Danube. Trent had barely satisfied them, and the withdrawal to Bologna had once more thrown everything into confusion. If the Pope would undo that act, they were still ready to exert themselves to save the Church's unity. If not, he must take the consequences.

The Catholic remonstrance was read in the Diet before it was sent. After all the other opinions had been heard the Emperor gave his own. He expected that the Pope would comply, and he said he could not part with the hope that something might yet be made of the council, and that the Protestant States and princes would consent to be represented there. Their deputies should be under his own special protection. He engaged his honour that they should have fair play, with free speech in the council's sessions, and free permission to withdraw, if they saw fit, at any time.

A papal Legate was present at the Diet, and heard all that had passed there. Not a respectful word had been said of the Holy See. The Emperor seemed to have no consideration but for the Germans. The Legate thought that, if the council allowed themselves to be sent back to Trent like truant schoolboys, they would thenceforth have to do anything that the Emperor might order.

It seems to us now impossible that the Emperor's policy could have been successful; but he and the lay princes at the Diet probably knew better than we do the material they had to deal with, and they certainly did not think it impossible. The Electors personally assured the Legate that if their terms were complied with, the unity of the Church in Germany might be preserved. Charles bade him tell his master that, unwilling as the Diet were to consent to a council where he presided, they were so anxious for peace that they would not refuse even this, provided the council returned to Trent. If the Pope rejected the offer now made to him, Charles said he would hold himself excused before God if he then tried other means.

Faintly the Legate again raised the English invasion project. If the Emperor would but leave the council alone and go and conquer England, the Pope would bless him, give him troops, money, ships, and the whole island for his own. The Emperor was insensible to the temptation. Germany appeared to have made its last offer to the Pope, for him to take it or leave it.

The Holy See has a right to consider itself an object of supernatural care. Many times it has seemed on the verge of ruin. It has not been saved by extraordinary personal holiness either in Popes or cardinals, or even by what man calls honour or honesty. But a mingled feeling of fear and reverence has paralysed the hands which have been raised to strike. It has been as the air invulnerable, and man's vain blows malicious mockery. If the council had been difficult to manage when composed of a handful of bishops, three parts of whom were the Pope's own creatures, the task was not likely to be more easy when it was reinforced by German heretics, and overshadowed by a determined Emperor passionately bent on Church reform; yet overshadowed it would be if it was forced back to Trent against its will, and the humiliation was the least part of the possible mischief. Paul was ill, Cardinal de Monte meant to be his successor. If Paul died while such a council as would then be constituted was sitting far off at Trent, it might elect someone else at Charles's bidding, who would be his humble servant. Any course seemed safer than to yield to German menace. In bad health as he was, the Pope gathered up his courage. He replied that the council had moved to Bologna of their own accord, and were not to be coerced. He was preparing even to dare Charles to do his worst, and to call the fathers from Bologna to Rome itself. Diego de Mendoza, who happened to be at the papal court, heard of it, demanded an audience, and asked the meaning of the rumour which had reached him. The Pope raged and stormed, accused the Emperor of impiety, and the Spanish bishops who had stayed at Trent of schism. The most that Mendoza could get from him was, to agree to leave the question of going back to the bishops themselves. He referred Mendoza to them, and he told the bishops they must consult the Holy Spirit. Father Paul says that the Holy Spirit usually inspired the

Legate with the Pope's wishes, and the bishops with
the Legate's wishes.   The fathers at Bologna had made
continual, ineffectual efforts to induce the Spaniards
left at Trent to join them.   They replied now to the
Emperor, that the removal to Bologna having been
lawfully decreed, and the Spanish bishops having con-
tumaciously persisted in schism and pretended that
they alone were the lawful council, they would compromise their right if they were now to return and join
the recusants.   The Spanish bishops must come first to
Bologna and make their submission.   They would then
consider whether they would go back to Trent or not.
One condition they must insist on : that the council
should remain under the Pope's presidency, and that
the German demand for a revision of the past decrees
should not be listened to.   The answer had been drawn
up by de Monte.   It was forwarded through the Pope,
and the Pope was entreated to stand firm and defend
the liberties of the Church.

  With the Bologna council at his back Paul was
able to reply to the remonstrance of the German
Catholic princes.   He said he had done his best to
please them in calling the council to Trent.   Not one
German prelate had attended, and under such circumstances the fathers had a right to remove.   He had not
advised it.   They had acted for themselves, no doubt
under the direction of the Holy Spirit.   He could not
believe that the Emperor intended violent measures, or
that the Catholic princes would support him should he
attempt them.   If he was mistaken in this, he could

not prevent anything they might do any more than he could prevent rain from falling or wind from blowing; but he bade them remember that Peter's house was built on a rock, and that they, and not the Holy See, would be the sufferers if they lifted a hand against it.

Mendoza waited on Paul to learn what he was to say to the Emperor. Paul said the bishops at Bologna had decided, and he could not interfere with them. He trusted, therefore, that the Emperor would order his subjects who had remained at Trent to join their brethren.

A scornful retort sprang to Mendoza's lips, but he checked himself and reported the Pope's answer. The Emperor saw how it was; but, as the responsibility had been thrown on the fathers, to them he addressed himself. He sent two Spanish canonists, Vargas and Velasco, to Bologna with a letter. He declined to call the fathers a council. He addressed them as a convention. The messengers were proud and insolent. Mendoza had threatened to throw the Legate into the Adige. Vargos told the Bologna bishops that they were shadows and not a council at all. Henry VIII. or Elizabeth never addressed an English Convocation more imperiously. He told them the Emperor ordered them to return to Trent, and his orders must be obeyed. The plague had gone, if plague there had ever been: once for all the Emperor would not allow the Church to be ruined by the Pope and an illegal synod.

De Monte said that threats would not move them.

The fathers backed him up, and Velasco, seeing that
nothing could be got out of them, read a formal protest,
in which it was stated that religion being convulsed,
the morals of the Church corrupted, and the greater
part of Germany broken off from the Catholic communion, the Emperor had called successively on Leo X.,
Adrian, Clement VII., and, finally, on the present Pope
to summon a General Council. At last, he had succeeded. He had brought the Germans to agree, and
was expecting a happy issue, when the Legate and a
part of the fathers had, for an insignificant cause, adjourned their place of meeting to the Pope's territories.
He had required them to return. They had given a
vain, captious, and insincere reply, which the Pope had
thought fit to approve. Their excuses would not be
allowed. Had they been honest, had they been really
forced to leave Trent for the cause which they alleged,
they ought to have moved deeper into Germany. The
Germans would never consent to a meeting at Bologna.
The Emperor by his office was protector of the Church.
He felt it his duty to extinguish religious discord, and
reform the lives and morals of churchmen throughout
his dominions. Once more, therefore, he called on them
to retrace their steps. Forty Italian dependents of the
Pope could not be permitted to legislate for countries
of which they knew nothing. Their arguments were
mere illusion. Infinite injury might now fall on
myriads of human souls, and on them the responsibility
would lie. The Emperor must make such provision as
he could. In what he might be obliged to do he would

spare the Holy See so far as the necessary measures would allow.

The protest was delivered in writing. The bearer required that it should be entered in the proceedings. De Monte stood valiantly to his text. The Emperor, he said, was the son of the Church, and not its master. They would all die sooner than allow a secular prince to command a council.

A similar scene passed at Rome. While the Castilian doctors lectured the bishops at Bologna, Mendoza delivered the same message to the Pope and the Sacred College. To the Pope he was moderately respectful. To the cardinals he sternly said that since they had refused to assist in the reformation of the Church and the restoration of peace to Christendom, they and their master would be answerable for all the ill that might ensue.

Mendoza was heard in dead silence. Not a voice replied, and he retired as he had entered. A few days after Paul sent for him privately and assured him of what Mendoza knew to be untrue, that he had not himself advised the leaving Trent. He said he would re-examine the circumstances, and if the reasons alleged for it had been insufficient, perhaps something might be done. But it was not to be supposed that the Holy Spirit could only speak at a single place. The secular and spiritual power had each its own province; one must not trespass on the other. He could not believe that the Emperor had really sent so hard a message.

Mendoza assured him that he had used the Emperor's own words.

The bishops at Bologna might talk of dying rather than surrender, but they had a wholesome fear of Charles coming down on them with a German army. They were doing nothing; why could they not be suspended? The Pope said that they might break up of their own accord if they liked it. He would not interfere with them. But this would not do either. If they separated, the Spanish bishops at Trent would then claim to be the council, and would act as the council. The Spanish bishops were an ugly spectre. Paul again sent them orders to rejoin their comrades. They referred him to the Emperor, and suggested that meanwhile their comrades might rejoin them.

All was going wrong with Paul. He had given the duchies of Parma and Piacenza to his bastard son Lewis. He had no right to those duchies. Lewis had been murdered. Upon this the Emperor had occupied Piacenza, and refused to restore it. Paul appealed to the Venetians. The Venetians would not interfere. He appealed to France, but France would not move without money; and though Paul had been showering out indulgences, the market for such wares had fallen, and his own treasury was empty. Still, yield about the council he would not, and Charles had to let him alone, and see what he could do himself to restore order in his own dominions. The decrees at Trent had exasperated Germany. It was easy to talk of toleration. Each of the States into which Germany was divided had a religion of its own. The Protestant States had dispossessed the Catholic minorities, seized the Church property, and forbidden the Mass. In the Catholic States the Protestants were disallowed their services. I must repeat that religion on both sides was not an opinion, but a *law*. There could not be two laws in the same country. When men felt with intensity, the step was short from convictions to blows; and wherever the free exercise of different creeds was tried, as it was tried in France, there was civil war in miniature in every district. The Emperor had been struggling to preserve the outward forms, restored to the old Church model, and to leave men free to think for themselves on mysterious points which no one could understand. The Pope had baffled him with his dogmas and anathemas. The Protestants had become violently doctrinal, too, and peace was impossible while a second religion, or indeed half a dozen doctrinal religions, were allowed to challenge and insult the old Catholic traditions.

Flanders had caught fire from Germany. There, too, anarchy was breaking into violence. As the government was Catholic, the Protestantism of the people took the aggravated form of Calvinism and Anabaptism. The whole of the Low Countries would have been on fire if they had been allowed their own chapels, and their preachers had been allowed unlimited license of speech.

The mischief came from dogmatism—Catholic dogmatism or Protestant dogmatism. Each was driving wedges into society and splitting it to pieces. In

England Henry VIII. and the Parliament were obliged
to pass a Six Articles Bill—to say to the people that if
they did not agree with what was established, they
must hold their tongues and keep their thoughts to
themselves. Charles had to try something of the same
kind in Germany and the Low Countries, till the
council could be brought into working shape again, and
be made to behave itself. At Brussels, in his own
dominions, he issued a very severe edict against
Protestant incendiaries, the more severe because he
knew how hardly he had been fighting the Pope and
the dogmatists on the other side, and he justly thought
his own people need not make his task more difficult.
The wildest legends were told afterwards, in the civil
war, of the cruelties which had been exercised under
this edict.

Charles was no ideal sovereign. He was an honest
mortal doing the best he could with refractory materials.
He had no sympathy—not the least—with Protestant
theology. Already Anabaptism had broken into rebellion. He was, perhaps, more severe with it than perfect
wisdom would have recommended; certainly he was so
in the terms of the edict, for which he may not have
been personally responsible. Any way the edict was in
force only for a year; and in keeping tongues from
wagging it may have saved the country from more
suffering than it caused.

In Germany the task was harder, for the authority
was less. The council for the present had failed.
The Emperor saw clearly that while Paul survived

there was no more hope, and to the end of his life he charged Paul with having deceived him. But Paul was eighty years old, and a change could not be far distant. For the time, with the help of the Diet at Augsburg, the Emperor adopted his own celebrated Interim, a scheme of formulary and discipline which he thought could be accepted by all parties, till a satisfactory council could be held. No one knows by whom it was drawn. It was perhaps the work of many hands. It consisted of twenty-six articles which could be interpreted in various senses as Catholic or Protestant influence predominated. The Mass was re-established, but with a difference, as in Edward VI.'s First Prayer-book. The Cup was allowed to the laity. The marriage of the clergy was permitted, but was permitted reluctantly, as by our own Elizabeth, on the ground that it could not be prevented. The Interim itself was presented to the Emperor by the most moderate of the German princes. The articles were revised by the Imperial Council, and accepted by the Catholic bishops, with a proviso that they should be submitted to the Pope.

To the Pope, the interference of a lay Diet with religion was itself heresy. The Dathan and Abiram theory was the first article of the papal faith. Paul glanced over the clauses, only to find them worthy of their origin. Original sin and justification were provided for without reference to the Trent decrees. Ignorance was visible to Paul in every sentence. Works of condignity were not properly distinguished

from works of congruity. The need of a visible head
of the Church was unacknowledged; obedience to the
See of Rome was not insisted on. The '*jure divino*' of
the bishops, which they had fought so hard for at
Trent, was admitted, to the ruin of discipline. The
Cup to the laity was destruction to the orthodox belief.
The Interim, in fact, was a child of rebellion, born in
sin and hateful in all its parts—a concession to the
fatal principle that the laity were to have a voice in
the constitution of the Church.

He felt his way with France. Francis I. was dead.
His son, Henry II., was biding his time for a chance
of a fresh stroke at the Emperor. To support the
Holy See would be a creditable pretext. The French
Ambassador advised Paul to be firm. Let him show
that he was really resolute, and France would stand
by him. But the Pope's courage failed him. He
would and he would not. To ally himself with France
under such conditions would be a last mortal affront
to the Emperor and to Spain. Yet the Interim was
a monstrous proceeding. Who could have believed
that a Catholic prince would have ventured it ? The
cardinals cried 'Actum est de re Christianâ.' De
Monte, brave as Julius II., advised Paul to go himself
to Bologna and gather the council about him, or if he
was too infirm, to call the fathers boldly to Rome, put
out his arm, and strike the schismatic Spaniards at
Trent with his lightning. Paul was past such adventures. He drew back, and France drew back also
when he was seen to hesitate. The Pope decided at

last not to notice the Interim, to treat it as a political *modus vivendi*, not as a scheme of religion; in fact, not to meddle either way. The Nuncio at Augsburg was instructed to make no opposition.

The Interim was read in full Diet. The Archbishop of Mentz thanked the Emperor in the name of the Catholics. The Lutheran deputies were silent, but did not openly object. The success, if incomplete, seemed to imply that an arrangement was not impossible. Separate measures were introduced for the reform of the morals of the clergy, for the reform of the hated ecclesiastical courts, for the reasonable restraint of the Church officials. Father Paul says that never was law code devised by man so just, so clear, so impartial. If the rules had been drawn by churchmen themselves, they could not have been more favourable. Even Pope and cardinals would have had little to complain of save in the limitation of indulgences and dispensations.

The scheme was printed, and was left for consideration preparatory to the next meeting of the Diet. Before they separated the Emperor expressed his hope that the council would soon meet again at Trent, and that all his subjects, Protestant as well as Catholic, would then be represented there. The decrees which the fathers had passed so hastily had been ignored in the Interim. It was presumed that they would be treated as non-existent when the council could again be opened.

Charles had spoken fairly; but compromises are only possible when both sides are anxious for peace.

There was evident anxiety among the German laity
to maintain unity if possible, yet the Emperor would
perhaps have found his task an easier one if he had
taken the Pope at his word and broken with him.
Altogether the Interim looked well on paper. In
practice it would not work. The Lutheran pastors
refused to celebrate Mass and had to be deprived.
They said they would as soon be Papists at once as
Mass-mongers.

Papal agents were busy throughout Germany offering easy terms of reconciliation. Middle courses are
always difficult and often dangerous, and the people
everywhere were reported as wildly minded. Luther's
teaching had kindled them into genuine enthusiasm.
Middle courses do not suit enthusiasm. As long as the
Pope was to be president, as long as there was no
distinct promise that the decrees should be reconsidered,
the prospect of the council brought no comfort to the
Protestant mind, and the present Interim was unbearable. The princes might be satisfied of the Emperor's
intentions, but the free cities were obstinate. They
called the Interim an institute of Popery. They bade
the Emperor take their property if he pleased, but
leave them their conscience. They asked him why he
imposed a creed upon them which he did not hold
himself? They resisted, some to be crushed, some to
submit under protest, some with open and stubborn
defiance. Magdeburg stood out in open rebellion, and
local wars began again, which broke out spasmodically
and would not be extinguished.

The Interim was not understood. Like our own articles and rubrics, it was not intended to force consciences. It was meant only as an elastic form which men of different opinions could agree to use. Some supposed that the Emperor intended to reimpose the authority of the unreformed Church of Rome. That he had no sinister purpose of that kind he gave the clearest proof. Maurice of Saxony had shown himself at the Diet of Augsburg to be the most antipapal of all the German princes. To Maurice Charles gave the command of the Imperial army in Germany. But the only effect was that Maurice was himself distrusted. Ambiguous formularies were then a novelty. They were designed to allow men of piety and character who differed on trifles to unite in a common worship, in a common confession of the moral obligations of religion. It was a dream, a dream of the Ivory Gate, but yet a generous dream. It is not conceivable that if the Emperor had the designs attributed to him by Protestant tradition, he would have selected to carry them out the prince who, of all others, was most certain to resist and disappoint him.

One person in Europe at least understood Charles, and that was the Pope. Paul had broken up the council, and had refused to restore it. He was left to the confusion which he had created; to wear out what was left to him of life in trying to exorcise the spectre of the Spanish bishops at Trent. A guilty conscience told him, and told the cardinals, that if he died, these bishops might elect his successor. He again appealed

to the Emperor.   The Emperor would not listen.   De
Monte advised him to excommunicate the Spanish
bishops. He did not excommunicate them, but he
summoned them to come to him at Rome, under pain
of his displeasure.   The Spanish bishops answered
quietly that they were obliged to disobey him.   They
forwarded his summons to the Emperor.   Mendoza
was instructed to wait on the Pope, and ask how he
could have ventured such an act without the Emperor's
permission.

Permission ! Permission from an Emperor to a
Pope who thought himself another Gregory VII. !
The angry old man said that the Spanish bishops at
Trent were a conventicle, a portent hanging in the
face of Europe.   Remain there they should not.   The
Emperor had demanded a reform in the morals and
discipline of the Church.   A reform of that kind could
be carried out at Rome, and at Rome only, and to
Rome the Spanish bishops should come.   He required
their advice, he said, with pleasant irony, and could
not do without it.

So he stood defiant to the last.   But the struggle
was too hard for his aged body.   France could not
help him, or would not.   When he was elected he was
not expected to live a year.   He had reigned for
fifteen in storm and strife, and carried his flag to
the last in front of the battle.   Pallavicino calls
him *clarissimœ memoriœ princeps.*   He had found
the Church a *cadaver,* says the Cardinal.   He left
it almost recovered to life.   In the opinion of his

biographer, he had but one fault: he was too much attached to his bastard children.

If it be a merit to have baffled the honest efforts of a Catholic Emperor to clear the impurities from the Church of Rome, and preserve the unity of Christendom, Paul III. had more than earned the praises of his encomiast. He began his reign with an affectation of being himself a reformer. If he was honest in his desire, he made the accomplishment of it impossible by his arrogance and obstinacy. He died on November 10, 1549. Cardinal de Monte, who had been his fellow-conspirator in the removal to Bologna, was chosen with little opposition to succeed him, and became henceforth known to the world as Julius III.

LECTURE XII

THE GERMAN ENVOYS

IN the sixteenth century on the accession of a Pope additions were usually made to the Sacred College, and the selections were watched with curiosity as indications of the disposition of the new ruler of the Church. Paul III. made a cardinal of his grandson, who was a boy of fourteen. Pius IV. elevated a youth scarcely older. Cardinal de Monte, on becoming Julius III., made the still more singular choice of a lad whom he had admired on the stage, had adopted into his family, and employed in keeping his monkey-house. Seasoned as they were in such experiences, the members of the Sacred College did on this occasion express some astonishment when their new colleague was introduced to them. They enquired by what merits he had earned his elevation. 'Merit!' said de Monte. 'Why, you elected me Pope; what merit did you see in me?'

In bringing the council to Bologna, de Monte, while legate, had carried out Paul's orders faithfully and dexterously, and had himself professed to approve. Having obtained the object of his ambition, however, he seemed to be anxious for peace to enjoy himself, and in announcing his accession to the Emperor, he intimated a readiness to meet Charles's wishes and to send the fathers back to Trent. After the attitude which the Court of Rome had assumed, and after the part which the present Pope had personally played, there would doubtless be an appearance of humiliation. But circumstances had changed in the interval.

The Emperor had tried his Interim and had not succeeded with it. The council alone could help him to the objects which he had in view, and he was too eager to see it recalled to insist himself on stipulations. He doubtless thought, as he had thought all along, that if it was reassembled and the German Protestants were represented at it, he could force it to do as he wished. Julius had been taught by his experience as legate that Charles's threats were less dangerous than they sounded. The circumstances of the time, and the temper perhaps of the bishops, better known to him than they can be to us, may have satisfied him that the risk might be run without serious consequences.

With very great difficulty the Emperor had extorted from the German Diet and Duke Maurice a consent that the experiment should be tried. Since the flight to Bologna the Diet had ceased to hope for honesty either in Pope or prelates. The Germans expected little, and they made their acquiescence conditional on an engagement that the articles of faith already defined should be re-examined, as an admission of the right

of the Protestants to be consulted; that the deputies
whom they might send should vote in the council as
well as speak ; and that, while the Pope might continue
to preside, it should be acknowledged that the Pope,
like any other bishop, was subject to the council.

The Emperor foresaw that these terms, if formally
demanded at Rome, would be refused, or that, if allowed
in appearance, they would be evaded.   He complained
that the Diet was obstinate.   But he undertook that
the reforms in the Church so long talked of, so long
demanded, must and should be carried out, and the
reforms once carried through would involve all the
rest.   He left the Imperial army still under the command of Maurice, though Maurice had been the most
determined in defending the Protestant view.   The
Diet consented reluctantly that deputies should be
sent without the formal stipulation, and both sides
were left to the obscurity of an understanding which
was to clear itself when the council should re-
assemble.

There were still preliminary skirmishes between
Pope and Emperor to secure advantageous positions.
The council was to meet again in May 1551.   The
Bull for the reopening was issued in the previous
November, and the Pope introduced into it the asser-
tion that he alone had power to convoke, preside over,
and direct General Councils.   Before it was published
a draft of it was sent to the Emperor, and Mendoza,
Charles's ambassador at Rome, was ordered to object
to language which gave the Protestants an excuse for

refusing to take part. The Pope frankly admitted that this was his real object. He said it would be disingenuous to use ambiguous phrases. In the end it would only infuriate them, and he did not wish to find himself fighting with a mad cat. Mendoza said that, if the Pope had the rights which he claimed, it would be better to leave them unexpressed. The object of the council was to recover Germany by gentle measures. It was imprudent to begin by exasperating it. Julius was the old de Monte still. Truth, he answered, must be spoken, let who would be offended. The Pope was Christ's Vicar, earthly head of the Church and light of the world. The successors of St. Peter never stooped to artifice.

Not a word of his Bull would Julius modify; so, as plain speaking was to be the order of the day, Charles read the draft in the Diet himself. The Lutherans were amused, finding things were just as they expected. Maurice said he would have none of the council unless the Protestant divines were to vote in it. The Catholic princes asked in disgust if the Pope was to challenge a supremacy which half Europe disallowed him. The Emperor passed it off as the folly of a vain old man. The Pope, he said, might talk of directing the council. If the Diet would send representatives, he undertook to go himself either to Trent or its close neighbourhood, and take care there was no direction. Something must be done to restore peace in Germany. He had tried the Interim. He had tried to reform the Church's morals. Both attempts had come to nothing, and the council seemed to offer the only resource. If that failed too, there would be universal anarchy.

The Emperor was evidently honest, and the Diet believed him. He had maintained from the beginning that if the Germans were once in the council, they would bring the Pope to his bearings. He pledged his honour that if they would consent, every German, Catholic or Lutheran, should be free to say what he believed to be true. He drew up a safe-conduct for the Protestant representatives to be free to go to Trent, stay there without interference, and leave when they pleased. The Diet finally agreed that go they should, and that if they were fairly used, Germany would abide by the result.

The opening of the council was to be on May 2. On April 29 the Italian bishops arrived and rejoined their Spanish brethren. A fresh detachment of the latter had come in from Castile to strengthen the Imperialist party; and Doctor Vargas, who had lectured the prelates at Bologna to such purpose, was sent with them to keep guard. May 2 came. The Italians were eager to begin and get done with their work. Vargas had to tell them that there were points still to be settled about the appearance of the Lutherans, that no more must be done till they had arrived, and that business must be prorogued till September. Such was the Emperor's pleasure. Charles doubtless meant to make the fathers feel the bridle after the Bologna escapade. They were, of course, furious. Were they slaves, they asked, that they must take orders from a secular prince ? Cardinal Crescentio, who had succeeded de Monte as president, tried in vain to soothe them. They refused to be comforted, and they passed a resolution that they would not be prorogued. Unsupported this time by the Pope, they found their resolution would not help them, and they had to digest their mortification as they could.

The summer months went by. At that season the climate was bearable, but Trent at its best was a dreary residence. Visitors dropped in. The Prince of Spain, afterwards Philip II., passed through on his way to Naples. His cousin Maximilian, Ferdinand's son, came a little later, and there were mild festivities; but neither Philip nor Maximilian could throw light on the intentions of their respective fathers.

French bishops were expected, but none arrived. Instead of bishops came a letter from the French King addressed to ' the convention,' which he would not dignify with the name of a council. The King said he had not been consulted about their meeting. He regarded them as a private synod got up for their own purposes by the Pope and the Emperor, and he would have nothing to do with them. Cold comfort to the fathers who were looking for French support against the imperious Charles.

Meanwhile the Germans were preparing leisurely to keep their engagement. Melanchthon drew up a body of Lutheran doctrine which was to be submitted to the council. Several of the Catholic German bishops, the

three Archbishop Electors at their head, made their
way to Trent in the course of the summer, and at
length Maurice informed the Emperor that the Protestant divines were ready to start. There was still,
however, a preliminary question to be settled about
their safe-conduct. Trent was occupied by troops
under the council's orders. These divines in the eyes
of the Church were condemned heretics liable to seizure
and execution. The Emperor had given them a safe-
conduct, but Sigismund had granted John Huss a safe-
conduct at the Council of Constance, and yet Huss was
burnt. Luther came to Worms with a safe-conduct,
and the Roman cardinals and bishops had urged
Charles to disregard it and burn Luther also. Very
naturally, therefore, and as will be seen with excellent
reason, Maurice required security in the name of the
council itself.

Impatient of delay, and provoked at what he considered needless preciseness, the Emperor nevertheless
bade Vargas and Mendoza obtain what was wanted.
The hesitation in granting it showed how necessary
Maurice's precaution had been. The question had to
be referred to the Pope. The Pope in evident em-
barrassment paused upon his answer, and September
came, when business was to open, before he could
decide what to say.

Another prorogation would have driven the fathers
into rebellion, and they were permitted to take up their
work where they had dropped it two years before. A
long address was read from the Pope of the usual kind.

The bishops were told that they had been reassembled to recover sheep who had strayed. It was a momentous duty, and God was watching them as a spectator and a judge. The next point was to consider their own position in view of the refusal of France to recognise them. Could a council be regarded as ecumenical, as representing γῆν οἰκουμένην in the absence of so important a member? There was a division of opinion about this. The papal party carried it in their own favour, but there was an independent minority, not unimportant, who still doubted whether they really were a council.

Reform came next, of course at the Emperor's insistence. 'Bishop's residence' had been left unfinished in consequence of the Spanish demands. Cardinal Crescentio introduced proposals, with the '*jure divino,*' on which the Spaniards had so insisted, still unrecognised. The old clamour broke out again. The Pope had no intention of parting with a single function which he had usurped. The bishops said that it was useless to force them to reside till their powers had been given back to them. They could not administer their sees. Priests and laymen were alike taken from their control by papal dispensations. Causes under trial in their spiritual courts were advoked to Rome, and criminal clerks threw themselves on the Pope's protection. They had nothing to do, and they did nothing. The Bishop of Valence said afterwards he had seen as many as forty of his brethren at once, amusing themselves, through enforced idleness, in the dissipations of Paris.

The council passed excellent resolutions of amendment, but was not allowed to provide means for carrying them into effect. The Pope stopped the way. The debate was a scandal, and the Legate was as pleased as his predecessor when he could change the subject and go off on heresy.

The Sacraments were again to be considered, especially the Eucharist. In opposition to the Protestant heresies, the change had to be insisted on which was produced by consecration, in the substance of the bread. It was admitted that the change was confined to the substance; that the accidents were not changed, whether separable or inseparable; and what substance was, independent of its accidents, independent of colour, form, extension, or natural properties, incapable of motion, and subject to conditions neither of time nor of space, metaphysicians found, as they still find it, difficult to say. Berkeley and other modern philosophers conclude that when all the attributes are thought away, there remains only an idea in the mind of God.

An idea with corporeal presence is again an enigma.

The discussion was protracted into endless refinements which do not touch the purpose of these lectures. A few practical points only need to be mentioned. The sense of the mysterious nature of the consecrated elements had not secured a reverential treatment of them, and the administration of this Sacrament was often scandalously indecent. Money was demanded for it in direct contradiction of the canon. At the churches in Rome, each communicant was required to carry a lighted candle, to the bottom of which some coin was to be attached as the priest's perquisite. Decrees of council could do little to correct disreputable customs so long as the disposition remained which led to them. If one practice was forbidden, another like it would take its place. The fathers, however, could express their disapproval, and were perhaps the more willing as Rome was the chief offender. They ordered, further, that when the Host was carried through the streets, everyone should kneel and uncover, that the Sacrament should be kept in each parish church, and that a lamp should burn day and night before it.

All this, however, was not the purpose for which the Emperor had brought the council together. His object had been to reconcile differences, and he had created a force which would do nothing but pass definitions which made reconciliation impossible. Every avenue was now almost closed. The Legate, with an affectation of liberality, consented to leave open, though only for a few weeks, the allowance of the Cup to the laity.

'Many Catholics,' says Pallavicino, 'had a fond opinion that, if indulged on this point and on the marriage of the clergy, the German heretics might be recovered to the faith.' This one subject, therefore, was left undetermined for a limited number of days to give time for Melanchthon and his friends to arrive. But the Legate declared peremptorily that he would wait no longer. If they had not appeared at the date specified, the decrees would be passed independent of them. He announced also, ostentatiously, that the work once done was done for ever, and could not be recalled. The Diet might talk of reconsideration and plead the Emperor's promise; Emperor and Diet ought to have known that when the Church has once spoken it never recedes.

Had Melanchthon and his companions been tempted to hurry to Trent by the inducement held out to them, very singular scenes might have been witnessed there. They were waiting for the council's safe-conduct, and the Pope and Legate were considering between them what sort of an instrument it was to be. That a safe-conduct should be granted by the council at all was, in Pallavicino's opinion, an enormous concession to German perversity and wickedness. In the eyes of the Church heretics were the worst form of criminals, and might be caught in traps if convenient, as legitimately as foxes or wolves.

The Emperor had gone to Innspruck as he promised, and was now established there, but with only his personal retinue. Differences had arisen between him and Maurice on the prolonged imprisonment of the Elector John Frederick and the Landgrave of Hesse; but they had not been of a kind to shake the Emperor's confidence, and no change was made in the command of the Imperial army. Maurice was left with the control of the only organised force in Germany, and yet his attitude about the council had been consistent and undisguised. He had said from first to last that he would never submit the Protestant cause to the council merely for it to be condemned. It may therefore be assumed that so far Maurice and the Emperor understood each other. It is equally clear from the Emperor's urgency, and from the anxiety of the Pope and Legate, that both he and they anticipated serious consequences from the presence of the Protestants at Trent. The Diet had not been hopeful; they had consented only to please Charles, and after the doctrinal campaign on the sacraments, and the declaration that the past decrees were irrevocable, they would doubtless have preferred, like France and England, to refuse to recognise the council at all. The Emperor, however, was persistent. The council had been his favourite remedy, on which he had fixed his hopes and credit. He clung to his conviction that with the presence of the Protestants there all would be changed

The legates had replied at last to Mendoza's request for a safe-conduct, with a haughty indifference assumed to conceal their uneasiness. They sketched out something, probably by the Pope's direction, which seemed sufficient on the surface. It was sent to Germany for approval, and when examined was found studiously worded so as to be no protection at all. If Melanchthon and the other Protestant ministers were to attend at the council they had required not only security to go and return, but the right to use their own religion in their own houses while they remained at Trent, and of this no notice had been taken at all. The Diet did not mean to trust their honoured pastors in the lion's jaws

Ambassadors were sent by Maurice and the Duke of Würtemberg to demand on the spot more sufficient security.

It was now the beginning of January 1552. The fathers had affected to consider that to listen to heretics at all was a condescension which approached a fault. The ambassadors when they arrived had to teach the fathers that they had mistaken their position. They declined to wait on the legates, lest they should seem to recognise the papal supremacy. They exhibited their commission before the council itself. They gave in a copy of the Confession of Augsburg, and desired that it might be examined by indifferent judges who had not been sworn to the Pope, a condition which excluded the legates and bishops. As to the safe-conduct, they defended their preciseness by referring to the decree of Constance that faith need not be kept with heretics — an odious slander, Pallavicino says, the Church's doctrine being merely that ecclesiastical judges were not bound by the engagements of secular princes.

It was exactly this which had made the Diet so particular. The bishops pretended to be indignant that their good faith should be doubted ; some of them thought that no safe-conduct should be granted at all unless the Diet bound itself to submit to every decree of the council past or future. The legates referred back to Rome, and an interesting correspondence ensued between them and the Pope. The College of Cardinals were asked for their opinion. The cardinals thought generally that the Church ought not to go out of its way to please rebels, but a direct refusal might irritate the Emperor too far. A safe-conduct might be made out for all Germans, lay or ecclesiastic, without specifying the Lutherans. If trouble arose afterwards, it might be contended that only Catholics were meant, since no others were named. Also the council might introduce the qualifying phrase, 'So far as their power extended.' The Pope would thus be left free to punish any faults which the heretics might be guilty of while at Trent.

The Pope liked the advice, and drew a form on the lines recommended, which was sent to the council and was read in session. By this document the council was to grant, *so far as lay in its power*, security to all Germans, secular or spiritual, of what degree, condition, or quality soever, to appear at the council, assist in its debates, propose, treat, and even, if they wished, dispute with the fathers, provided it was done with decency, as well as to withdraw at any moment if they should think fit.

Such a safe-conduct might have seemed sufficient, and the Germans might have overlooked the phrase which concealed so sinister a meaning. Constance, however, had made them suspicious. They observed the words. They again referred to Augsburg, and the Diet agreed unanimously that the safe-conduct must be further amended.

The fathers, supposing that they had extricated themselves from the difficulty, went on with their

ordinary work. They defined the power of the keys
as committed exclusively to priests. Priests had it,
however wicked; laymen had it not, however holy.
Absolution was a judicial act, not a mere declaration,
and contrition was of little value without it. This was
all easy sailing. Reform went less smoothly A proposal that benefices should only be conferred on persons
of suitable age fell through, because it would deprive
the bishops of the means of providing for their young
relations. There were daily skirmishes between the
bishops and the legates over papal encroachments.
Both, says Father Paul, protested that they sought
only the glory of God, when they were merely fighting
for their own interests. The bishops repeated that
they could keep no discipline as long as monks and
seculars could buy dispensations to live like laymen,
with one foot in the world. The Pope would not have a
limitation of his dispensing power. The friction between
the bishops and their father at Rome was evident on
all occasions. There was only peace when they were
hunting heresy together, or resisting secular interference.

The Emperor was close by at Innspruck. The
ambassadors of Saxony and Würtemberg were in the
town watching the council's performances and waiting
for their instructions. But the Pope seemed to think
that he had now everything his own way, and need not
disturb himself about either Emperor or ambassadors.
To strengthen his position he created thirteen new
cardinals, and he sent up fresh batches of Italians to
increase his majority.

All now pointed to a crisis. Temper in Germany was rising. The equivocation in the safe-conduct had been discovered and exposed. Evidently Popes and bishops were still of the old material, with no honest meaning in them. People began to think they were betrayed, and even the Emperor's good faith was distrusted. Disturbances broke out in the Lutheran States. The French began to make overtures to Maurice in case the war broke out again, and outwardly Maurice seemed to listen, as if he too was not entirely certain of the Emperor's intentions. Yet, though warnings were sent to Charles to be on his guard, he continued to show the same unbounded confidence in Maurice's fidelity. He went on as if nothing was the matter, observing the council, sending directions to Mendoza to support the Protestant ambassadors, promising them that, if they would be patient, all would yet go well.

Orders came at length to the ambassadors to apply for an alteration of the safe-conduct to the presiding Legate in person. Crescentio was difficult to approach. They had been told to be conciliatory, and the Cardinal of Trent being on better terms with them than the rest, they asked him to procure them an audience. On their arrival, they had themselves refused to wait on the Legate. They were told now that they could not be received till they had stated what they wanted. They said their business was to demand a safe-conduct with no doubtful meanings in it, and to present again the Lutheran confession of faith, which their theologians would defend when they arrived.

The Cardinal of Trent carried the message to the Legate, and the Legate broke into most unapostolic rage. He said he would have no heretic articles of faith presented or defended in a holy ecumenical council. There had been disputes enough, and he would allow no more of them. The business of the fathers was merely to examine and condemn the opinions advanced in heretical writings. If the Protestants would state their difficulties in a spirit of humility, and with a willingness to receive instruction, the council would teach them the truth; but he said he would rather forfeit his life than permit strangers to advance doctrines of their own in a synod of Christ's ministers. As to the safe-conduct, the ambassadors' language was an insult to the council's honour; all had been granted that could be granted, and every Catholic would resent a demand for further security as a personal outrage.

The truth was now coming out. The legates had never intended that the Protestants should be heard in the council at all. The Emperor had promised that they should be heard. The council itself had seemed to promise it in the sham safe-conduct which had been offered; but all was illusion. The Church was still not to be bound by the engagements of secular princes, and the council's promises were conditional, and were to have been set aside by the Pope.

The Cardinal of Trent had to soften the Legate's language in conveying his answer to the ambassadors. He told them, however, that they could not defend their views before the council. The Legate at present was angry about the safe-conduct, and would not see them. In a few days, perhaps, it might be different, if they approached him in a proper manner.

The storms of thirty years had taught nothing to the Court of Rome. Pope and cardinals were still unable to recognise that they were mortals bound by the common laws of faith and honesty. Jean Ziska's drum had been the answer to the treachery of Constance, but Ziska's drum had been forgotten, and they were ready as ever to play the old tricks. The Emperor had distinctly promised the Protestants that they should be heard in the council. The council itself had been brought together in order that they should be heard; but who was the Emperor that he should dictate to anointed bishops?

The ambassadors asked Mendoza what they were to do. The Legate could not refuse an audience to the Spanish Minister. Mendoza went to him, reminded him of the Emperor's wishes, and told him that the Protestants must be admitted. He must alter the safe-conduct, and be prepared to reconsider the decrees. The Legate affected mere astonishment. What did Mendoza mean? Were a set of miserable sectaries to question the honour of an ecumenical council? The decrees were irrevocable. The sectaries might have an audience, but that was all. They had dared to ask that the bishops should be absolved from their oath to the Pope. To cancel the oath would open the bags of Œolus. He would rather die than do it. **If** such demands were persisted in, he would dissolve the council.

Mendoza reminded him that the Emperor was a dangerous person to trifle with. The Roman churchmen, however, seem to have thought, after the failure of the Interim, that the threats of falling back on the Diet were only talk. They thought that the Emperor had found he could not do without them, and that they were masters of the situation. Mendoza brought the angry Legate at last to promise to re-ceive the Protestant ambassadors in congregation; but suspend the past decrees he would not, not for a day, not for an hour. He had the Pope's orders, which he meant to obey. He felt on reflection that he must yield something about the safe-conduct. He asked Mendoza what form of safe-conduct would satisfy them. The Bohemian heretics at the Council of Bâle had exacted protection for life and limb, a deliberative voice in the council, the free exercise of their own religion in their own houses, while the council was in session, and a patient hearing for their doctrines. The German Diet required the same for their own divines.

The Legate, with an angry snort, said that he would consult the fathers, and the fathers, it appeared, had not all parted with their senses. The general feeling was that, in the Church's eyes, these Protestants who were coming were excommunicated infidels. To admit such persons among them would be a scandal, and to let them vote would be monstrous. The only fit relation between an ecumenical council and heretics was that of an acknowledged ruler willing to grant pardon on their submission to penitent sinners. Still, the Emperor wished them to be allowed to defend them-selves. The Emperor was dangerous, and was close at hand. It might be unwise of the council to stand too absolutely on its rights. Mendoza undertook that the Emperor would be satisfied if the treacherous clause in the safe-conduct was omitted, and if the council would promise to hear the Protestant deputation with courtesy and attention.

The papal party struggled desperately, pretended scruples of conscience, and entered protests in the register. They had thought it no crime to contemplate deliberate treachery towards heretics. They shuddered at the enormity of a discussion with them on equal terms. Prudence, however, prevailed. The bishops, Spanish and German, who were the Emperor's subjects, were afraid to disregard his wishes. The Italians held out longer. The Legate was the last to yield, and still meant to fight on every point of detail.

The safe-conduct, however, had to be given, and without the words which were to have enabled the Pope to disregard it. Mendoza imagined that the victory had been won. The Protestants would attend, and all would then go as the Emperor desired. His only fear was that they might presume too much on their success. He was afraid that they would begin with pressing for a renewal of the declaration of Constance that the Pope was subject to the council.

This would set everyone quarrelling, and he begged them to be careful at the outset. The rest would come right in time, if they would be patient and moderate.

Charles had said the same all along. If once Lutherans and Catholics could meet in the same assembly, Charles was convinced they would make up their differences, over the Pope's body. It might be so, but the Germans were still wary. The new document was not yet granted on the Bâle model. There had been an attempt to deceive them once, and Melanchthon must not run his head into a noose because the Emperor had an enthusiastic confidence in the justice of his own views. They observed that the safe-conduct was in general terms only, that it did not run in the name of the Pope and council. Nothing was said in it giving them the deliberate voice nor securing them the use of their religion during their stay. The Legate vowed that he would make no more changes. Mendoza thought the present scruples needless. But his order from Charles was to support the Protestants. He advised Crescentio to leave them no excuse for further objections by following the Bâle pattern exactly. If this was too great an indignity, the Legate might give the ambassadors the audience which they had asked for and hear what they had to say.

Again Crescentio kicked against the pricks; but having yielded once he could not now draw back. The ambassadors were to be heard, and heard in full congregation before the assembled fathers. The occasion was felt to be momentous. In all Church history there had been nothing like it. The foreign ministers attended in their robes of state. The fathers of the council sat ranged along the benches, hiding thoughts in their tonsured heads which few of them would have dared to utter. The ambassadors—plain, honest, German laymen—were introduced into the splendid assembly, and did not seem to have been particularly awed by it. One of them, Leonard Badehorn, spoke for the rest.

He began by addressing the fathers as 'Reverendissimi Patres ac Domini.' He would not call them a council, for Germany had not yet recognised them, and France had disputed their title. Mendoza had cautioned him against touching the papal supremacy. It was the heart of the matter, and Badehorn went at once to it. He said that the States of Germany had intended from the first to send representatives to a General Council, but it was to be a council where Scripture was to be the rule of controversy, where all persons present were to have liberty to speak, and where the head of the Church was to be called to account as well as its members. They had hoped that the time had come when these conditions would be fulfilled. Unfortunately the time had not come. The Council of Constance had ruled that safe-conducts granted to heretics need not be respected. The safe-conduct offered to themselves was insufficient in the face of such a declaration. Until that difficulty had been removed, the divines of the Augsburg Confession could not attend, and, in their absence, he and his brother ambassadors protested against further definitions of doctrine.

He had been told that the definitions already made were not to be revised. He refused to accept that conclusion. Those definitions were full of errors, and sixty bishops were not to suppose that they could legislate for Christendom. At Constance and Bâle it had been ruled that in what concerned faith and morals Popes were subject to councils. It was but reasonable, therefore, that the prelates whom he saw before him should be relieved of the oath which the Pope had extorted from them. He was speaking, he said, and he desired the fathers to mark his words, as the representative of the Elector Maurice of Saxony. In the name of that prince he required the bishops present who were Saxon subjects to regard that oath as no longer binding, and he invited the rest to reaffirm their superiority to the Pope. The Church was notoriously corrupt. The Pope had resisted all attempts at reform, and nothing could be done while the hierarchy were his sworn subjects. If the Pope now on the throne would set them free, he would be acting like an upright man. The council would then be a real council, and its decision would carry authority as being the free judgments of free men. He bade them take in good part what he had said. Prince Maurice was careful of his soul, loved his country, and was seeking to secure the peace of the world.

Language so bold and so unusual on such occasions

implied a belief, no doubt well founded, that, so far as the Pope was concerned, half the bishops present were on the speaker's side. It must have been equally certain to the Legate that, so long as Maurice was left in command of the army, the words used in his name were the Emperor's as well as his own. What was to be done? An anxious consultation was held at the Legate's house. The speech was a flat invitation to mutiny. If Protestant theologians were to be admitted to the council, and were to speak there like Badehorn, St. Peter's bark would be among the breakers. It was concluded to yield on the safe-conduct, but to retire on a second line of defence.

Trent was now full of soldiers in the council's service. The next day there was a grand military display at the cathedral. Visitors had crowded in, in large numbers, from a sense that great matters were in the wind. Mass was said, and then was read the reply of the council to the ambassadors' demands. It began by an enumeration of the efforts made by the fathers to induce the Protestants to join them. To satisfy their scruples, the safe-conduct had been twice recast. It was now brought into a form to which no objection could be raised. All Germans, lay or cleric, might attend the council, speak, propose resolutions, present articles of belief, dispute and defend them. They were not to be liable, while residing at Trent, to be called to account for any offence against religion which they had committed or might commit, and if anyone committed an offence, either at Trent or on the way to it, which

would forfeit his right to protection, he was to be tried
by his own people. The Protestant deputies and theologians should have the freedom of the town, send and
receive letters, and have absolute security during their
stay and on their journeys. They might leave when
they pleased without prejudice to honour or liberty.
In conclusion the council pledged its faith that the
safe-conduct should be honourably observed, the decree
of Constance notwithstanding; and if any wrong was
done and redress refused for it, the council consented to
be regarded as promise-breakers and as having incurred
the infamy of violated faith.

Now at last the victory did seem to have been
really won. In yielding, the Roman party had shown
that they did not dare to resent the language of
Badehorn about the Pope. But behind the emphasis
of the partial concession were still concealed certain
fatal reservations. Nothing had been said about the
right of the Protestants to vote, nothing about the
revision of the dogmatic decrees, without which their
attendance would be a mockery.

With these points of vantage firmly held, and
judiciously made use of, the Legate felt that he might
still defy the malice of the enemies of the Apostolic
See.

LECTURE XIII [1]

SUMMARY AND CONCLUSION

IT is in the nature of speakers and lecturers to magnify the importance of their subject, but to magnify the importance of the Council of Trent I believe to be impossible. | On the action of that assembly was to depend whether modern Europe was to have one religion or many, whether the creed which for so many centuries had shaped the characters of mankind was to continue to speak as the united judgment of all wise and good men, or whether Christendom was to split into factions which would rend and tear each other in every segment of the globe, till the very faith for which they were spilling their own and others' blood, was to fade away out of their hands, fade away from the most absolute of certainties into a disputed opinion. |

[1] The first twelve of the lectures on the Council of Trent were delivered to a class of undergraduates and other members of the University, but the last lecture of the series was by request given publicly. The recapitulation in the first part of Lecture XIII. was therefore unavoidable.—ED.

I will briefly repeat the circumstances which occasioned the council's meeting. Charles V. at his accession had found the laity of Germany and the north of Europe in revolt against the depravity and tyranny of the spiritual orders. Inflated by privilege, corrupted by wealth, and fooled by the imagination that they possessed supernatural powers, they had forgotten the purpose of their existence, and despised the lessons which they professed to teach.

The scandal reached its height when an Alexander VI. or a Julius II. claimed to be spiritual sovereign of Christendom as the successor of the fisherman of Galilee. The laity awoke, awoke at the call of Luther, to demand that the absurdity should end. The movement at first was not against the doctrines of the Church, but against immorality and tyranny alone. The Church had replied with excommunications and curses, and when it was able with axe and stake. Naturally the teaching came to be enquired into which produced results so portentous. This article of its faith was questioned, and that article, and religion being the nearest of all things to the hearts of serious men, religious truth the most essential, and religious error the most hateful, there was discord and confusion everywhere threatening to turn to civil war.

The remedy was a council, an assembly of the best and wisest men from all parts of Christendom. There was no wish to destroy the Church. The wish was to save the Church, to purify its abuses, and if any errors had crept into the creed, to remove them. But the loudest of the Reformers did not presume to set up their private opinions against the general judgment. Luther offered to submit to a free General Council. The Diet of Germany were ready to submit to a free General Council; so too were our Henry VIII. and the English Parliament. There was only this difficulty, that all past councils had been composed of clergy alone; and at least for 1100 years had been presided over by the Bishop of Rome. In the present state of things the Pope and the clergy were the chief offenders, and could not be sole judges in their own cause. The laity claimed to be represented and to have a voice in the measures to be adopted. They must have a council, but it must be a free council, not a council in bondage to Rome.

The Popes, who could scarcely hope to escape even from a synod of bishops, knew perfectly well how they would fare before a mixed tribunal. They struggled, resisted, intrigued, stirred up wars, appealed to the princes to crush the Reformers down. But the princes of Europe could not in conscience use fire and sword upon their own subjects while the Court of Rome remained a sea of iniquity. Reluctantly, therefore, the Pope and cardinals had been forced to yield, a council had been brought together, and brought together, could the Pope have known it, with the utmost desire to shield them. Popery and the Roman Catholic creed are now synonymous—we do not separate them even in thought. In the sixteenth century at least half Catholic Europe, bishops and laity alike, distinguished between the creed and the See of Rome, and, while holding the faith in unblemished orthodoxy, they regarded the Papacy as a usurpation and an impertinence.

England was antipapal always. France under Louis XII. had all but broken off. Germany revolted openly, and even the orthodox Spaniards had sacked Rome and taken Clement prisoner. Charles V. had as little fear of the Pope's curse as his uncle Henry of England, but from his youth he was a person of singular piety. His mind was moulded in Catholic forms. No saint ever observed more scrupulously the discipline of his religion. A part of every day was set aside for prayer. In his most severe campaigns he withdrew at intervals into retreat. When still young and newly married he agreed with the Empress that they two would spend the evening of their days in a religious house. As a man he had no faith in new opinions. He believed with all his heart in one Catholic and Apostolic Church, under one visible head. Other princes would have been content, like our Henry, that each nation should have a Church of its own, as it had its own laws. Charles, who perhaps understood better the power of religion over the minds of men, foresaw that out of such an arrangement there would arise only endless discord, wars and confusion. He could not leave the Pope and clergy as they stood, unreformed, with all their sins about them. His hope, his dream was that the Church itself might reform itself and remain unbroken. The decisions of a council which fairly represented the wisdom of Christendom all the world would respect. The Court of Rome, the Pope himself, might be mended, after the ancient models. The subtler problems of theology, free will, justification, the power of the keys, the mystery of the sacraments, might be left as they were, undefined to individual conscience, and the outward and even inward unity of Christendom might remain unimpaired, defended by the three creeds. This had been the advice which Erasmus had given when Charles consulted him. This was Charles's own conviction, and in the faith of it he had laboured on, driving his two unwilling horses, the Pope on one side, the German Diet on the other, till at length he had got his council together. The Pope presided still. The bishops alone had votes. To the Reformers such a condition of things appeared an absurdity. England and France refused to recognise a body so composed. The German Diet were long equally obstinate. Both to England and to Germany, however, Charles said that this arrangement was only for the outset. The bishops had no love for the Pope. Let German and English deputies present themselves at Trent and claim admission. They would not be unsupported, and they could then remodel the council as they pleased. It was thus that Charles always represented the position. France and England refused to be persuaded. The Diet unwillingly consented, and to encourage their confidence the Emperor charged Pope and Legate both, that till the Germans could be present the council must address itself solely to the great question of moral reform, and

the correction of the notorious scandals which had
provoked the revolt.

But the Emperor had to deal with an antagonist as
determined as himself and a great deal more subtle.
Paul III. had no intention of being reformed; he knew
well enough what would happen to him if the bishops
began upon reform and were reinforced by rebellious
Protestants.   He knew that his own bishops resented
his encroachments, and resented the oath extorted from
them of obedience to the Papacy.   He had packed the
council with Italians, but with all his skill he could not
prevent spurts of mutiny.   The bishops alone he might
still hope to control, and, therefore, since a council there
had to be, all his efforts from the first had been to
make the coming of the Lutherans impossible.   His
legates directed the proceedings, and scarcely touched
reform with the points of their fingers.   They played
on the appetite of the fathers for doctrinal discussions.
Disregarding absolutely the Emperor's orders, they had
hurried through decree on decree, definition on definition, on the points on which the Lutherans were most
sensitive.   These once settled, the legates hoped that
the Lutherans might refuse to appear, or that if they
did come, it would only be to find that all was over,
and that they were committed to the council's
decisions.

The Emperor had been baffled, but would not give
up the struggle.   The Diet naturally urged that, if
they were to be represented on the council, the decrees
must be re-examined.   To ask for such an engagement

beforehand he felt would be useless, but both he and his brother Ferdinand were still persuaded that, if a body of learned German laymen were once received at Trent, all would be altered. Perhaps they were right. They had their own ambassadors at the council. They had their own subjects among the bishops, and probably were aware of their feelings. They besought the Diet to waive its objections, and it was agreed that Melanchthon and a party of their ablest theologians should actually go.

Entrenched among their doctrines, the papal party might have considered themselves safe, but the coming of the heretics among them was still a frightful prospect, and must be prevented if possible.

Catholics were burning heretics wherever the secular powers would allow them. There was a Catholic army in Trent under the council's orders, and Lutherans could not venture into such a hornet's nest without a safe-conduct. The Emperor undertook for their security, but the recollections of Constance and the fate of Huss were still fresh. The Diet, therefore, required a safe-conduct from the council itself. The Emperor approved. He was eager to have Melanchthon on his way. He instructed his ambassadors at Trent to obtain the necessary documents; so earnest he was that he undertook to go to Innspruck himself to ensure Melanchthon fair play. He even intimated as his own opinion that the decrees might have to be reconsidered.

If the danger was to be escaped, the legates needed

the best weapons in their arsenal. Perhaps they had seen enough of the Spanish bishops and knew enough of the Spanish character to be satisfied that the Emperor would not dare to use force with them. The Castilians hated Rome, but they hated heresy worse. The legates' best resource, therefore, was in the safe-conduct. It is not likely that they contemplated a second Huss tragedy; but if the Protestants came, they meant to receive them not as equals, but as criminals brought up for condemnation. They had, therefore, to be careful how the document was worded. At first the presiding Legate refused any safe-conduct in the council's name. Finding that the Emperor would not tolerate a refusal, he consulted the Pope and the Sacred College, and their combined ingenuity produced a document apparently complete, but with an intentional equivocation, to enable the Pope to disregard it. The Protestant Ambassadors at the council observed the ambiguity and understood its meaning. They required that the safe-conduct should be redrawn. The Imperial and Austrian Ambassadors backed them up. The legates, detected in deliberate fraud, took refuge in affected indignation that their honour should be doubted, but in the discussion which followed the truth came out. Never, they said, should heretic laymen be allowed to debate on equal terms in a council of the Church. The attitude of the Church towards such men was that of teacher to humble suppliants for truth, or of judge to impenitent sinners. If the German heretics would come submissively to be instructed in the doctrines of the Church, the Church was willing to teach them.

But debate with them, permit them to argue questions of high divinity in a sacrosanct council, the Legate said the council never would. He himself would rather die than allow it. In the safe-conduct he would make no alteration. The Lutherans might take it or leave it. As to reconsideration of the decrees, the Church never reconsidered; a resolution once taken was taken for ever. The extension of the Cup to the laity had been left open for a time in deference to the Emperor's wishes; but with this, too, the council intended immediately to proceed.

The Legate was perhaps trying what is called brag. At any rate he said more than he could maintain. The Emperor was close at hand observing all that passed, and with agents on the spot who would do his bidding. Pressure was laid on. The Legate had said the safe-conduct should not be altered. He was made to consent that it should be altered. He had tried treachery and had overreached himself, and the Protestants had raised their demands on the discovery. The safe-conduct they now claimed was not only to promise them a hearing in the council, but was to permit them to debate, argue and make propositions, and to have the free use of their own religion while they stayed.

On this a fierce altercation had followed. In the course of it the Protestant ambassadors claimed to be heard in congregation. Leonard Badehorn, their

leader, spoke for the rest, and spoke in the name of
Maurice, a name which by this time the legates'
wisdom might have learnt to fear.   Surrounded by a
ring of scowling faces, the unmoved Saxon described
with pitiless sincerity the purpose for which the council
had assembled, and the ill use to which it had been
turned by the Court of Rome.   Briefly, contempt-
uously, he alluded to the trick which had been tried
with the safe-conduct.   He protested in his master's
name again against the precipitate definitions of doctrine.   He appealed to the bishops present to reassert
the decree of Constance, that the Pope was subject to
the council, not the council to the Pope ; and he urged
them to repudiate the oath which they had been
unjustly compelled to swear.

A strange speech to have been heard in such an
assembly, and stranger still the reception of it.   The
fathers might have been expected to have risen in
indignation, and to have bidden Badehorn and his
companions depart to their own place.   They did not
rise.   They did not protest.   They became apparently
the meekest of meek assemblies.   They granted the
new safe-conduct.   They promised in it that, if the
Lutheran divines came to the council, they might
propose, answer, speak, debate, present their own
articles of faith, do all which the Legate had said he
would sooner die than permit.   They might have their
own religious services while they were at Trent, they
might depart when they thought fit, and the fathers
consented to be held infamous as promise-breakers if

the engagements so made were broken in the smallest point.

Why the legates, why the Italian bishops so suddenly gave way on points which they had defended so obstinately, was variously explained. It was generally set down to the Emperor. But, in fact, they had only retired on their inner lines. The Church of Rome does not risk defeat in indefensible situations, and Cardinal Crescentio had secret instructions to avoid an open quarrel. If the Protestants were refused admission, and if the council failed through the Legate's action, the Emperor might after all fulfil his threat, and call a national synod in Germany. The temper of the bishops on the Roman supremacy was too critical to be depended on, and it was necessary to yield something; since, therefore, the coming of the Protestants could not apparently be prevented, the Pope had directed the Legate to receive them courteously and allow them to say what they liked, provided only he could keep them off the fatal question of his own prerogative. On this, and only this, Crescentio was to be firm. Short of it, he might promise anything and venture anything. The primacy of the See of Rome left untouched, and the canons already passed being maintained as irrevocable, the Pope thought, and the Legate thought, that they might still defy the worst which the Protestants could do.

The outworks thus abandoned and the garrison withdrawn to their vital defences, Crescentio was now all graciousness. Nothing more was said of judges and criminals, and the meek willingness of penitent sinners to receive instruction. He professed the utmost readiness to receive the Protestants on their own terms, only with the understanding that the work done was not to be impeached.

The new safe-conduct had to be referred back to the Augsburg Diet. Weeks, months perhaps, would pass before Melanchthon could receive his final commission. The interval was the Legate's own. He had only to add fresh decrees, to increase the difficulty of revision, forge link on link, till the catena of doctrine was complete. The Protestants might then come if they pleased. Nothing would be left for them to do or say. Thus, all other business set aside, the fathers plunged again into theology, piling canon upon canon. The Protestant ambassadors asked Mendoza what it meant; Mendoza complained to the Legate, but no longer in his old peremptory style. The Spanish bishops, loyal as they were to the Emperor, and stern as they had been in their demands for reform, were perhaps as unwilling as the Legate to admit heretics into doctrinal consultations with them.

The Emperor was again baffled. He was no match for the Pope in diplomatic management. There was no remedy but force, and force he could not use. Badehorn appealed to him to check a haste which would turn Melanchthon's coming into a mockery. He did what he could. He wrote to Cardinal Crescentio. He sent an express to Rome to require the Pope to stay the Legate's hand. He commanded the German and Spanish bishops to take no further part in doctrinal decrees, and to protest if the Legate persisted. Father Paul says the Pope bade the Legate wait long enough to save appearances and then hurry forward again. Order his bishops as he might, the Emperor was obliged to recognise that in matters of faith he could not count on their obedience.

The council had been Charles's passion. A reform of the Church by itself, and the moderation of its system of doctrines, so that all pious reasonable men might remain in a single communion, had been the cherished object of his life. Divided religions meant internecine war, and of all wars a religious war was the most detestable to him. The Pope had urged him to force back the recusants with fire and sword. He had aimed at a happier solution by a free assembly where argument could be met with argument, and the common sense of all might hold in awe the fretful spirits. He had persisted through obstructions which would have exhausted the patience of a less admirable prince. All the resources which unreason has at command to thwart the welfare of mankind—calumny, treachery, hypocrisy, open opposition and secret intrigue, self-will, superstition, fanaticism—all had been tried against him, and he had fought on through a long life, and would not believe that he could fail. The final manœuvring at Trent was forcing him at last to see that he had failed. In younger life when the storm first broke, and he was in the vigour of his manhood, then with a firm hand he might have won the

battle. Rome was prostrate, the Pope a prisoner in
St. Angelo, and none more scornful of Church and
churchmen than his own Spaniards.   The idol had
fallen, and he might then have swept it away with the
thanks and approval of all honourable men.   He had
preferred milder methods.   He had waited till Romanism and Protestantism had hardened into irreconcilable
antagonism.   He saw it all at last.   In the council he
had created a force which he could not govern, and
which had become an organised manufactory of discord.

In the midst of their professions of willingness to
receive the Protestant deputies, the fanatics at Trent
could not keep their own counsel.   A foolish Dominican
preached in the cathedral on the parable of the tares.
The heretic tares might be endured for a time, but in
the end they were all to be burnt.   Pope and legates
had satisfied themselves that, hampered as he was by
his Catholic subjects, Charles could not interfere.   It
did not occur to them that, if Charles could not move
himself, there was another prince who might move
instead of him.   They would have been wiser if they
had paid more attention to what Badehorn had said
to them.

The relations between Maurice of Saxony and
Charles V. are among the perplexing problems of
Reformation history.   It was with the help of Maurice
that the Emperor had broken up the Schmalkaldic
League in the war of 1547.   The Emperor and the
German moderates were hoping for a reconciliation
with Rome.   The Elector John Frederick and the

Landgrave of Hesse desired no reconciliation, and wanted spiritual independence. Luther had cautioned them against violence, but they had taken arms in spite of him. They had failed, and since Mühlberg, they had both been prisoners in the Emperor's hands. Maurice was the Elector's cousin, and had been brought up at his cousin's court. He was the Landgrave's son-in-law. He was as determined a Protestant as either of them. But, like Charles and like most of the Lutheran princes, he feared what would happen to Germany if it was broken up into separate sects. He had tolerated the Interim if he had not approved of it, and when the Interim would not work, he had agreed to give the General Council another chance. But he had insisted that, if the council was to succeed, it must be free in fact as well as name. The laity must have a voice in the discussions. The work which had been hurried through before the flight to Bologna must be reviewed by Catholics and Protestants conjointly, and the bishops must be relieved of their oath to the Papacy. There was no mistake about the attitude of Maurice. He was loyal to the Emperor, and believed in his sincerity. The Emperor believed in Maurice, and with Maurice's help had recovered the confidence and the obedience of the Lutheran States. The blot on Maurice's character, if blot there was, had been his having deserted and turned against his cousin and his father-in-law. None were dearer than they to the friends of German liberty. They had been kept prisoners ever since the war, and Maurice was held responsible. The Emperor had refused to give them their freedom because they had remained in stubborn opposition to his own policy. They had rejected the Interim, and by their influence had helped to make it a failure, though they were promised liberty if they would agree to it. They declined to advise their countrymen to assist at a council where the Pope was to preside; and at large, and restored to their rank, they would have been troublesome opponents. Germany, however, was impatient for their release, and Maurice himself had pressed it. Hitherto the Emperor had refused, but his confidence in Maurice generally was as strong as ever; nothing seemed to shake it. The army that had been employed in reducing the towns which had rejected the Interim was still left in Maurice's command, and all the operations were trusted to him.

Magdeburg had stood out. The siege had been dilatory. The Catholics had complained that the Protestant general was wasting time, and had no heart in the enterprise. Rumours spread that Maurice was secretly treating with France. Magdeburg surrendered at last, but on terms so easy that the Protestant garrison enrolled themselves in Maurice's legions; yet Charles showed no uneasiness, and still expressed unbounded trust in Maurice's fidelity. He remained himself at Innspruck, in the passes of the mountains, without more protection than the ordinary guard, while to Maurice was left the negotiation with the Council of Trent for the reception of the Protestant deputies.

The reasonable inference is that Charles now despaired of being able to control Pope or legates by ordinary influence, and could only hope to keep them in order by leaving the force of the Empire in the hands of a leader whom the council might fear. He could not conveniently use force himself on account of his own fanatically Catholic subjects. But he had promised that the Protestants should be heard even if the papal supremacy went down in the struggle. He knew that the Protestants would not be admitted unless the council was made afraid to refuse. He was bent on having the experiment tried, and, as long as Maurice was willing to let Melanchthon attend, he preferred to leave him in full power.

When the safe-conduct was at last extorted, the object seemed to have been gained. But the advantage had been neutralised by the precipitation with the doctrinal canons, which revealed the continuance of the old determined opposition. The shuffling over the safe-conduct and the Legate's insolent language about the council's position towards heretics had already exhausted German patience. Badehorn had given the council fair notice of what might follow on their persistence in so imperious an attitude. The papal party had appeared to yield, but only so yielded as instantly to revive their pretensions in another form; and Maurice, and the Diet, and the Emperor had had enough of it. The council had been called to reform the Church. A genuine reform conducted by the Church itself might have reunited Europe.

The Pope and the legates had determined to have none. Decrees on points of complicated doctrine aggravated discord and hardened innocent differences of opinion into cries of battle. It was now clear that nothing else would be got out of the council, and that the longer it sate the more mischief it would do. The refusal to revise the decrees was fatal to a sincere settlement. An insincere settlement would be worse than none. It was time for the farce to end.

To the Emperor it was the disappointment of a life. The action of Maurice, when it came, is represented generally as a piece of treachery by which Charles was taken by surprise. It is hard for me to think that two experienced statesmen like Charles and the Chancellor Granvelle, who was with him at Innspruck, were as unprepared as the world is asked to believe. It is impossible to think so. Personally Charles was a devout and even passionate Catholic. The supremacy of the Pope was then no article of the Catholic faith; a visible head to the Church might be a desirable form of government, but it was not then of the essence of the creed, and the papal administration might be reformed as well as any other administration which forgets its duties. About this Charles could judge for himself; while his belief was the belief of Catholics, not of Protestants, the belief of the Church before it had been corrupted by the Court of Rome. Once already in his reign a Spanish-German army had sacked the Holy City and made the Pope a prisoner. He could not, perhaps would not, himself sanction a second armed interference with Pope or papal council, but he was evidently determined to spill no German blood in their defence. Two courses alone were open to him if he intended to act; either to fall back, as he had so often threatened, on the German Diet, and lead the revolution, or raise a Catholic army in the Pope's interest and begin a desperate civil war. Spanish orthodoxy, and perhaps his own religious feeling, forbade the first. The second he had many times declared that he would not do. There was nothing left for him, therefore, but to turn aside and let events take their course.

Maurice, in all that he had hitherto said or done about the council, had been frank and undisguised. He wore his colours in his cap. The language of Bade-horn at Trent was his own language, and was not spoken in a corner. The Emperor and the Chancellor could not have understood its meaning, and his conduct after he had resolved to move shows as little sign of purposed treachery. Before the first active step was taken he left his troops. He went to Linz to hold a private consultation with Charles's brother Ferdinand. If he had meant to attack Charles, this was the very last thing which he would have ventured. Of what passed at this interview only so much is known as Maurice or Ferdinand chose to reveal. It was given out that the object of the visit was the release of the Elector Frederick and the Landgrave. If this was all, Maurice could have spoken with more effect remaining at the head of his army.

His stay at Linz was short. He himself rejoined his forces, while Ferdinand hastened to Innspruck to communicate with Charles. Again the avowed object was to intercede for the prisoners. But by this time Maurice's intentions had ceased to be a secret. Pressing messages were sent to the Emperor to beware of him, yet Charles contented himself with the old answer that he was perfectly satisfied with Maurice; and he remained where he was, in a defenceless city, making not the slightest attempt to gather a force about him. Events hurried on. Maurice on returning from Linz issued a manifesto saying that he was taking arms to secure the Protestant religion, to defend German liberty, and deliver the Elector and the Landgrave. By a rapid march, for which we are told to believe the Emperor was utterly unprepared, he forced the passes through the mountains, dispersed the scanty force which defended them, and advanced on Innspruck. Maurice entered the town at one gate while the Emperor left it at another. Had the war been meant in earnest, he might have caught Charles without the least difficulty. But there was no sign that, as against the Emperor, it was meant in earnest at all. Maurice said that he had no cage for so large a bird. Charles with his family retired into Carinthia. There was no pursuit. His quarters were plundered by the German troops, quite possibly to maintain appearances and prevent suspicion of collusion. The Elector, whose imprisonment was the pretext for the attack, declined the freedom which was offered him, and preferred to continue at Charles's side.

Never was so powerful a prince sent flying with so little effort, or with such slight sign of wish afterwards to revenge the insult. So far as outward symptoms explained his conduct, he permitted his hand to be forced in disgust at the council, and interested himself no further in its fortunes.

At Trent, and at Trent alone, the effect was felt, and felt immediately. From Innspruck to Trent there was a broad road, an easy march of three days. The unfortunate fathers were like a gang of coiners surprised by the police. They had painted heretics to themselves as frightful monsters fit only for the flames, and here those monsters were close upon them and in arms. To their frightened imaginations Maurice was another Frondsberg carrying a rope with him to hang the Pope or at least a cardinal. The bishops gathered their effects together and fled for their lives. Couriers galloped to Rome for instructions. The Pope had no instructions to give, save to suspend the council. When his message arrived none were left of that venerable body save the Legate Cardinal Crescentio, the Nuncio, and a few Spaniards who had more courage than the rest. By these a hurried vote was passed that all their decrees, those already sanctioned and those that waited for the Pope's approval, should be held valid for ever. This done, they locked the doors and went their several ways. The Legate, broken down with terror and excitement, died in a few days strangely haunted by the spectre of a black dog, not forgotten by Protestant tradition, and the council, the child of so many hopes,

which was to have restored peace to Europe, vanished
into space, with its last act making peace impossible.
It met again ten years later, but in purpose and nature
a new assembly, with which I have no present concern.
It met no longer with a pretence of desiring peace, but
to equip and renovate the Roman communion for the
reconquest of its lost dominions. It met to split
nations into factions; to set subjects against their
sovereigns and sovereigns against subjects; to break
the peace of families, to fight with and trample down
the genius of dawning liberty.

The history of Europe for a hundred years was the
history of the efforts of the Church, with open force or
secret conspiracy, with all the energy, base or noble,
which passion or passionate enthusiasm could inspire,
to crush and annihilate its foes. No means came amiss
to it, sword or stake, torture chamber or assassin's
dagger. The effects of the Church's working were seen
in ruined nations and smoking cities, in human beings
tearing one another to pieces like raging maniacs, and
the honour of the Creator of the world befouled by the
hideous crimes committed in His name. All this is
forgotten now, forgotten or even audaciously denied. I
will mention but one illustration connected with the
subject of these lectures.

The decrees of the Council of Trent were not
received in France, and when the gutters of Paris were
running with Huguenot blood after the black day of
St. Bartholomew, and the unhappy country was shud-
dering with horror, the guilty King tried to excuse

what had been done by charging the Huguenots with political conspiracy. This is the explanation now commonly given by those who wish to defend the French Government, and at the same time to defame its victims. Pope Gregory XIII. rebuked the modesty of the son of St. Louis, and forbade him to explain away an action so pious and so glorious. He held processions and thanksgiving services at Rome in honour of the destruction of the infidels. He sent Cardinal Orsino to France with his congratulations, and the expressions of his hope that after such an evidence of the piety of the King and the nation, the decrees of Trent would now be introduced. The Cardinal on reaching Avignon found the Catholics excusing the massacre as an unfortunate accident. He invited them to an attitude more worthy of themselves and of the signal services which they had rendered to the truth. At Lyons there had been a massacre only second to that of Paris. The Cardinal (I quote from De Thou, the greatest of the French historians, who was in the midst of the scenes which he described) sought out the leader of the Lyons butchery, and gave him his blessing and his absolution. At Paris afterwards he urged Charles to claim openly the credit of a deed achieved for the glory of God and the honour of the Holy See, so he said future ages would know that no personal fears or feelings had led him to consent to the slaughter of his subjects, but zeal for the Catholic and Apostolic Roman religion which the Council of Trent had purged from heresy, and which now required the extermination of the Protestant sect.

This was the spirit in which the Roman Church began its wars with the Reformation, and it was met with a courage equal to its own. The Church pretended that outside the pale of the faithful human virtue was impossible. As if to repel the insolent assumption, new and noble races grew out of the fight for freedom. Before the Reformation the nations of Europe had been the mere subjects of kings and priests and nobles. The people rose everywhere, elevated by their cause to the level of their rulers. English, Scotch, Dutch, Swedes, Germans, were heated in the furnace and hammered in the stithy, till the iron in their blood grew to steel. France might reject the light, but it came back to France in the Revolution as forked lightning. The annals of mankind were enriched with splendid names. No Plutarch, no Pindar ever told or sang of grander men than those who fought and bled in the long battle for European liberty. So has Nature worked in the training of our race that we may prize the spiritual freedom which it has cost so dear to win. Yet with a little more wisdom, a little more good-will in the Roman Pope, mankind might have been spared so bitter an experience. The council which Charles V. had brought together might have peacefully accomplished the same results. It was wrecked only on the determination of the Church of Rome to resist the reform of abuses which the Church itself could neither deny nor excuse.

The advance of Maurice on Innspruck was in May 1552. The peace of Passau followed in July, and toleration was established in Germany, to last till the Thirty Years' War. Charles himself took no part in the settlement, and interested himself no further in the quarrels of Pope and Protestant.

Of what remains of Charles's career I may have more to say to you hereafter. One only observation I have to make in bringing these lectures to a close. The Reformation is now said to have settled nothing. I wish you to recognise that every one of the 'hundred grievances' of Germany, every one of the abuses complained of by the English House of Commons in 1529, has been long ago swept away, and so completely that their very existence is now forgotten. I called the movement at the outset a revolt of the laity against the clergy. Everywhere, in Catholic countries as in Protestant, the practices have been abandoned which the laity rose then to protest against. The principles on which the laity insisted have become the rule of the modern world. Popes no longer depose princes, dispense with oaths, or absolve subjects from their allegiance. Appeals are not any more carried to Rome from the national tribunals, nor justice sold there to the highest bidder.

The clergy have ceased to pass laws which bind the laity and to enforce them with spiritual censures. Felonious priests suffer for their crimes like unconsecrated mortals. Too zealous prelates cannot call poor creatures before them *ex officio*, cross-question them on their beliefs, fine, imprison, or burn them at the stake. Excommunications are kept in bounds

by the law of libel.   Itinerant pardon-vendors no
longer hawk through Europe their unprofitable wares.
Cardinals cannot now add see to see that they may
have princes' revenues, or private clergy buy benefices
as they would buy farms, and buy along with them
dispensations to neglect their duties.

These scandals against which the laity cried so
loudly are gone, and the devoutest Romanists would
not wish to revive them.

And there has been one more victory as real, if less
obtrusive.   In the intercourse of daily life, in the joint
discharge of common duties, men of different opinions
have at last found it possible to live together without
regarding each other as natural enemies.   They have
been obliged to recognise that truth, honour, purity,
justice, manliness are neither the growth nor the
privilege of a belief in special formulas; that men can
disagree in religion without wishing to destroy each
other.

The doctrines of the Council of Trent may still be
held by half the Christian world to be the true interpretation of the mystery of existence.   But the
anathemas have been silently repealed, and something
has been gained for poor humanity.